Jim Larson looked at th[...] [...]pression. "I got a call from someone who works with my wife, Carla. She told me that my wife was expected at a meeting this afternoon"—his voice dropped almost to a whisper—"but she never made it."

The officers studied the disturbed husband intently. "Are you hesitant about telling me something, Mr. Larson?" the deputy prodded.

Jim said that he couldn't understand Carla's disappearance. "We—my whole family—have all become extremely watchful, but especially Carla ever since—well, let me explain."

The detectives exchanged glances.

"My sister, Sonja, was one of the students at the University of Florida who was murdered in August 1990, along with four others. A crazy man, a serial killer, named Danny Rolling killed them. I'm sure you remember that."

The two detectives and the deputy sat stunned.

Do we remember the case? Detective Weir thought. *The whole country remembers the case.*

BOOK YOUR PLACE ON OUR WEBSITE AND MAKE THE READING CONNECTION!

We've created a customized website just for our very special readers, where you can get the inside scoop on everything that's going on with Zebra, Pinnacle and Kensington books.

When you come online, you'll have the exciting opportunity to:

- View covers of upcoming books
- Read sample chapters
- Learn about our future publishing schedule (listed by publication month *and author*)
- Find out when your favorite authors will be visiting a city near you
- Search for and order backlist books from our online catalog
- Check out author bios and background information
- Send e-mail to your favorite authors
- Meet the Kensington staff online
- Join us in weekly chats with authors, readers and other guests
- Get writing guidelines
- AND MUCH MORE!

**Visit our website at
http://www.kensingtonbooks.com**

EVIDENCE OF MURDER

SAMUEL ROEN

PINNACLE BOOKS
Kensington Publishing Corp.
http://www.kensingtonbooks.com

PINNACLE BOOKS are published by

Kensington Publishing Corp.
850 Third Avenue
New York, NY 10022

First Printing: September 2003
10 9 8 7 6 5

Printed in the United States of America

For Marcia

ACKNOWLEDGMENTS

The writing of a book devoted to a specific true crime requires authenticity and accuracy in the reportage of the occurrence. Only then is the re-creation a valid presentation.

This work has been so guided. Acknowledgments are recorded here of persons who gave me their cooperation and firsthand knowledge of what transpired with their experience in this case, without which this work could not have been effectively completed.

Jim Larson, husband of victim Carla Ann Larson, and his mother, Ada, graciously provided detailed accounts of the ordeal of horror that they lived. I am also grateful to Ada Larson for her permission to reprint her column printed in the *Orlando Sentinel* on Thanksgiving Day, 1997.

Detectives Cameron Weir and John Linnert of the Orange County Sheriff's Department contributed their time, recollections and behind-the-scenes knowledge, John's coming via e-mail from Boston, where he now resides.

Assistant State Attorney Jeff Ashton served brilliantly in this double-featured courtroom battle. Jeff took time for many interviews and telephone calls to give me the aspects of the state's case. He was especially helpful and considerate.

Public defender Bob Wesley cooperated with an interview on the defense of the accused.

Former prosecutor Ted Culhan accounted some of the background preparation of the case against the accused.

Seminole County Sheriff Donald F. Eslinger cooperated importantly, providing official accounts of Huggins's criminal record and relative information to crimes he had committed.

Seminole County Sheriff's Department Lieutenant John Thorpe and Public Information Officer Steve Olson, complementing Sheriff Eslinger's cooperation, provided critical matter relative to the subject.

Orange County Sheriff's Department Officers Tom Woodard

and Tom McCann and Public Service Officer Jim Solomons contributed substantially with information.

Gainesville, Florida, former Chief of Police Wayland Clifton Jr. arranged for information about the University of Florida campus crimes related to the Orlando story.

Several others considerably helped in various capacities that assisted in the preparation of the book.

I am entirely appreciative of the efforts of editor-in-chief Michaela Hamilton for her priceless contribution and improvements to this book.

Kathleen Waltz, publisher of the *Orlando Sentinel,* cordially authorized information, photography and great cooperation of the paper's reportage and personnel.

Jim Leusner, longtime reporter with the *Orlando Sentinel,* provided detailed information regarding the Huggins case and the Gainesville killings.

Tom Burton of the *Orlando Sentinel* furnished special photos contiguous to the story.

Attorney Hal Roen reviewed the story approach with a legal, editorial eye.

Sara Roen Brady opened doors in Seminole County to interviews with officials relative to the procedures used in this book.

Attorney Leah Roen Wiederspahn supplied significant computer research on Huggins's Web site.

Mike Moore, computer specialist, kindly provided important technical help and information.

Philip Russell and Angie Folks of Office Depot were helpful in making photo reproductions and copies for the book.

A special acknowledgment of Gary S. Roen, who served his father as literary agent, critic and reader throughout this project.

A very special acknowledgment of Marcia Roen, my wife, who worked as editor, collaborator and prime consultant.

PROLOGUE

On Tuesday, June 10, 1997, Carla Ann Larson, a lovely thirty-year-old blue-eyed blond engineer, was deeply engrossed in her design work for Centex Rooney Construction Company on a new project: the luxurious Coronado Springs Resort on the fabulous Walt Disney World properties in Orlando, Florida. Hungry, Carla checked her watch to discover that it was the lunch hour.

Carla decided to go to a nearby supermarket, where she could pick up something for her usual speedy lunch, telling fellow workers that she would return shortly, asking if she might bring something back for them.

As she drove along in her white Ford Explorer, she smiled and waved to several other Centex Rooney employees as she sped off the Disney property.

But Carla Ann Larson failed to return to work. She vanished. . . .

CHAPTER 1

James Larson sat at his desk at home and stared at the phone. For the past several hours, he had steadily grown more concerned.

He scanned the charming, comfortable room that he and his wife, Carla, had so lovingly furnished and decorated, noting all the little touches, yet not really seeing anything. His mind jumped from one memory to another.

He thought back to breakfast, remembering how Carla had smiled as she offered, "More coffee, honey?" How she kissed him and waved happily as they both left for work in their separate cars. *Dear God, was that only this morning?*

Jim rolled a pencil between his thumb and forefinger and remembered back to the time when he met the beautiful girl with whom he fell in love. He drew circles on a scratch pad as he reflected on how pretty and vivacious she was, with such an engaging smile—that smile could always light up his heart.

He remembered how he and his coworker Dan Thomas had traveled all over the eastern United States with the Goodyear Tire & Rubber Company ground crew, offering rides to the general public on the Goodyear blimp. They became close, enduring friends.

One day Dan looked at him and said, "You know, I've been thinking."

"What have you been thinking—or maybe I shouldn't ask," Jim replied with a smile.

"I've been thinking that you should meet Carla."

"You mean your sister?"

"Uh-huh. I think you would be good together. Perfect for each other," he declared.

When Jim met Carla Ann Thomas, he immediately knew she was the girl who would change everything about his life.

He reminisced how they began going together, and it was quite a while before he discovered that Carla was only sixteen years old.

He smiled at the memory of that and his subsequent conversation with Dan.

"Hey, Dan, what is this? You told me your sister was eighteen and she admitted to me that she's only sixteen."

And how Dan had burst into a howling laugh and declared, "What does a number mean? She's a super girl and I was sure you would like her. And she'll be eighteen in two years—just think of that."

By this time the die was cast, and he was in love with Carla Ann Thomas. Nothing would change that, and he would not give her up just because she was sixteen.

Jim recalled with warm pleasure that after Carla graduated from high school in Pompano Beach, Florida, she enrolled in the University of Florida to earn her degree in architecture as well as a master's degree in building construction. How proud he was of her achievements.

Jim stared at his desk, remembering when he and Carla were married on December 1, 1990. After Carla graduated, she was hired by the Centex Rooney Construction Company in Atlanta, Georgia, the same corporation where Carla's father, also an engineer, worked for many years until his retirement.

Jim was still with Goodyear, but he came to the conclusion that the traveling was great for a single guy but it sure didn't fit with married life. After fourteen years with the company, he resigned his position and moved to Atlanta with Carla. He enrolled in the Port Folio Center College to study graphic design, illustration and art direction. He also took a part-time job.

He smiled, recalling how happy they were there. It was a magical time. They were young and in love and living in a big city. They had fun exploring and enjoying all the excitement of a major metropolis. It was like a perpetual honeymoon.

Then came the opportunity for Carla to transfer to the construction project at Disney World in Orlando, to work on building the new, posh Coronado Springs Resort hotel. They were both ecstatic with that chance and happy to be moving back to Florida, where they could be closer to their families.

Then to make their lives complete, Carla became pregnant and they had Jessica, the light of their lives.

Mostly he remembered the laughter, Carla's bubbly sense of humor and their silly private jokes.

He thought forlornly, *Where are you, Carla?*

There's no choice. He sighed finally and dialed the Orange County Sheriff's Department (OCSD).

In a strained voice Larson hesitantly told the answering officer, "I . . . I need to report my wife missing."

The officer asked Larson to stay on the line while a transfer could be made.

In the following moments James Larson reported a brief account of the disappearance of his wife, Carla. He gave his address, phone number and a few specifics of identity. He was in turn advised that an investigator would be dispatched to his residence.

The communications officer who received Larson's call contacted the on-duty deputy in Jim's area. He passed the information on to Deputy Tom Woodard, in whose district Larson's address fell.

Immediately the heavily built 6'1" patrol deputy headed off to the Larson residence.

Driving into the College Park section of Orlando, Woodard looked over the area as patrol officers do automatically. The streets were named after prominent colleges throughout the United States: Yale, Harvard, Princeton, Vassar, Amherst, Smith. College Park, more than fifty years old, had in recent years become popular with young professionals, who purchased the older homes, then remodeled and upgraded them. Woodard noted the well-kept homes with their beautiful, tidy lawns and shrubbery as he passed and thought, *College Park is certainly not a high-crime area.* He hoped that the missing woman was not a victim of some criminal act.

The patrol officer arrived at the Larson home and made a quick study of it and its surrounds. All seemed quiet. He approached the front entrance and pressed the doorbell.

The deputy studied the man who opened the door. He observed a man of neat but average appearance at 6' or possibly 6'1" and a trim 180 pounds. He had a lean face with a sparse mustache. His blue eyes looked concerned, and his dark brown hair dangled where he had brushed it back anxiously. In the normal sequence of his daily life, Jim Larson was a nice-looking guy with a pleasant personality who went about without disturbing anyone or drawing special attention. Now he appeared obviously shaken, like someone who had lost everything.

"Hello, I'm Jim Larson. Please come in." Larson led the deputy into the dining room.

Deputy Woodard said, "Just take your time and tell me what you know about this situation as best you can."

Larson looked at the deputy with a bewildered expression, unsure how to begin. After a moment, he offered, "I should start at the beginning. I was at work—uh—I work at Home Depot—when I heard my name paged over the loudspeaker. When I got on the line, the caller identified herself as one of the Centex Rooney workers at Walt Disney World. You know, someone who works with Carla. She surprised me when she asked if I knew where Carla was." He stopped abruptly, clearly returning in his mind to the call.

Tom Woodard, who had seen every imaginable situation in his years with the sheriff's department, studied the man and said, "Just take it easy. . . . Take your time."

Jim Larson took a deep breath and continued. "Well, the woman told me that Carla had taken off shortly after noon, headed for the Publix supermarket that's in the proximity of the Disney work site." He brushed his hair back with his hand and added, "She said Carla was going there to pick up some stuff for lunch and some fruit for a meeting in the afternoon."

Jim swallowed before continuing. "She told me that my wife was expected at an engineers' meeting this afternoon"—his voice dropped almost to a whisper—"but she never made it." Shaking his head in confusion, he repeated, "She never made it to the meeting."

Woodard asked, "Did anyone, any of her other fellow workers, hear from Mrs. Larson? Did anyone see her, anyone that you know of?"

Jim Larson slowly shook his head.

"What did you do after you talked to the woman from your wife's job?" the deputy asked.

"I don't know. I was confused, upset. . . . I didn't know what to think. I was worried that something happened to her. I didn't want to think about that. I just waited, thinking, and then I asked for permission to leave work. I wanted to get home; maybe my wife might be there, maybe she came home sick, or maybe I could find some answer to this whole thing." He paused, shaking his head again.

The patrol officer studied the disturbed husband intently. "Are you hesitant about telling me something, Mr. Larson?" Woodard prodded.

"No, I'm just trying to reconstruct what I did then. After I left work, I drove over to the day-care center to pick up our little girl, Jessica."

His face changed as a thought struck him. "My God, what do I tell my little girl, why her mommy isn't home for her? She's only a year old."

"Don't do this to yourself, Mr. Larson. We're going to find answers for you."

Jim Larson continued, searching for the right words to tell the deputy. "Anyway, I took Jessica home, fixed her dinner and tucked her into bed. I didn't know what to do. I made call after call to everyone I could think of, my mother—actually, she's my stepmother—in Pompano Beach, all our friends, anyone who might know where she is. I even called the hospitals to find out if maybe she was in an accident and been admitted."

He slumped back in his chair and said that he had reluctantly called Carla's parents, also living in Pompano Beach. "They were stunned. They hadn't heard from her today. I promised to keep them informed."

Woodard asked Larson if he would like to take a break, but Jim said that he would go on. He continued, saying, "I thought that I should call the Centex Rooney site and see if they found out anything more. That was about six o'clock. The woman I spoke to told me that they heard nothing. She said they thought that Carla might have left for a doctor's appointment or something. I just don't know. There's just no explanation. Carla is a most reliable person, and it is certainly not like her to have missed an important engineers' meeting."

"There's just one more thing, Mr. Larson, and I'm sorry to have to ask you, but did your wife have an illness, either physical or mental? Was she depressed?"

"Oh, no, absolutely not. She is fine, in perfect health."

"How about your marriage? Were you two having problems?"

"No, oh, no. Nothing like that. We are very happy."

"Could she have gone off with another man?"

"What?" Larson was shocked. "No!"

"Are all of her clothes and belongings still in your home?"

"Yes, as far as I can tell."

Everything appeared normal to Woodard on the surface.

So it wasn't logical for a young, healthy, happy mother to leave her family voluntarily and just take off.

"Mr. Larson, would you object to my looking over the house, going through it room by room?"

"Go right ahead. But please don't disturb Jessica. She's asleep in her room."

Woodard nodded. The officer inspected and found nothing amiss.

He returned to Larson, who was sitting quietly at the table and staring blankly at the wall.

"Mr. Larson, I think it would be a good idea if I could talk with Mrs. Larson's parents."

Startled by the suggestion, Larson said that he could not see the necessity of involving the Thomases. "They are going through the worst thing that ever happened to them, worrying about where their daughter is, and I don't know if they are up to talking with someone in your position with the department."

"Suppose you just call them on the phone, introduce me, and let me have a few words with them."

Larson reluctantly agreed to make the call, but he cautioned Woodard to be brief and not too intensive about the facts of their daughter's disappearance.

In his conversation with Phyllis Thomas in Pompano Beach, Woodard asked her if Carla had any problems with her husband, Jim, or if she had any plans to leave him.

Mrs. Thomas told the deputy that she did not know of any problems. She was very upset, but she promised to call him if she thought or learned of anything that might be relevant. Woodard assured her, "I will do the same."

The deputy also spoke to Ada Larson, Jim's mother, on the phone. She expressed great concern and told him that she was going to come to Orlando to be with her son and granddaughter.

When he concluded, Woodard turned to Jim Larson. "Do you have a recent picture of your wife that we can have?"

"Sure," he answered, "let me get one for you."

In a few moments he returned and handed a photo to Woodard. The deputy studied the picture of the lovely young woman. Carla's expression, blue eyes, cheerfully smiling face and long blond hair all added up to an appearance of bursting vitality.

"Can you give us a description of your wife?"

"She's five-eight and weighs one hundred thirty pounds."

Taking notes, Woodard asked, "About the car. What year, what model is this car of hers?"

"It's a four-door 1995 Ford Explorer," Jim answered. "The license number is TGX-99V."

"All right, sir, I'll call this in and we'll get the department started on it right away."

Woodard briefed the department's watch commander, Eric Viehman, requesting assistance in the area where Carla Larson was last seen.

After hanging up the phone, Deputy Woodard looked at the despondent Jim Larson and wondered, *Is this guy as nice a fellow as he appears to be? Or is he a very good actor?*

The Orange County Sheriff's Department entered Carla Ann Larson's description into NCIC/FCIC as a missing person. The report listed her as 5'8", 130 pounds, braided long blond hair, blue eyes, wearing a red sleeveless shirt, Gap blue jeans and brown work boots when last seen. The information on her automobile was also entered into the teletype system.

At 8:30 that night Corporal Ken Glantz drove to the Publix on International Drive, Kissimmee, and met with the store manager. The personable man told the corporal that Centex Rooney coworkers had already contacted him. They described her disappearance to him and asked him to search the store's daily receipts for any transactions that might be traced to Carla. The manager had complied readily.

"We found a credit card receipt that had Carla Larson's signature on it," he told the corporal. The receipt showed that Carla Larson used her Discover credit card on the purchase of $8.63 worth of food items at register two, and the operator of the register was listed as Kim Hall. The itemized purchases were cherries, pita bread, grapes and pretzels.

Corporal Glantz asked the Publix manager for a copy of that receipt, and the man gave it over.

Joined by Deputy Ric Voelker, Glantz tracked down cashier Kim Hall and questioned her about Carla Larson.

"Do you remember seeing her? Very pretty young woman with blue eyes and long blond hair in a braid. She came here for some stuff around lunchtime," Corporal Glantz asked Hall.

The clerk looked blankly at the two officers. She tilted her head trying to match Glantz's description with an earlier customer. Finally she answered, "I really can't recall the woman. You know, we have hundreds of customers all day long, so it's hard to remember individuals."

Glantz thanked the clerk and turned to leave, but Hall called out, "Just a minute, Corporal, you might check with our manager and ask him if this woman is on our surveillance camera."

"That's a good idea, thanks," Glantz said. He turned to Voelker. "Let's find the manager again and get him to check the surveillance tape."

The two officers caught up with the manager, who readily agreed to check the tape. The surveillance camera, though, was trained in the area of the Presto ATM machine and did not show Carla Larson. The manager gave Glantz the videotape anyhow. "I don't know if it will be of any use, but if it could be important, it's yours."

Corporal Glantz thanked him and the officers returned to the Disney construction site.

Deputy Voelker spoke to two Centex Rooney employees who told him that they saw Carla Larson entering the Publix market parking lot shortly past noon.

Other Centex Rooney men, traveling west on Osceola Parkway in the early afternoon, saw a vehicle resembling Carla's Ford Explorer coming out of a wooded area. They pinpointed the location south of the Caribbean Beach Resort, north of Osceola Parkway and a quarter of a mile west of Route I-4.

"Did you get a look at the driver?" Deputy Voelker asked.

One of the witnesses answered, "Yes, it was a man, a white man. I got a good look at him and saw him looking down at the floorboard on the passenger side of the vehicle as he sped out of the woods."

Voelker said, "Describe the guy as best you can."

"I'd say that he was in his mid or late thirties and he had dark hair. I can't do much better than that."

A deputy was posted near the area where the vehicle was seen, treating it as a crime scene in preparation for the more intense search, which would begin shortly.

CHAPTER 2

Fourteen-year veteran investigator Detective Cameron "Cam" Weir of the Orange County Sheriff's Department shifted his medium-size body, a solid 175 pounds in a 5' 9" frame, trying to get comfortable in his chair in the family room of his home. He focused his sharp chestnut brown eyes on the television set, hoping to luck upon a program that would hold his interest, take his mind off crime and his daily serious pursuits. The ringing telephone interrupted his channel surfing.

"Would you take that, honey?" his wife called from the next room. "It's probably for you anyway at this time of night."

The detective picked up the phone and heard the voice of the dispatcher from the sheriff's department. "There's a report of a missing woman, an engineer who works on a project at Disney World."

The dispatcher continued briefing the detective with the basics that Deputy Tom Woodard had reported. "Woodard's waiting for you at the Larson house."

"I'm on my way."

Behind the wheel of his official OCSD vehicle, the detective called his partner, Detective John Linnert, and advised him of the situation. They both hoped it was something simple like a flat tire or a dead battery or a late meeting. They arranged to meet at the Larson home.

Weir and Linnert had worked together on many investigations over the years and were members of the Sheriff's Offices Dive Team (SODT). They also developed a close friendship outside of work, and their families socialized together in their off-hours. The men worked well together, brainstorming ideas and techniques. In interview situations they sensed each other's direction and played off it. Each had great respect for the other's opinions and ability. They were a successful team.

Weir glanced at the dashboard clock and saw that it was 10:11 P.M. By 10:37, he arrived at the Larson house. In a quick scan of the residence and its surrounds, the detective judged it to be a comfortable upper-middle-class home that fit in nicely with this well-kept neighborhood in Orlando.

Deputy Tom Woodard greeted him at the door and apologized. "Sorry to get you out at this hour of the night. Here's what I found out so far." He proceeded to fill in the details surrounding the disappearance of Carla Ann Larson.

Following the briefing, Woodard introduced Weir to Jim Larson, and Weir appraised him with a polite but scrutinizing look.

With his many years' experience, it became almost second nature for Weir automatically to observe and to be aware of any indications or hints of anything that might be important to an investigation. In this case he kept an alert eye on James Larson.

Detective Weir addressed the distraught husband. "Mr. Larson, I would like you to give me your account of what transpired. I know that you went through this with Deputy Woodard, but I'd like very much to hear it directly from you."

"Sure, sure, I understand," Larson said.

Before he could start, they were joined by Weir's partner, Detective John Linnert, a fourteen-year veteran with the sheriff's department. He was thirty-nine years old, 6'1", 155 pounds, medium build, with brown hair and brown eyes.

"Sorry it took so long. I got here as quick as I could," the detective apologized.

"You're right on time, John." Weir welcomed Linnert and introduced him to Jim Larson. "Okay, Mr. Larson, please proceed."

"I hope you understand that I'm very upset, but I'll try to tell you as simply as possible from the time I got that phone call while I was at work."

It was clear to the investigating detectives that Jim Larson was distressed, but he seemed to be overly cautious. Weir studied the man and his emotional demeanor just as attentively as the words he spoke. He silently wondered, *What is there about this man? There's something not quite right. I have an uneasy feeling about him. I think he'll bear checking.*

"We understand, just start at the beginning," Linnert encouraged.

Larson recounted briefly the information he had previously given to Deputy Tom Woodard.

Continuing with his story, Larson said that while he was trying to figure out something else that he could do, someone rang the doorbell at his home. "It was one of the women workers at Centex Rooney. I was surprised to see her, and I thought that she might be bringing me some good news about my wife. I invited her in, but she said that she was on her way home and only came by to drop off Carla's briefcase that she left at her desk at work."

Larson recalled for the officers, "I sat with the briefcase lying on my knees and stared at it, wondering, just wondering. And that's when I called the sheriff's department."

He said that he couldn't understand her disappearance, that Carla Ann was supercautious and careful. As he continued to speak, the detectives perceived something that was not apparent initially. The tone of his voice changed as he spoke hesitatingly. "We—my whole family—have all be-

come extremely watchful, but especially Carla ever since—
well, let me explain."

The detectives exchanged glances, silently wondering
what Larson was about to disclose. "My sister, Sonja, was
one of the students at the University of Florida who was assaulted and murdered in August 1990, along with four others. Do you remember that case? A crazy man, a serial killer,
named Danny Rolling killed them. I'm sure you remember
that. The whole country was shocked by this horrible crime."

The two detectives and the deputy sat stunned, speechless
as Larson stopped and looked at them questioningly.

Do we remember the case? Weir thought. *The whole
country remembers the case.*

"Yes, Mr. Larson, we do remember the case. Please go
on," he encouraged.

"We were all devastated by my sister's death. Especially
Carla. Ever since, she has been supercautious about everything,
the meeting of strangers or unknowns. Just about everything
in daily life. We all realized that we could not be too careful."

The lawmen remained silent, astounded by his story.

Jim Larson loosened his tie, allowing him to breathe
more easily while he recalled the devastation he suffered
seven years ago. His younger sister, Sonja, a freshman at the
University of Florida (UF), was brutally assaulted and murdered along with four other students in the fading days of
August 1990.

*The calm and poetic setting of the university and the city
of Gainesville exploded into a resounding shock wave that
shook the city, the state and the nation. Dread struck his
whole family, especially him and Carla.*

*Christina Powell's parents repeatedly phoned the apart-
ment shared by Christina, seventeen, and Sonja Larson,
eighteen, but their calls were not answered.*

Fearful, Christina's father called the Gainesville Police Department and requested that his daughter's apartment be checked.

Jim Larson remembered all too well what the Gainesville police discovered when they opened the door of Christina and Sonja's apartment.

It was one of the most horrific murder scenes ever witnessed anywhere.

At 4:00 P.M. Sunday, August 26, 1990, Christina's nude body was discovered lying on the living-room floor, mutilated, stabbed repeatedly, her breasts carved with the nipples excised. The walls were splattered with her blood.

In an upstairs bedroom lay the naked, beaten and murdered body of Sonja Larson, the second victim of a crazed killer.

The news of the murder spread wildly across the campus; then it rocked the city even more as another coed who had suffered an even more brutal slaying was discovered.

Christa Hoyt, nineteen, a chemistry major at the nearby Santa Fe Community College, met her death in what had to be a frenzied killing. Her torso was gashed open from her pelvis to her chest, then sexually posed. In a final hideous degradation, her head was hacked off and mounted on a bookshelf in a ghoulish display.

These three deaths stunned the Gainesville Police Department and the Alachua County Sheriff's Department. Ironically, victim Hoyt had been a well-liked member of the sheriff's department, working there as a clerk before enrolling at the college.

Soon thereafter, another shocking murder struck the Gainesville student population. Two more bodies were discovered in an apartment complex. University of Florida undergraduates Tracy Inez Paules, twenty-three, and her friend Manuel R. Taboada, twenty-three, both from Miami, were found stabbed to death in their adjacent off-campus Gatewood apartments.

At a staff campus meeting, university president John Lombardi told the gathering, "It is clear that this part of the country has some maniac on the loose."

These five murders evoked the memory of serial killer Ted Bundy, who had killed, among a number of others, two female students at Florida State University in Tallahassee in January 1978.

With five students mysteriously dead in forty hours, the question was, "Who's next?"

Fear overshadowed the university and the entire community. Hundreds of panicked students left the city to return to the safety of their parents' homes.

In droves, the remaining students flocked to local hardware stores purchasing new secure locks, bolts and door bars. Others bought guns, rifles and knives of all descriptions for protection.

On the two campuses, most of the activities usually taking place at the beginning of a new term were canceled.

At the Gainesville headquarters Chief of Police Wayland Clifton Jr. led round-the-clock work with his detectives, crime scene technicians and other specialists executing one of the most comprehensive criminal investigations in the history of the department.

The chief declared, "The murders are the most horrific I've seen in thirty years of law enforcement."

Clifton, pulling out all stops, called for assistance from the Florida Department of Law Enforcement (FDLE), the Alachua County Sheriff's Department (ACSD), the Florida Highway Patrol (FHP) and certain high-tech specialists from the FBI.

To crack this horrible, bizarre case, the chief incorporated more than one hundred investigators, analysts, specialist technicians and prosecutors from city, state and federal government to create one of the most qualified forces ever organized in the state.

Despite the trauma that engulfed the campus and the en-

*tire Gainesville community, President John Lombardi an-
nounced that classes would not be canceled, but he also said
that students would not be penalized if they went home.*

At the same time the investigation turned up an odd UF
student as a possible suspect. Reports stated that he was
seen in the vicinity of the crime scenes. While several possible suspects were being questioned, this man seemed to be
the prime suspect.

On Thursday, August 30, the probe shifted to Brevard County,
where this student was arrested for beating his grandmother.
An assistant public defender told the press, "The gentleman
seems to be a suspect in some pretty serious crimes" in
Alachua County (Gainesville area). The investigation reported that he entered his grandmother's home about 12:00
A.M. on Thursday, found his grandmother sitting in a chair
and allegedly began beating her. By the time the police arrived, the victim was covered with blood. The suspect was
taken into custody.

Reports disclosed that the suspect was not a stable person, that he had emotional problems, but there was nothing
solid linking him to the campus murders.

On campus, rumors freely blurred facts and fantasy together concerning this 6', more-than-two-hundred-pound,
unstable freshman. The suspect was brought into the Brevard
County Sheriff's Department (BCSD) for questioning from
3:00 P.M. Thursday to 3:00 A.M. Friday.

Sheriff C. W. "Jake" Miller declared that this guy's "hol-
lering, screaming, crying and ranting" was what brought attention to him.

The young student suspect was held on a million-dollar
bond on charges of assaulting his seventy-nine-year-old
grandmother, but he was not yet implicated in the college
homicides.

Meanwhile in Gainesville, Chief Clifton was pleased that
the expanding investigation now included the Brevard
County Sheriff's Department.

The press, print and electronic media throughout the state devoted their full effort to seeking leads and assistance to help the investigators solve the multiple murders.

Funeral services were held in Jacksonville for Christina Powell, in Newberry for Christa Hoyt, and in Pompano Beach for Sonja Larson. In Miami hundreds gathered to bid a solemn farewell to Tracey Paules and Manuel Taboada.

Back in Brevard County, authorities questioned the student suspect's brother. He insisted, "There has to be another person, a killer, who had to be the perpetrator of these terrible crimes. My brother has problems, but he does not have the mental ability to plan and to execute such an involved murder scheme." He recounted the origin of his brother's problem. "My brother was in a severe automobile accident, which destroyed his ability to function properly mentally. And I assure you that in no way could he possibly have planned and executed these five victims."

The investigation labored on for months with little progress, but Chief Clifton remained firm in his determination to discover the Jack the Ripper–type killer.

Then out of the sites of the murders, the crime scene technician specialists came up with proof that someone other than the student suspect had committed the campus murders. Quietly, the advancing breakthroughs moved ahead with no disclosures to the media.

In Gainesville 9,317 possible witnesses were questioned, over 5,000 leads were followed and about 3,000 possible suspects were pursued.

A task force of 466 officers and specialists united to pursue the investigation.

On Thursday, January 24, 1991, reporters barraged John Joyce of the FDLE with questions. They somehow got word about a Louisiana man who reportedly attempted to kill his father, a police lieutenant. Joyce stated that he could not possibly discuss any aspect of an ongoing investigation.

The next day, the new suspect was identified as thirty-six-year-old Danny Harold Rolling.

The media were quick to reveal what facts they uncovered about Rolling. He was arrested in Ocala on charges of armed robbery of a Winn-Dixie supermarket. There were strong indications of his being tied to a triple slaying in his hometown of Shreveport, Louisiana, committed in November 1989.

Although this curious individual was not charged with the murders in Louisiana, the Florida law authorities saw overwhelming similarities between the two sets of murders. Julie Grissom, twenty-four, one of the victims, a student at LSU, was found with her nude body sexually posed after her stabbing death, similar to the victim in Gainesville.

Danny Rolling was not charged in Shreveport, but the case was still open and strong leads indicated him as the prime suspect.

The Gainesville investigation found that Danny Rolling was registered in a Gainesville motel in August 1990. He later camped out in the woods not far from the living quarters of the campus murder victims. At the camp site the police found numerous items that tied Rolling positively to the murders. Among them was a screwdriver that they believed he used to break into the apartments; they also found a pubic hair that was matched to Christa Hoyt.

On the first day of March 1992, Danny Rolling, wearing a ski mask, robbed a Gainesville bank. Unknown to him, the money contained a concealed dry pack that exploded dye on him. He was swiftly arrested and charged.

Chief Wayland Clifton Jr. said, "I never met anyone like this man Rolling. When I saw him, I could not believe that this individual was what we determined. He just did not look like a cunning murderer. In our interrogations Rolling would not talk directly to our investigators. He would not even look at us. Instead, in response to questions, he turned and gave his answers to his fellow prisoner Bobby Lewis, who relayed whatever this accused killer wanted to be his answer."

Clifton stated that this procedure was strictly unusual. On May 21, 1992, a Gainesville hearing before Judge

Maurice Paul on the bank-robbing charges revealed Danny Rolling's criminal past, which included repeated arrests for armed robberies in Louisiana, Georgia and Florida dating back to 1972.

He previously confessed that in May 1990 in his home state of Louisiana he got into a violent argument with his father, a former police lieutenant, over putting up the windows in a car as it began to rain. As the quarrel heated up, the senior Rolling fired shots into the air. Danny followed his father into his house, shouting, "Okay, old man, you want to shoot it out?" He shot his father in the face, then ran to a neighbor's house, where at gunpoint he demanded money and fled.

Rolling's record showed that he burglarized a home in Missouri and stole the identification of a deceased family member. He used that ID in several Florida cities, including Tallahassee, Sarasota, Gainesville and Tampa.

Detective LeGran Hewitt of the Alachua County Sheriff's Department, who had dug out Danny Rolling's record, stated that the subject ran down a deputy while fleeing from a grocery story robbery in Tampa.

In his appearance before Judge Paul, Rolling told of his newfound devotion to the Lord. This fell on the unsympathetic ears of Judge Paul, a tough and distinguished jurist, who sentenced him to life in prison.

After long legal processes, Rolling was incarcerated in Florida State Prison.

Seated in his cell at the prison in Starke, Florida, in June 1992, Danny Rolling pleaded not guilty to the five student murders in Gainesville.

In September Circuit Judge Stan R. Morris set a trial date for Rolling of September 1, 1993, a year ahead. He was charged with five counts of first-degree murder, three counts of sexual battery and three counts of armed robbery.

In the following months both sides prepared for the court date. The media paid little attention to the upcoming trial, until one newspaper printed an exclusive story.

A reporter wrote of an interview he obtained with Bobby

Lewis, a convicted murderer serving a life term. Lewis said he became a prison buddy of Danny Rolling's, who confided in him that he killed a woman, her father, and her nephew in Shreveport. Rolling said he stalked the woman and bragged that he was never charged with those three murders.

Lewis said that Danny Rolling also admitted to him that he killed the five students in Gainesville as part of a vendetta against those who had abused him since his childhood, especially his father and his ex-wife. Rolling married at the age of twenty, but the union ended in divorce after three years. Lewis said the ex-wife would not let Danny see his daughter after the divorce, which embittered him.

Lewis said Rolling told him that he devised his plan while he was incarcerated at Mississippi State Prison serving a sentence for armed robberies. Rolling's plan was to kill one person for each of the eight years that he spent behind bars.

Danny told Bobby Lewis all the gory details of the Gainesville murders.

Lewis said the killing rampage began on August 24 at 3:00 A.M. when Danny Rolling, dressed in a black ninja suit and wearing a ski mask, pried open a door to apartment 113 and stood over Christina Powell, who was sleeping on a downstairs couch. He left Powell and tiptoed upstairs, where he stabbed and killed Sonja Larson. Returning downstairs, Rolling taped Christina's hands and feet, cut off all her clothes and forced her to perform oral sex on him. At the conclusion he raped her and stabbed her in the back while uttering, "Take the pain. . . . Take the pain."

Lewis said that Rolling then calmly walked into the apartment kitchen and ate an apple and a banana from the refrigerator.

Lewis stated that late the next day, August 25, Rolling went to Christa Hoyt's duplex. He spied on her as she dried herself after stepping out of the shower. Later, he broke through a sliding door with a screwdriver and lay in wait, shocking Hoyt as she returned from a racquetball game about 10:00 P.M.

Rolling subdued Christa, taped her mouth and hands, cut off her clothes, sexually fondled her, then gutted open her torso. He cut off her head and displayed it on a bookshelf. Finally he arranged her nude body in a sexual pose.

Rolling returned to his nearby campsite, where he discovered that his wallet was missing. He returned to Hoyt's apartment, searching for it. Unsuccessful, he called 911 and reported his loss, using the name of Kennedy.

On August 27 Rolling assaulted Manuel Taboada at his Gatewood apartment. He stabbed Taboada repeatedly, but the young UF student, a strong former football star, fought back. They struggled until both fell to the floor, where Taboada bled to death.

Tracey Paules, Taboada's friend and neighbor, in an adjacent apartment, heard the commotion and investigated only to see him collapsed from the stabbing. Terrified, she turned, ran back to her apartment and locked the door. But Rolling smashed it open and grabbed her. He duct-taped her mouth and hands, raped and stabbed her several times with a replica of a U.S. Marine Corps KA-BAR knife. He dragged her dead body to the hallway, where he wiped her face clean with a washcloth, then raped her a second time.

At the opening of Danny Rolling's murder trial in Orange County, in a change of venue, on Tuesday, February 15, 1994, Public Defender Rick Parker stunned the assemblage with his announcement that his client, Danny Rolling, pleaded guilty to all counts of murder and all other charges as well.

Subsequently in a Gainesville court on Monday, March 7, 1994, the jury met again, this time to determine the sentence for Rolling.

Photographs of the murdered, mutilated and violated victims were shown to the jury in graphic detail, producing gasps of disbelief.

State Attorney Rod Smith described what the killer had done to his young victims and demanded the death penalty for the drifter, stating there was no other course of action that they could recommend.

On Thursday, March 24, the twelve-member jury deliberated five hours, voting unanimously for the death penalty.

In the final accounting, bringing Danny Rolling to justice cost the taxpayers of Florida in excess of $6 million.

Jim Larson told the Orange County investigators some of the effects of the tragedy. "Carla was so affected by Sonja's death that she instigated a safety program. She bought a rottweiler dog for protection. She never drove without locking her car doors; she insisted on the installation of a home security system. She avoided strangers. No one took more safety precautions than Carla after the murders.

"Our wedding date was set when this happened and we decided to postpone it. But family members and friends insisted that Sonja would not want us to delay the wedding we planned for a long time."

Tears rising in the corner of his eyes, Jim went on. "It was so soon after Sonja's funeral, but some of her friends wanted her to share in the joy of our marriage, so a group of them came to the ceremony for her."

The lawmen were silent, not knowing what to say.

Larson continued his explanation. "So you see, gentlemen, why our whole family, especially Carla, was so supercautious."

Weir answered, "We had no idea. Of course we knew about that case. But we didn't make the connection." Weir walked over to Jim Larson and extended his hand. "I want to express our sympathy to you."

"Thank you," Jim Larson said softly.

Deputy Woodard looked at Larson and thought, *I'm looking at Jim Larson, not as an officer of the law, but almost as a friend in my sympathy. I feel close to him.*

Detective Weir turned to his partner. "I think we're about done here, don't you?"

Linnert nodded. "Yes, I think so."

The lawmen knew that the investigation activity was already started at the Disney site and were anxious to get out there.

Weir explained, "We have to get going. But be assured, Mr. Larson, we're giving this investigation top priority. We'll get back to you with any developments."

Larson nodded gratefully. "Thank you, Detectives, for whatever you can do. I'll be waiting to hear from you."

The lawmen left the Larson home. As they approached their parked cars, Weir remarked, "Holy jeez, I sure as hell never expected to hear anything like that!"

"Neither did I," Linnert agreed. "I was just stunned when he told that story."

Like any seasoned homicide investigators, the detectives each developed a certain level of cynicism and jaded emotions. But they were both shaken by what Jim Larson had told them. Certainly they were familiar with the case, but they hadn't made the connection of Jim Larson to one of the victims.

"You never know what to expect," Weir mused, shaking his head. "Maybe that explains why he seemed to be acting strange. I had a feeling he was hiding something."

"Yeah, me too. Of course we always look at the spouse first in these kinds of cases."

"True." Weir paused, then added, "We'll still have to check out his whereabouts today."

"Right."

The detectives got into their separate vehicles and drove off to the Disney World area. Deputy Woodard returned to his regular duties.

CHAPTER 3

Upon their arrival at the building site of the Centex Rooney project, Weir and Linnert were met by company workers and several of the sheriff's department personnel.

With a small group of three or four sheriff's members guiding them, they walked through the area, observing the terrain. They were dismayed by the vast overgrown surroundings, the roadways, the narrow almost hidden paths and the small lakes and ponds in the section. A massive search would be arduous through all that undeveloped wild property.

The search was already in progress with sheriff's men and Centex Rooney employees swarming over the area, armed with flashlights. It was now early morning, dark and not conducive to their work, but the men were determined.

Cam Weir and John Linnert talked briefly, summarizing what they saw and learned.

"We have to assume that Carla Larson didn't leave voluntarily. There's the possibility she was snatched for ransom, but that doesn't seem likely. The Larsons have good jobs, but they don't seem to be rolling in dough. So what does that leave? I don't like this. I have a really bad feeling about it. And the more time that passes, the more uneasy I get," Weir said.

Linnert nodded. "I feel the same way. She's been gone too long for it to be something simple. The search will go on all night, and it will be light in a few hours, so that will help. Maybe we'll get lucky."

After the investigation began, Deputy Tom Woodard returned to the Larson home. Beyond his official duty Tom Woodard was concerned for the man, his missing wife and his daughter.

The deputy was struck by the tragic case into which he was drawn. He thought, *How could something like this happen to a family more than once? What are the odds on that? They must be astronomical. The Larsons seem like such a nice family and certainly don't deserve anything like this. But then, who does?*

The Larson house was now the focus of the College Park neighborhood with coworkers, friends, nearby residents and acquaintances crowding into the home. All were concerned for Carla and Jim.

When the crowd thinned, Deputy Woodard took Jim Larson's arm and suggested that he try to get some sleep. "You've got to be strong for Jessica."

Long before the sun broke across Orlando, Cam Weir and John Linnert were headed to the Publix market in Kissimmee, the site of Carla's last known whereabouts.

In the car traveling along the major highways toward the store, the two men noted the growth and development of the area.

"I haven't been out this way in a while," Linnert commented. "I can't believe what's happened here. And so fast. This used to be all orange groves and cow pastures. Now look at it."

"Yeah," Weir agreed. "At the rate it's growing, the town of Kissimmee and the city of Orlando will just merge into one huge metropolis. Not many cattle ranches left out here anymore. Newcomers can't believe that Kissimmee was once a 'cow town,' the cattle capital of Florida."

"Well, the land became too valuable. There's housing developments everywhere. But that's not as bad as the rest, wall-to-wall motels and dozens of tourist attractions side by side. Hundreds of new businesses to support them. All of it as a result of one man's dream and ambition—Walt Disney."

Weir added, "Walt's probably spinning in his grave. They're just the kind of places he hated, the kind that spring up around his theme parks. He said that's why he bought so much land here for protection—thousands of acres—and it still happened."

"Plus all the crooks and scam artists that come with it," Linnert grumbled.

"Well, look at it this way, John. It keeps us busy."

When they arrived at the Publix market, they carefully examined the area around the building, the large parking lot and its busy surrounds. At the conclusion they drove back to the Centex Rooney building sites.

Cameron Weir, now designated the command officer in charge of the investigation (he and Linnert shared that position equally, changing every Friday), called the OCSD people together.

"Fellows, we have a major job here," he stated. "What we have to do first is go over everything that we know." He ticked off on his fingers. "We know our missing person Carla Larson drove off from work in her white Ford Explorer. We know that it was just minutes after noon. We know she went to the Publix market. We also know that a vehicle similar to hers was seen later that afternoon driven by a man. What we don't know at this time is what happened to her after she left the store. And we don't know where Carla Larson is now. That's the big question facing us. That's the big question we have to answer. And time is not on our side."

Linnert told the group, "So far we have a helicopter searching the area and we're sending in special K-9s as well as cadaver dogs. We're also setting up ground unit specialists and more search parties to comb all of this area, which will be pretty hard going. You can see how thick the scrub is all through here. The search began just north of the Osceola Parkway and I-4 intersection near the Publix market, which is where Mrs. Larson was last seen, and fans out. Okay, let's get to it."

Weir and Linnert had been told that Dora Landscaping worker Milton Johnson had some information that might be helpful to the investigation. The detectives met Johnson at the wooded area off Osceola Parkway.

"A group of us working out here yesterday stopped for lunch." He referred to his watch. "It was just twelve-forty, I remember." Johnson looked over at the parkway and turned toward I-4, fixing the location precisely into his account. "We frequently eat lunch by that little pond"—he pointed to a small body of water—"just east of the dirt path running into the woods." Johnson explained how the path forked and then stretched out two ways, to the east and to the west. He stated that while they were eating their lunch, one of the fellows, Lavon Brown, pointed out a white Ford Explorer going past them. It went on toward a drainage canal at the far eastern end of the path.

Linnert asked, "Did you see the driver? Can you tell us what the driver looked like?"

"Hmmm. He had dark hair; he was a white man."

"Was he alone?"

"I didn't see anyone with him. It didn't take him very long until he was speeding back in the other direction. I didn't pay much attention to him. I just thought it was a Disney security vehicle."

He said his supervisor, Barry O'Hearne, arrived with fellow employees David Maderano and Francisco Morales and they ate lunch together.

"Anything else?"

"Yeah, David Maderano and I started walking the path back to the Osceola Parkway, picking up discarded soft-drink cans, when the car came out of the woods from the west side of the fork traveling south toward us, traveling twenty to twenty-five miles per hour, which seemed fast for the driving conditions."

Trying to provide an accurate picture, Milton Johnson explained, "I was on the east side of the path and Maderano was walking on the west when the vehicle raced between us, going like a bat out of hell. I turned my head and this car was right over by me and I got a better look at the driver. He was in his mid-thirties, medium build, maybe one seventy-five to one hundred eighty pounds. He had dark hair and a fuzzy mustache and he was wearing those aviator-style sunglasses."

"That's great," Linnert encouraged.

"I can tell you something about that car. It was a Ford Explorer with gray trim around its bottom edge and it had lightly tinted windows and factory 'mag' wheels." Shaking his head, Milton Johnson repeated, "The guy was driving the car too damn fast."

"Mr. Johnson, we're going to put you in touch with our department artist and you can give him the description of the driver so he can make a drawing. You've been very helpful," Linnert stated.

The detectives interviewed David Maderano and Lavon Brown, who told the detectives that they had seen the white Ford Explorer, which they described with gray or silver trim around the bottom of the body. But they were not able to provide a physical description of the driver.

The two detectives interviewed David Gust, a building superintendent at Centex Rooney, also David Lewis and a number of other Centex Rooney employees, all who saw a man driving the Ford Explorer out of the woods that day around lunchtime.

Weir and Linnert also talked with Barry O'Hearne, project manager for the Dora Landscaping team. He told the officers that he saw the vehicle from approximately seventy feet away heading back to the main fork of the path. He estimated that it was traveling at thirty-five to forty miles an hour. O'Hearne caught a glimpse of the driver and described him as a white male with a mustache, wearing sunglasses, with dark hair pushed up.

In a discussion at the department crime scene office, the investigators decided that the original receipt that Carla Larson signed at the Publix market, rather than the copy they were given, could become a piece of evidence as the case expanded.

"Carl," Weir told Sergeant Carl Head, one of the key members of the department's crime scene unit, "we need to confirm that Carla Larson was at the Publix market and made some food purchases."

Head, whose specialty is evidence, anticipated. "You want me to go to the Publix and get something for your file on this case."

"Right. We've already got a copy of her credit card receipt, but we need the original. They have been most cooperative and I'm sure that they'll help you."

"No problem. I'm on my way."

At the huge supermarket Head met with the assistant manager of the store and explained his mission.

"It would be helpful to the case if we could have the original receipt with Carla Larson's signature on it for the evidence file."

"Well, I'll have to go back into our records and root it out. It may take some time, but I'll do it now if you want to wait."

"That would be fine."

In short order the assistant manager produced the receipt and gave it to Detective Head.

Back at headquarters Carl called Detective Weir and told him that his trip was successful. Weir asked Head to deliver the receipt to Crime Scene Detective Ron Weyland, who added it to the growing evidence file.

Meanwhile, Detective David Callin went to the Home Depot building supplies store and met with one of the office personnel.

Callin asked to check the work schedule of James Larson on June 10. The records verified that Larson clocked in to work at 6:00 A.M. and checked out at 3:03 P.M. It was noted that he took a break at 9:41 A.M. through 10:40 A.M. Callin obtained a copy of the time sheet.

Later that afternoon, Detective Linnert conferred with Weir and reported his findings. "I checked the Visa Bank of America credit card and also the Discover card in the Larsons' names. There was no new activity reported on either card. I had the accounts flagged and the companies will notify us of any subsequent use of either of the two credit cards."

"That's good. Callin got Larson's work schedule for yesterday and it checks out. But I'd like him to take a lie detector test."

"Do you think he will?"

"I don't know. We'll ask."

Weir phoned Jim Larson and asked if he would take a lie detector test.

"Sure, any time," he agreed.

"Good. I'll set it up and get back to you."

"Fine. I'll wait to hear from you."

Weir contacted polygraph examiner Richard Keifer and arranged for him to administer the test, then called Larson and asked him to come to headquarters, where it would be done.

At the conclusion of the examination, Richard Keifer advised Weir and Linnert that James Larson passed the examination, showing no signs of deception.

When the investigating detectives received the report, Weir told Linnert, "Keifer passed Larson with flying colors. He's in the clear."

"I'm glad."

"Yeah, so am I. Poor guy's had enough bad luck."

Weir and Linnert continued their investigation with an interview with John Ricker, a Centex Rooney Company employee.

Ricker worked with Carla Larson for five years. Both were with the building company in Atlanta, where Centex Rooney had an assignment under construction, and both happily accepted the opportunity to move on with the company when the project at Walt Disney World in Orlando became a possibility. They moved in December 1995 and began work on the Coronado Springs Resort at Disney.

Weir asked Ricker, "Did Carla Larson have any problems when she worked with you, either here or in Atlanta?"

"No, none, not at all. Carla is one of the most dependable persons you'd ever meet. No, she had no problems; she is always very conscientious about everything, especially her work."

"What do you remember about yesterday, whatever you can recall?"

"Well, like the other guys, we were all taking our lunch break. I was with Ray Walby and Freddie Kitchens. We all work together. We left the job in Ray's company truck and drove east on Osceola Parkway. As we were driving, we saw Carla, who was also driving along the parkway, heading in the same direction. She was driving her white Ford Explorer. When she got to International Drive, she turned right, heading south toward 192. She was alone; no one with her," he emphasized. "She gave us a big smile and waved as we passed."

"Is there anything else that you can recall?" Linnert asked.

Ricker replied, "I sure as hell was shocked when I heard around six-thirty that she was missing. I was stunned. I had just come out of a meeting and returned to the office when I heard secretaries calling hospitals, looking for Carla."

With a mournful expression on his face, John Ricker said

that he learned from some of the other Centex Rooney people that Carla never returned from lunch. "Some of the guys
went out and spoke to the Publix manager. Ray Walby and I
went out to check the wooded area behind the market."

Weir and Linnert concluded the session and returned to
their vehicle.

"Are we making any progress, do you think?" Linnert
asked.

"Well, I think we're headed in the right direction. But
we'll have to dig deeper. We still don't know what happened
to Mrs. Larson after she left the grocery store. And the clock
is ticking."

Later that afternoon, the detectives interviewed Centex
Rooney employees Ray Walby and Freddie Kitchens, who
confirmed John Ricker's account of seeing Carla shortly before noon in her vehicle, going to lunch.

Cindy Garris at the Centex Rooney construction trailers
was eager to talk to the detectives. "I've known Carla for
about a year and a half. And we're good friends. She is always so considerate," Garris volunteered. "Only yesterday
Carla came up to Deborah Brooks and me at the front desk
and told us that she was going out to lunch. She asked if she
could bring anything back for us. We thanked her but told
her that we were going out, too. I asked where she was going
and she said to Goodings supermarket. We told her to go to
the Publix. It's closer. And we gave her directions because
she had never been there." Cindy looked away as she thought
about the suggestion that they made to Carla.

Aware that Publix was reportedly the last sighting of
Carla, Linnert's lips tightened. He asked, "Anything else?"

"Well, at about twelve-fifty Deborah and I left for lunch
taking the same route that Carla would have if she followed
our directions. We didn't see any sign of her or her vehicle."

Cindy shifted her eyes from one detective to the other.

"About two-thirty, long after we returned from lunch, Deborah came up and said, 'Everybody's looking for Carla.' 'What do you mean?' I asked her.

"She said that several different people had been looking for Carla and they couldn't find her. Nobody seemed to know anything about her. Deborah said that they tried to reach her by radio, thinking that she might be out in the field."

Weir was alerted. "What do you mean, about the radio?"

"Oh, we maintain contact with workers in the field by radio. Deborah said that Carla never responded to the radio attempt. We became concerned but thought maybe she had been delayed. We decided to wait to see if she turned up for her three o'clock meeting."

Cindy explained, "Carla isn't like that; she would not miss a meeting. She just wouldn't. I couldn't get Carla Ann off my mind. It didn't make sense. Deborah and I couldn't just sit there and do nothing. We talked about what we could do and decided to call Carla's husband and find out if she was at home or if he knew where she might be. But we didn't want to worry him unduly."

"Did you talk to Mr. Larson?"

"Oh, yes, Deborah did. She asked him if Carla was at home or if he knew where she was, and he told her that as far as he knew, she was at work. Deborah asked if Carla had, like, a doctor's appointment that she might have kept. He said that he didn't know of any appointments."

Cindy said that she and Deborah were more disturbed after her talk with Larson. "We thought that there had to be something really serious if Jim Larson didn't know anything more than we did."

Cindy brushed back her hair and continued. "We were scared; we sat staring at each other. We were at a loss as to what we should do . . . what we could do. Finally I suggested to Deborah that it might be a good idea for us to go out to the parking lots of Publix and maybe Goodings, too, to see if we could find out something. So we drove over to both places, but it was fruitless."

Weir asked, "One final thing. Can you give us a description of Carla as you normally saw her? You know, how she dressed, anything that might take special attention."

"Well, she's very pretty with long blond hair, which she wears in a braid. The last time I saw her, she was wearing a red sleeveless shirt with a rounded collar. She usually comes to work in blue jeans. Gap jeans. She also wears brown work boots; they are just a normal part of her."

Cindy thought a moment and then added, "Carla always wears nice jewelry, like her diamond stud earrings. And her diamond engagement and wedding rings, of course. Also she always wears her Centex Rooney five-year pendant on a chain; she is very proud of that. She usually carries a brown purse, which I'm sure she had with her when she went to lunch."

The detectives made notes and absorbed the information. Weir wanted to discuss the jewelry with Linnert when they were alone, but as they were leaving the telephone rang. Cindy answered and called to Detective Weir, "Sir, there's a call for you. You can take it here."

"Thank you." He said into the phone, "Detective Weir."

"Detective," Jim Larson began, "I've been wondering if you found out anything yet."

"Mr. Larson," Weir explained gently, "we're doing everything that we can. We are investigating and following through on everything we find. But so far we haven't found your wife."

"Detective Weir," Jim said in an apologetic tone, "I don't mean to put any pressure on you. I'm sure you understand our concern. I wouldn't have called, but my mother is here and so are Carla's parents. They drove up from Pompano Beach and they are naturally anxious, as I am, to know if there has been any progress in your investigation." Larson paused. "Have you learned anything about Carla's disappearance?"

"Mr. Larson, I understand what you're going through and I am sympathetic," Weir answered. "Let me assure you that we are entirely devoted to finding your wife." He explained, "Solving crimes requires patience. We just keep digging until we find the answers. I've been in criminal investigation for fourteen years, and I can tell you that there is no quick way to solve a complicated case like this one—"

"Detective Weir," Larson interrupted, "I didn't call you to make any problems for you or to question your handling of the investigation. It's just that our whole family is so concerned, I just thought I would check with you to see if you have learned anything yet."

"I certainly understand," Weir told the distraught husband. "And when we find some answers, you certainly will be told. We won't hold back on you in any way."

"Thank you. There's one more thing. I've been wondering about your men searching the area and I would like to be out there helping them, if it's all right with you."

Cam thought about this request. *It might be a good thing for him to be out here. Then he can see what an intense job we're doing, that no one is just sitting around eating doughnuts and talking about the weather. He'll see for himself what's going on. And maybe it will help him if he feels he is participating in the search.*

"Mr. Larson, if you'd like to do that, I have no objections."

"Thank you, sir."

CHAPTER 4

Detectives Cameron Weir and John Linnert sat with several other sheriff's department detectives and special investigators. Their discussion centered on the lack of progress in finding Carla Ann Larson.

"To bring you all up to speed," Weir said, "so far all our search efforts have resulted in nothing." He shook his head in disappointment. "No trace of her or her vehicle. The helicopter, the dogs, the foot search, all negative. It's as though Carla Larson disappeared into thin air. And we know that's not possible. Somewhere out there are the answers we need. We're just going to have to dig deeper for some leads."

Linnert took over. "We also have divers exploring several lakes, ponds, retaining pools and canals on the Disney lands. And we're fine combing the whole area. We're bound to find something. But we'd better do it soon. It's been too long already."

The gathered personnel understood the urgency and all departed with renewed determination to find some answers. Weir and Linnert returned to the Disney site to oversee the search.

The hours passed slowly and the weary searchers, on foot and in vehicles, who worked in shifts throughout the night—

shining their flashlights through the woods, examining the brush, each bush and tree—were exhausted. They rested only a few hours, fortified themselves with strong coffee and sandwiches, and returned to their arduous task. Daylight made the search easier, but there was so much territory to cover.

As the day progressed, the reports on all of their efforts began coming back to the detectives. They were negative. No sign of the missing woman. No sign of her automobile.

Weir looked at Linnert, shook his head and muttered one word, "Nothing."

While Weir and Linnert pumped up the spirits of the investigative personnel, as time passed with no results, their apprehension grew. Their hopes of finding Carla safe were dwindling.

Linnert asked, "Have you considered the possibility that maybe Carla Larson isn't out there? She may be long gone."

"Of course I have. But I keep coming back to the question, why was that white vehicle, possibly hers, seen out there in the woods? And with a man driving it. I can't get past that, and my gut tells me we should keep looking in this area."

On Thursday, June 12, Deputy Heather Mason sat facing the stack of reports at her desk at OCSD headquarters. She looked at the clock, realizing that the afternoon was practically over and it would soon be time to go home. Her phone rang, and when she answered, she was told to report without delay to a location near the Coronado Springs Resort/Centex Rooney work site.

Racing to the designated location, the deputy wondered, *Why have I been called out? That's where the search is going on for Carla Larson. The detectives are out there handling that. Why the call to headquarters?*

When she arrived at the area, Deputy Mason learned the shocking details of a discovery that was made on the Disney properties. "I can't believe this," she muttered. Mason immediately called dispatch. "Notify Detectives Weir and Linnert. Tell them to get out to the Centex Rooney building site ASAP. Tell them it's urgent!" She repeated, "It's urgent!"

The detective team immediately responded and, upon their arrival, Deputy Mason greeted them. Her face was ashen and she was obviously agitated.

Concerned, Weir asked, "What's up? What's so urgent?"

Mason indicated several Centex Rooney employees grouped together. She pointed to one, explaining, "Mr. Munson can tell you more than I can."

The puzzled detectives turned to the man for clarification.

"We found a body," came the stark statement.

The cool early-evening air only partially explained the chill that gripped both detectives. "A body? Where?" Linnert asked, stunned. Yet, in his mind it was what he had expected and dreaded.

Weir sighed, turned his face toward the sky, then focused on the man and requested, "Can you take us there?"

"Of course," assured Michael Munson.

In the group Weir and Linnert recognized John Ricker, one of the men whom they had met the previous day. Ricker walked over to Weir, held out his hand and said sadly, "This is probably the break you were looking for, and not wanting to find."

There was something unsettling in Ricker's remark; the detectives nodded.

Ricker, along with Munson, led the pack like a cluster of bear hunters in the foothills of the Rockies. They slowly wove their way through the scrub brush that they had trudged through for practically the entire preceding day and night, as well as all day today. It was difficult struggling through the thick underbrush and wild untamed growth.

Finally the leaders stopped abruptly. Ricker pointed wordlessly to a swatch on the ground. Wedged into dried, burned palmetto debris lay a nude body, curled up and partially covered with a faded discolored blue towel. A piece of torn tattered carpet stretched partially across the remains of a decomposing human being, much of which was already devoured by the bugs, worms and other insects in a feeding frenzy.

"Holy jeez," Weir whispered. He brushed his hand across his forehead and exchanged horrified glances with Linnert.

This was what they dreaded. As experienced investigators, they expected the worst but always hoped that it would not occur.

The officers and personnel who came with the men stood quietly in shocked silence.

"It appears to be a white female body, young. But it's in such bad shape we can't assume that it's Carla Larson," Weir stated in a careful tone. "We can't even identify her by the clothing. Where are her clothes? Let's get some help out here and have this location cordoned off. We need this place secured and protected."

If this body turned out to be Carla Larson—and in his gut Weir knew that it was—then this was no longer a missing-person case but murder. Now it was vital to see that nothing contaminated the area.

"Notify the ME. We need him here right now," Linnert directed.

Almost magically, Jim Larson appeared with Carla's rottweiler at the site. With a dismayed, horrified expression, he looked at the battered remains of the unrecognizable female. Overcome by the sight of the body, he stood frozen, his eyes flooded with tears, until one of the sheriff's officers gently took Larson's arm and led him away.

While awaiting the technical and medical people, Weir and Linnert moved off to the side to question Ricker and Munson about their exploration of the area in which they found the body.

Ricker began, "Mike and I have been on this search with no stop for, I guess, most of two full days." His eyes showed his weariness. "We started about five P.M. on Tuesday when we first heard Carla was missing. First we went through that overgrown mess behind Publix at 192 and International Drive. Then we went through the section west of Osceola Parkway, the place where the white car was seen."

Ricker took a deep breath. "We were part of the search party that was briefed about where the vehicle was seen leaving the woods. Because of that information Mike and I decided to recheck the area off Osceola Parkway where it was sighted. We followed the dirt path off the parkway and searched the south section of the fork to the canal. We went over the trails, through the woods, back to the highways over and over again, just looking for something, anything. We were pretty worn out and were tempted to give up and go home." He recalled conversations he had with Munson and their deep regard for the young engineer. "But we work with Carla and we think very highly of her and we sure didn't want to give up on the search if there was any chance at all for success." He added sadly, "But we didn't realize what success meant."

"So you guys kept on with the search?"

"Yes. We just didn't want to give up. There was something in both of us that kept urging, 'Stay with this' and we just couldn't give up—no matter what. We went deeper into the woods just combing, combing through the brush. Off and on there were others who were also scouring through the woods, fellow workers at Centex Rooney, various persons from the sheriff's department, and even Jim Larson. We watched Jim, poor forlorn guy. He just groped along silently with Carla's rottweiler; he looked so troubled. No one really knew what to say to him." He paused and shook his head. "What can you say to the guy at a time like this? Then we met a fellow, Tommy Sparks, who works for Disney security and we talked with him, explaining what we were doing. He said that the other day, I guess he meant June tenth, he was surprised to see a white vehicle parked amidst the trees and bushes back behind a pond. He pointed out very specifically where he had seen the white vehicle.

"Mike and I figured that there might be something to that, so we walked around that section. Pretty soon we got an uneasy feeling. There was something in the air and then it became really pungent. It was a foul odor and was overpowering. I said, 'What's that awful stink?' I couldn't remember ever smelling anything that bad. And Mike said, 'Something's dead.' And I said facetiously, 'Or someone.' He looked at me and I was afraid to think what was in his mind. I didn't want to project or speculate in my own mind." He shook his head.

"We couldn't locate where it was coming from, so Mike lit his lighter. I thought that was a pretty smart thing to do. He watched the flame, judging the direction from which the wind was blowing, carrying that foul smell. Mike motioned to me, indicating the wind course. We turned and followed the flicker for about twenty feet, until we came to a huge spread-out palmetto bush. We stopped and I said to Mike, 'You go around that side and I'll circle around the opposite way.' And that did it."

Ricker's expression changed as he recalled their shock at what they saw on the other side of the brambly brush. "I couldn't believe it. I didn't want to believe it. But there it was, the body. Mike came up and stood beside me. He couldn't speak. And I didn't know what to say. It was like a nightmare where you couldn't move or talk or do anything. It was one of those moments when you wished that you could magically be somewhere else."

Munson said, "I never saw anything like it in my life. I could see that the body was naked and there was an old raggedy blue towel thrown over her. Her hair was over her shoulder and she lay there facedown." He stopped and swallowed. "We just couldn't stay there; we had to get away."

"That's when you called us?" Weir asked.

"No," John Ricker corrected, "we were so upset that we rushed back to our car and sped off to our office." His face reflected the horror he felt with their discovery. "Your headquarters was then called and notified about our discovery."

By this time a horde of OCSD personnel spread out over

the critical section, securing it with the yellow stretch tapes restricting it to authorized officials only.

Shortly after 11:00 P.M., medical examiners Dr. Shashi Gore (an ME with long experience of seeing bodies of every size, color and origin in every conceivable condition) and Dr. Max Blue arrived, along with their investigator, Dean Smith.

With the aid of improvised lighting provided by the Orange County Fire Department, ME Gore examined the body. The doctor professionally noted that the white female body had blond hair and there were signs of marbling on the stomach and abdomen.

With a grim expression, Dr. Gore studied the destructive injuries that the victim suffered. Her face, her eyes and her head were so shatteringly beaten that this woman was truly unrecognizable. Her neck showed severe bruise markings that indicated extreme violence; it was discolored, battered brown and blotched. There were numerous bruises and marks of brutality indicating severe attack and molestation in sundry places of her body. Although there were strong suspicions, it was not conclusive that she was raped.

Dr. Gore, extremely cautious and determined to avoid any errors, carefully refrained from any definite pronouncements as to the injuries or the cause of death. He commented sorrowfully, "Not a pretty sight. She took some terrible beating in her losing fight for life."

Weir asked, "Can you venture the cause of death?"

Shashi Gore stared through his black horn-rimmed glasses. "Cam, what I tell you now is only a projection, not an official judgment. It looks like her killer worked on her neck to cut off her breathing. Strangulation is how I see it now, but I don't want to make that official until we can make a thorough examination. And I'm afraid," he said, "that the ID will have to be made through dental records."

Watch Commander Eric Viehman notified Deputy Tom Woodard and directed him to the Larson residence with the dreaded news about the female body.

"There is a strong possibility that this might be the missing Carla Larson," he advised Woodard. "I hate to put this on you, but since you already have rapport with the family, we thought you should be the one to tell them."

But when Woodard arrived at the Larson home, a swarm of news media personalities were all around and the family had already heard the disheartening report.

In minutes Jim Larson, with tears streaming down his cheeks, entered his home. "He was very upset," Woodard observed. "And as he stood rigid before his family, he unhesitatingly told them, 'It's Carla.' He was devastated by his own words."

Larson said that he had seen the body in its frightening condition, bruised, battered beyond belief, wrapped in the dog's blanket he recognized, taken from the back of Carla's Explorer. As he spoke, tears rolled from his eyes.

Recalling the scene later, Deputy Woodard said, "Jim knew it was Carla. The family, sharing the distress and tragedy with him, was upset. They were stoically maintaining composure as well as they could. I guess that they already pretty much gave up hope since Carla was missing too long. I stayed for another hour or more trying to do what I could to console Jim, his family and friends."

Woodard recalled that Jim made an attempt to be strong, but it was an effort. He told Tom softly, "She was my whole world; I don't know what I'll do."

The two mothers shared their tragic bond. "If you don't have family supporting you, I don't know how you could go on," Ada Larson said. She had lost her daughter, Sonja, in the University of Florida killings. "We have to support Jim and each other now. It's like the light of my life is gone. What else can they do to me? They've taken the gut out of me already. I don't think people who haven't gone through this can understand."

"She was just such a beautiful child," Phyllis Thomas mourned. "How could this happen to her?"

Deputy Woodard recalled, "It hit me pretty hard, even

though I became resigned to the fact that she probably wouldn't be found alive. I just felt it was awful that someone took an innocent life of a person who showed so much future promise as a wife, mother and all-around good person. I never met Carla Larson, but I felt that I knew her. I saw all the family photos and heard stories told by her family of what a good daughter, wife, mother and friend she was."

His voice softening, this man, whose career dealt with some pretty low individuals, confessed later, "I was planning to attend the memorial service, but I just couldn't bring myself to go."

CHAPTER 5

In the area of the body discovery, Crime Scene Detective Ron Weyland set up a command post with several units, in order to collect all relevant evidence.

"Hey, wait a minute," Weyland asked as a thought occurred. "Are we in Orange County or Osceola County?"

All activity stopped abruptly. Various members of the department expressed their opinions and comments about this unexpected consideration. Within which county's boundaries was the body discovered? With that determination rested jurisdiction.

"We can't do anything until that is established," Weir stated.

In a meeting of officials from both counties, maps were consulted and the opinions of authorities sought.

In addition, an OCSD helicopter, piloted by Sergeant Ralph Glover, flew over the specified land, fixing the coordinates to establish the precise plot where the body was found.

"Come on, fellows, make up your minds," Weir grumbled at the delay.

In a final judgment it was concluded that the dead body lay inside the boundaries of Orange County.

Weir received the news with relief. "Finally. Okay, let's get moving," he ordered.

With jurisdiction established, Dr. Gore ordered the body removed to the morgue for his full examination and autopsy. Also he would pursue and establish identification.

"As soon as possible, Doc?" Weir cajoled.

"Yes, Cam, we'll get right on it," Gore said.

With some measure of order established, Weir exchanged views with Linnert. "I don't want to jump to a conclusion, and we're never supposed to assume a goddamn thing, but— it's a pretty sure bet that it's Carla Larson."

Weir thought about Jim Larson, wondering how he was taking the latest development. Weir also was not ready to let go of the lingering doubts he still had about this husband. The detective recalled that too frequently cases had unexpected twists. He hoped there wouldn't be any in this one.

Linnert sighed. "If the ID has to come from dental comparison, we'll have to wait to know for sure. But the indications are pretty strong that you're right."

"Either way, the investigation continues," Weir assured him.

In the morning Detective Ron Weyland and others from his crime scene unit began a zealous reexamination of the discovery scene and its surrounds. They scoured the area, gathering anything that might be evidence, and took black-and-white and color photographs from every conceivable angle, including aerial shots of the entire vicinity. They used divers to search ponds, lakes, barrow pits and canals for Carla's clothing, jewelry, purse, any other items of evidence, possibly even her Ford Explorer.

"We've searched every possible spot, Cam," reported Weyland, "and there's absolutely no trace of Ms. Larson's clothes, her jewelry, her purse or her vehicle."

"Well, we have to conclude that the Explorer, with her things in it, departed the Disney World area," Weir replied. "I guess when all those people saw the vehicle racing onto the parkway, it just kept going. We have APBs out on it, but so far nothing."

"Well, it's still pretty early. Maybe you'll hear something soon."

"What it looks like right now is that some vicious killer evidently snatched this young woman in broad daylight during the noon hour from a busy grocery store parking lot. All she did was go into that store to buy some stuff and she paid for that with her life. At least that's the way it looks right now. If it was a random kidnapping, she was just in the wrong place at the wrong time."

Weyland shrugged. "Happens all the time."

When the mutilated female body was discovered on the Disney properties, the *Orlando Sentinel* wrote a major story, displaying pictures of Carla Ann and her husband. The story carefully stated that this body was "probably" the missing Larson woman. The article quoted Lieutenant Mike Easton of OCSD saying that the body was partly covered with leaves and branches. He did not, however, reveal or describe the brutalized condition of the victim. Easton said she had been dead for forty-eight to seventy-two hours, which time frame fit with the actual disappearance of Carla Larson.

The local and national TV and radio stations carried the story, and the national print media ran articles.

Seated at their desks at department headquarters, Weir and Linnert discussed the media coverage.

"It's staggering, the exposure this case is getting," Linnert remarked.

Weir nodded. "Maybe we'll get a lead on the Explorer."

Weir's phone rang and interrupted them. While his partner conversed, Linnert busied himself with paperwork on his desk, but he saw a surprised expression cross Weir's face.

Weir hung up and looked across at John. "That was a producer for *America's Most Wanted*. They want to do the Larson case for their June twenty-eighth show. Can you believe it?"

"No fooling!" Linnert leaned back in his chair, his arms crossed behind his head. "Wow!"

"I don't know." Weir was dubious. "We can't let it interfere with our investigation. I don't want to make a gross error judgment with a case this important."

Linnert pointed out, "But on the other hand, it could be very helpful. That show generates lots of attention on the cases they present, and they have a great record of success in helping solve some of them."

"Guess you're right. Anyway, they also want someone from the department to be in their studio the night of the broadcast. Neither you nor I can possibly take time from the investigation. We'll have to send somebody else."

"When did you say the show goes on the air?" Linnert asked.

"Saturday night, June twenty-eighth."

"That soon?"

"That's what they said. So what do you think, John?"

"We'll have to send someone really good."

"Any ideas?"

"Let me think about it for a minute." Linnert sat quietly, deep in thought, drumming his fingers on his desk. "I know."

"Who?"

"Tom McCann."

McCann, a 6'2" detective, exuded confidence, experience and capability. He was with the OCSD for twenty-eight years, specializing in homicide for nineteen.

Linnert added, "McCann has a warm, friendly personality. He'll be a great representative for our department."

"Great choice. Let's get him in here and explain what we need."

When McCann arrived at the office, Cameron Weir asked him bluntly, "How'd you like to go to Washington?"

McCann looked at the detective. "The state or the capital?"

"The capital, of course."

McCann studied the detectives, thinking, *What are these guys getting me into?*

Finally he answered, "Okay, I guess. I haven't been there for a few years. But what's this about?"

Linnert said, "Cam and I were discussing who we should send to Washington to represent the department at the broadcast of a major television program."

"Tom," Weir added, *"America's Most Wanted* is going to do the Carla Larson murder case."

"Terrific!" McCann blurted out.

Weir and Linnert smiled at McCann's enthusiasm.

Weir continued, "We had a call—"

"From John Walsh," McCann interrupted. He was familiar with the program.

"No," Weir quickly corrected. "He didn't make the call. It was one of his producers."

"That's terrific," McCann repeated. "That certainly could be helpful to us." As a regular viewer of *America's Most Wanted,* McCann was familiar with the great success the program racked up, with credit for capturing hundreds of profiled fugitives.

Detective Weir continued his speech. "They were following the developments of our investigation and are convinced that this is a major murder case. It has important elements that interest them. First of all, the setting of the crime is Walt Disney World, which has worldwide interest; then the victim is a beautiful young woman engineer. Few women are engineers and this gives it a certain distinction. Also they know about the tie-in to the University of Florida murders by Danny Rolling, so it all adds up to an interesting presentation for them."

McCann asked, "What do you want me to do in Washington?"

Weir leaned back in his chair, pushing away from the desk. "The producers want a representative from our department to be there for the airing of the program, someone to be on hand to answer questions and to assist in whatever they need. John and I can't take the time away from the investigation. So how about it?"

McCann was pleased and his satisfaction was apparent. "Sure. Be glad to. When do I go?"

"The show is scheduled to be aired on Saturday, June twenty-eighth. The producers would like to have you there early that day."

Linnert added, "If there is anything pressing that you have, let us know and we'll work it out."

Tom turned his palms up. "No, no problems. I'm free to make the trip."

"Good," Weir said. "Transportation will have your flight tickets ready for you on Thursday, and you're all set."

McCann asked, "Are there any special instructions? Anything that you want me to do?"

"Nothing that we know of. You've been with the department long enough to know what's expected. Of course, if anything comes up that you feel you need some help from us, don't hesitate to call."

McCann nodded. "Okay, will do." He shook hands with the two detectives, who wished him a great trip, and he left, already thinking of possible suggestions he might make to the producers, should he be asked.

Detective Weir made arrangements for the sheriff's department to cooperate with the producers of *America's Most Wanted* and help in any way needed. They supplied information and guided the crews to the various places in the area that were involved in the case. The department was eager to help the TV people produce an accurate presentation, and they released information, including descriptions of Carla's missing jewelry.

Even before the *America's Most Wanted* TV broadcast, hundreds of responses, tips and reactions came pouring in as a result of the local and national stories, overwhelming the investigators.

Weir said, "Well, John, you got your wish. Now come the follow-ups."

"Yeah. Who said, 'Be careful what you wish for'?" Linnert answered.

The two detectives worked around the clock, dealing with the seemingly endless calls. The callers provided leads, tips and information, including various sightings of the Ford Explorer, all of which they followed through, but with no success.

The composite drawing of the possible suspect made by the department artist from the eyewitnesses' accounts was released and shown in daily and weekly newspapers, as well as broadcast on a number of TV stations.

As a result, a man called a local TV show, *Crime Line,* which asked the public for help in solving crimes by phoning in tips and receiving a reward. Brad Wilson, the caller, surprised the producers of the show, saying, "That drawing is inaccurate."

At his headquarters desk, Detective Weir learned that one of the *Crime Line* operators wanted to speak to him. She said, "A Mr. Brad Wilson of Centex Rooney has some information and is anxious to talk with you."

The two detectives discussed Brad Wilson's call to *Crime Line.*

"He claims that the drawing that's running now is inaccurate?" asked Linnert.

Weir nodded. "That's what he told them at *Crime Line.* If this guy knows something, we have to talk to him."

"Absolutely. I'll make the arrangements."

The detectives arranged to meet with Wilson at work at Centex Rooney and made the trip out to the site on Disney World property.

After introductions Weir stated, "Mr. Wilson, I understand you called *Crime Line* with some information about the artist's drawing being circulated."

"That's right. It's not accurate," he stated in a voice of absolute certainty, and then added, "I can provide the artist with a more detailed drawing to help you catch the guy. I saw the man in the white Explorer and can describe him."

The detectives were impressed with Wilson's confident manner. They learned that he worked with Carla Larson with whom he had a great, friendly relationship. It was evident that he was upset about Carla's fate, and that was the reason he was anxious to pitch in to help.

Weir and Linnert arranged for Wilson to meet with Detective Steve Fusco, the department artist, who would create a new drawing.

After Brad spent time with the artist, Weir and Linnert met with him at the OCSD office in the Cassidy Building.

"Mr. Wilson, how did the drawing session go?" Cam Weir asked.

"I think that it went great. The artist will give you his report. I think he did a super job. The drawing is definitely more accurate and should better help to identify that guy."

"Great. Now I'd appreciate it if you would give us a detailed review of what you witnessed or know," Weir said.

Wilson answered in his clear, confident voice. "It was that day, the tenth of June, and a group of us Centex fellows were returning to the job, you know, the Coronado Springs Resort. It was about one o'clock. I was with Gary Wilson." He smiled and then explained. "My Dad. He works for Centex Rooney, too. Also David Lewis and Dave Gust. We were on Osceola Parkway, going west, crossing the I-4 bridge. That's when we saw this white Ford Explorer coming out of the woods." He emphasized, "I don't think we would have been so observant about the vehicle, but it came racing out of the woods and it struck all of us that the driver belting that car that way was asking for trouble, that he should get a ticket." Brad paused and then said, "It was more than just plain speeding; the conditions of the road were terrible, and to drive that fast under such conditions just made no sense. We all commented about it."

Linnert asked, "About how far away were you from the vehicle?"

Wilson glanced away, his brow furrowed in thought as he figured. "I'd say about one hundred to one hundred fifty feet when we first saw it."

"Did you see or observe anything else of significance at the time?" Weir asked.

"There were two men in green T-shirts, carrying plastic bags, walking on either side of the path where that vehicle was traveling." He added, "I'm pretty sure that the Ford drove between the two of them."

Brad thought before continuing. "I remember very distinctly that we were in the left-hand lane of the parkway and the white car pulled directly up onto the roadway without even stopping. I couldn't believe it. And I thought that man should have his license revoked; that is, of course, if he actually has a license. Anyway, we followed the Explorer from behind, but I didn't take notice of the license tag." Brad then apologized. "You know, it's easy to think of what you should have done after it's over, but at that time we didn't have any reason to make note of the tag. I did see that there was a painted beige trim around the body of the vehicle, on the lower section.

"As both cars were heading westbound, we pulled alongside the Explorer, and that guy behind the wheel looked over at me and I got a good look at him."

"Was he wearing sunglasses?" Linnert asked.

"No, and there was something about his eyes—they were kind of bulgy. I couldn't put my finger on it, but he looked troubled."

"Describe him as best you remember. This is important, so take your time," Weir said.

"I think that I mentioned that he was a white fellow. I could see that he was outdoors quite a lot. He had a heavy tan. I felt that his tan wasn't the kind that a tennis player gets or one that you get on the beach. This guy looked like he got tanned working outdoors.

"His brown hair was sun bleached, too. He had a light mustache and a beard. Getting back to his hair, it struck me as being windblown back onto the top of his head." Brad paused and recalled, "He was wearing a green shirt similar in color to the shirts the two men walking along the path were wearing, but this one looked like it had been out in the sun too long—it was bleached; it didn't have a collar."

"How big was this fellow?" Linnert asked.

"I'd have to take a guess, but I think I'd be safe with one hundred eighty to two hundred pounds." He scratched his head as if to confirm his estimates and added, "He could have been two hundred ten pounds maybe. I'm not too good at guessing weight." He laughed apologetically. "They'd never hire me to guess weights at a carnival."

"You were with your group, your father and who else?"

"David Lewis was driving and my father, Gary Wilson, was riding up front in the passenger seat. Dave Gust was sitting in the left rear passenger seat and I had the right rear passenger seat, the prime seat to see the guy. In my position I had a real opportunity to get a good look at him."

Brad looked at the detectives and said, "After the news about Carla's body being found out there, it seemed logical to me that him coming out of that wooded section where Carla was found—and driving at such a crazy speed—might be something linked to her.

"I couldn't get that guy out of my thoughts. I just had to do something, especially after seeing that inaccurate composite on television. So I called *Crime Line.*"

Brad told the detectives that he insisted to the *Crime Line* person that the drawing presented on TV gave the subject a Hispanic appearance. "And the man I saw at close hand sure as hell was not Hispanic. In fact, outside of his hair, he looked like an average-looking American guy who you would pass on the street.

"His head was drawn too wide, the hair too dark, and when I saw him, he was not wearing any glasses." He also noted that the man had both a mustache and a beard and he felt that his face was more elongated, with a higher forehead.

"He made a hell of an impression on you," John Linnert commented.

"I'll tell you this, that man's face is engraved in my mind. I'll never forget it."

When the new drawing was completed by Detective Steve Fusco, it was distributed to the newspapers and television stations.

CHAPTER 6

On Friday, June 13, Detective Weir received a call from the offices of Dr. Stanley Asensio, a highly regarded forensic odontologist.

Weir waved at his partner and asked, "How superstitious are you, John? Today is Friday the thirteenth."

"Not very. What's up?"

"They want us at Dr. Asensio's office. He's doing the comparison work on our body's teeth with Carla Larson's dental records. Maybe he can make an official ID."

"Let's keep our fingers crossed."

During the drive to the dentist's office, Weir projected, "I don't think that we're in for any surprises. From everything that we know, this ID is simply a formality."

In his private office Dr. Asensio welcomed the two detectives. "Thanks for coming so quickly. I know you've been anxious to hear my findings," he greeted. "I have the identity of the body discovered at Disney World."

"That's good news. What did you come up with?" Weir asked.

"Let me show you." The doctor pointed to a stand on which were displayed several X rays of the dental makeup of the dead subject. The doctor directed their attention to the positive similarities of the structures compared with Carla Larson's dental records, then stated, "These dental records of Carla Larson positively match those of the deceased woman. She is definitely Carla Larson."

It was what the detectives expected. Neither said anything. Both were thinking of Jim Larson and they felt strong sympathy for him.

Dr. Asensio provided the detectives with an official document of identification.

The detectives thanked him for his help and silently drove back to their headquarters. They were relieved to have the positive identification that it was Carla Ann Larson, but saddened by the reality of that knowledge.

In the quiet atmosphere of Orlando's College Park United Methodist Church, more than two hundred relatives, friends and fellow workers of Carla Ann Larson's sat somberly on Monday, June 16, gathered in a memorial service for her.

Mourners wept freely as the church's pastor remembered Carla as a "precious jewel." Jim Larson sat stoically with his one-year-old daughter on his knee. His stepmother, Ada, and Carla's parents, Phyllis and Mert Thomas, sat beside him during the solemn services presented to the grieving gathering.

The pastor intoned, "There is nothing you can say about what happened to her. There is nothing we can do but pray and hope."

Following the formal service, in memory of Carla, friends planted a palm tree next to a huge wooden cross mounted in the yard behind the church. They laid white roses at the base of the graceful tree.

At the conclusion a throng of well-wishers hugged Jim and the members of the family and expressed their sympathy.

Friends established a trust fund for Jessica at a local bank, and Jim Larson asked that donations be made in lieu of flowers: "Carla left me a beautiful gift. I'll try to take the best care of raising her as I can. I hope she grows up smart like her mother."

There was a second memorial service the following day at the Trinity United Methodist Church in Lighthouse Point, near Fort Lauderdale, in the part of Florida where Jim and Carla met and previously lived.

Because Jessica was so young that she would recall very little about her mother, mourners filled notebooks to record memories of Carla for Jessica when she is older.

Two of Carla's close friends eulogized her during the hour-long ceremony. One of them, a friend since she and Carla were seven years old, read from a card that Carla sent her just two weeks ago. The card's theme was the joy of lifelong friendship.

In their continuing investigation Detectives Cameron Weir and John Linnert held regular strategy meetings with several of their fellow officers but also met alone regularly. In these meetings, with no others present, the two lead investigators discussed their progress and their plans, and they exchanged ideas, thoughts and evaluations.

"I don't know," Weir said dejectedly. "We sure seem to be going around in circles. Nothing breaking through, nothing leading us anywhere."

Linnert, equally distressed, agreed. "You know, Cam, we've talked to all those fellows who saw that white Ford Explorer coming out of the woods and racing away. But we questioned them in groups, and I think there was too much unanimity. I mean, they were just too eager to agree with each other."

"What are you driving at, John?"

"Just this. I think it might be productive if we talked to these guys individually. You know, now that they've had more time to think about it, they might very well remember little things that didn't seem important at the time. Sometimes those little bits can yield something substantive."

"It's worth a try. We haven't latched on to anything else

yet," Weir agreed. "You talk to one, I'll talk to one and we can go through that entire group—ten or twelve." He smiled. "Maybe one of them can come through."

The detectives drove out to Centex Rooney on the Disney properties and met with the building superintendent of the company, explaining their idea.

"We'll do anything and everything that we can to help you," the super assured him, and he arranged an area for the two detectives to conduct their meetings.

For the next several hours, Weir and Linnert interviewed the engineers, builders and their assistants, landscapers— anyone who saw Carla Larson on her fateful trip to the Publix market, or later saw her vehicle driven by a large white fellow with brown hair, wearing a faded green shirt.

They interviewed David Lewis and David Gust, employees of Centex Rooney, who were with Brad Wilson in the car when they all saw the Ford Explorer charging onto the Osceola Parkway without stopping. Lewis, who was driving, said he only saw the back of the driver's head. He stated that he exited on the Buena Vista ramp and did not notice if the Explorer continued westbound on the parkway.

David Gust also only saw the side and back of the driver of the Ford. But Gust noticed what appeared to be a canvas tote bag in the passenger seat next to the driver. He said the driver also seemed to be fidgeting with something on the floorboard area of the front passenger area.

When the detectives interviewed Gary Wilson, the fourth passenger in the car, he told roughly the same story. He did not get a look at the driver's face but noticed that he was tan and was wearing a green shirt. He said the man focused his attention on the passenger seat of the vehicle and appeared to be reaching for something on that side of the vehicle. Wilson made out that there was an item on the passenger seat that appeared to be a brown bag.

The detectives' interviews with Ray Walby, Freddie Kitchens, Lavon Brown and David Maderano produced nothing new.

When they concluded, Weir shook his head in disappointment.

Linnert, always more optimistic than Weir, tried to console him. "Well, that's what this work is; we just keep trying."

The two detectives continued working practically around the clock, checking each of the massive calls that came in after the new composite sketch of the possible assailant ran in the media.

"We've got hundreds of tips," Weir said wearily, "but so far nothing in any of them."

"Yeah, people get interested in a big case and want to help," Linnert said. "They see it on TV or read the newspaper. Their imaginations go wild and they call with a full story in complete detail."

"And we have to follow up on all of them." Weir sighed tiredly, stretching his arms. "We can't afford not to. And in answer to our bulletins and the description of the Ford, we're also getting reports from all over about it being sighted. Dozens and dozens. I didn't know there were that many white Ford Explorers in central Florida."

"Ain't that the truth!"

Weir and Linnert worked steadily, ploddingly, following through on every detail, but making no progress. Paperwork and growing files were the only outward signs of their labors.

"You know, there's something else we should pursue," Weir suggested, viewing the mountain of followed-up leads on their desks.

"What's that?"

"Carla Larson's jewelry. We were told she always wore some expensive jewelry and the only thing found on or near her body was her wedding ring. We might be able to track the rest. Maybe the killer tried or will try to get rid of the stuff."

"Good idea." Linnert leaned forward approvingly. "Let's get a complete description of the pieces from her husband."

Weir nodded, pleased that they had a new avenue to travel.

Following through, on Friday, June 20, the detectives called on Jim Larson at his home.

When Larson answered the door, Weir nodded and asked in a friendly tone, "Mr. Larson, how are you doing?"

Larson gave a faint smile and responded, "About as well as can be expected. Come on in. What can I do for you gentlemen?"

Weir, always sensitive in speaking to people close to homicide victims in cases that he worked over the years, hesitated before broaching this delicate subject. "We wanted to talk to you about your wife's jewelry—the things that are missing."

Jim Larson's face showed an unwelcome surprise. He evidently did not expect the subject of jewelry to be the reason for this visit, nor did he feel any pleasure in being asked to go back in his memory to the occasions of his gifts to Carla. Still, he replied, "Oh, sure. What can I tell you?"

"We need a detailed description of the pieces Mrs. Larson was wearing that day."

Larson recalled sadly, "She was wearing her engagement ring and her wedding ring, of course, which she never took off." He paused. "The diamond in the engagement ring was a distinctive pear shape, and it was three-quarters of an inch, in a gold setting."

"I hope you don't mind, but would you give us an idea of the value of the ring?"

"I don't mind. I'd say that it was approximately thirty-four or thirty-five hundred dollars."

"What other items do you recall?" Linnert asked courteously. He was aware that they were deep into the personal life of this couple, yet he professionally knew it was necessary if it might help the investigation.

Jim Larson rubbed his hand across his mouth. "Well, there were her earrings. They were diamonds, her favorites. They were round and also in a gold setting. Each one was half a carat, and I'd say that they were about two thousand dollars." He added, "She wore a gold chain that was sixteen inches in length, with her Centex Rooney pendant on it."

He paused, remembering how honored Carla was when she was awarded the pendant. "The pendant had a gold-and-black CR logo design with a small diamond set in." Larson stopped again and said apologetically, "I'm not too sure of the value, but I would take a guess, which I believe would be pretty close. I'd say the approximate value would be one hundred fifty dollars. There was another pendant—garnet, with six or seven stones and also two small diamonds." He faced the detectives and stated, "I'd put a hundred-fifty-dollar value on that, too."

Larson stood up and told the detectives, "I'm sure that I have appraisals on the engagement ring and the earrings. Let me get them for you."

He left the room, and when he was alone, the memory of Carla's jewelry brought tears to his eyes. Covertly he wiped his cheeks before returning to the detectives with the authenticating documents.

"Thank you, sir. We'll be in touch," Weir said.

In the car headed to headquarters, Linnert said, "I'll get this information distributed to jewelry stores and pawnshops. Maybe that will bring some results. We can only hope the guy tries to unload them." He stared through the window, thinking of the potential boost to their investigation if that happened.

CHAPTER 7

On Friday morning, June 27, when the ringing telephone on his desk took his attention, Cam Weir pushed away the stack of papers he was working on. *Who the hell is calling this early in the morning?* he wondered.

"Detective Weir, this is Deputy Todd Howard of the Brevard County Sheriff's Department."

"Good morning, Deputy Howard, what can I do for you?" he asked.

"I think it's more what I can do for you. We've got something over here in Cocoa Beach that we think will interest you."

Weir's curiosity spiked. "What's that?"

"We have a vehicle that's been torched beyond recognition—well, almost beyond recognition."

"Why call me about it?"

"We think it's a Ford Explorer." The phone went silent.

Lightning flashed inside Weir's head. *Ford Explorer? Can it be? It must be, why else would he call?*

"Are you there, Detective Weir?" Howard asked after a long silence.

"Yes, yes, of course. I'm sorry. What about that vehicle?"

"We have reason to believe that this burned vehicle is a Ford Explorer, and you have an APB out looking for one."

"Yes, we do. Why do you think that's the vehicle we're seeking?" Weir was cautious but hoped that there would be a tie-in with the Larson vehicle.

"Well, I'm not a hundred percent sure, but it is possible. It's so badly burned that the usual markings and points of identification have been destroyed by the fire."

Here come the doubts, Weir thought. *But don't close the door. This could be the break we've been looking for.*

"When did this happen?" Weir asked.

"Late last night, after midnight," Howard answered. He hesitated, then pointedly suggested, "We think you should come over and examine these remains yourself. You might see some leads here that we're not familiar with." But after studying the burned automobile, Todd Howard had a strong conviction that this was the vehicle sought by the OCSD, and he didn't want them to miss out on this discovery.

Detective Weir absorbed this unexpected development. Thoughts ran through his mind about how the Larson vehicle could have wound up in that county and why it was set on fire. They had followed up so many leads on the Explorer; each had sounded promising but led to nothing. Yet the Brevard deputy seemed so sure. Could this finally be the break they needed?

Quickly he assured the deputy, "My partner and I will get over there without delay."

"Thank you, Detective Weir. We'll be waiting for you. And I think that you will find your trip over here productive."

"I sincerely hope so, Deputy Howard. See you soon."

Immediately Weir called John Linnert. "Speed it up, John, we're off to Brevard."

Sleepily Linnert demanded, "What's so important that we have to rush over there at this hour? I haven't had my breakfast, not even a cup of coffee."

"Well, let me tell you," Weir retorted. "I got a call out of the blue from a deputy with the Brevard County Sheriff's Department. They have a torched vehicle over there and he sounded pretty damn convinced that it could be Carla Larson's Ford Explorer."

"I'll be with you in ten minutes," Linnert replied, his spirits soaring.

Weir drove and John Linnert sat in the passenger seat as the two detectives sped off on the approximately sixty-mile journey to the Brevard County Sheriff's Department on the east coast of the state. He stared at the passing scenery, deep in thought.

As he drove along the wide modern highway, Weir stared at the wide expanse of land, seeing the still undeveloped beautiful countryside, heavily wooded on either side of the roadway.

"You know, John," he began, reminiscing, "you always hear about change, especially here in central Florida, how this used to be and how that was."

"Yeah, so? Were you thinking of retiring and moving over here someday?" Linnert joked.

"No, I was just thinking about Cocoa Beach and what it is today compared to what it used to be. I've heard old-timers, longtime residents of the area, talking about how some forty or fifty years ago there were only a few cottages along the oceanfront there, pretty primitive, where occasionally people would come for a weekend, possibly for fishing or just to get away. But it wasn't any great vacation spot. There wasn't anything over there, no restaurants, no motels, no nice buildings, just some bait shacks and small country grocery stores. Most of all, the drinking water was abominable. It was eighty percent sulphur and smelled like rotten eggs. It was undrinkable. People had to use bottled water, even to make coffee."

"Well, they've come a long way, baby," Linnert quipped.

Weir mused, "The land back then was, to coin a phrase, dirt cheap. I mean big plots sold for as little as a dollar an acre. Imagine that. We all could have been rich as Rockefellers if we had just put a little money into land and let it sit."

"Hindsight is great. Who knew that space program would come along and change this entire part of the state?"

"Ain't that the truth? But I wonder, what did they do about that stinky water?"

As they approached the town of Cocoa, traffic became heavier, and when they crossed the bridge over the Banana River and neared Cocoa Beach, the area became congested. What had been a tiny coastal hamlet was now crowded with motels, restaurants, apartments and homes. With the advent of the space program and NASA coming to Cape Kennedy, barren land, which sellers couldn't give away, suddenly sold at premium prices. From Titusville and Cape Canaveral, south to Patrick Air Force Base, growth was rampant.

Linnert finally broached what was foremost in their minds. "You know, Cam, if that burned vehicle is really Carla Larson's Explorer, the guy must have driven it over to Brevard after he killed her. It's quite possible that he lives over there somewhere. Maybe Cocoa, Cocoa Beach, or even Melbourne, somewhere in the vicinity. He certainly had a reason for driving over there."

"You're right, John. If the car is actually the Larson Explorer, we have a good lead. Maybe we can track the guy down and find out why he came over to this county. And then we need to find out why the hell he torched the vehicle."

"Yeah, why do you suppose he did that?" Linnert asked.

"Beats me. But he must have had a reason. It still comes back to whether this is the Larson vehicle."

"Well, you said Deputy Howard and the others were pretty confident that the burned vehicle matched our APB."

"He sure was, and I hope they're right," Weir replied.

The detectives sat silent, each absorbed with his own thoughts and projections.

Arriving at the BCSD, the detectives met Deputy Todd Howard. "Glad you fellows could make it," he greeted.

He ushered the detectives into a conference room and offered coffee or cold drinks. The Orlando lawmen refused, impatient to get on with their mission. Howard introduced them to several of the Brevard officers, including Bruce Barnett. "He's with the homicide department. He'll update you on what we have."

Barnett shook hands with the Orange County detectives and offered, "Y'all can drive out with Todd and me to the location of the burned vehicle."

"That's fine," Weir agreed.

Traveling along Route A1A, with Weir sitting in front with Bruce Barnett, the Brevard detective stated, "You guys really got yourselves a big-time case out at Disney World."

"I guess that's right. It sure looks that way," Weir responded, "but we haven't yet figured out where it's going." He turned slightly to face Barnett and continued. "Hearing from Todd was certainly unexpected. And I'd like to add, most welcome. That is, if this is the Larson vehicle."

"I think you may be pleasantly surprised," he answered with a smile.

Arriving at their destination, Barnett pulled off the main highway and drove into a secluded setting, hidden away from the general view of the nearby highway and its heavy flowing traffic.

The remains of the vehicle were set deep into a surround of wild brush and junglelike trees and native growth.

"He sure kept this project out of view," Detective Linnert commented at the sight of the destroyed SUV. It was amazing that the secluded spot where the vehicle remained, just an incredibly short distance from the major highway A1A on the east, was almost completely secreted.

Facing the charred automobile, the detective team stared in amazed silence. The once-attractive gleaming white SUV was now burned beyond belief. Its fine white finish was a wild smear of charcoal, ash yellow, burned brown with touches of unexplained red and blue and a smatter of green, all mixed together.

The windows of the automobile were blasted out and the weight of the entire remains settled into the burned globs that were once tires. The raised hood at the front end displayed the burned engine remains. Nothing in this effort to destroy was left to chance. The interior of the vehicle was soaked thoroughly with a burning agent, probably gasoline, and ignited to ensure the automobile's total destruction.

After minutes of careful study, Weir turned to Deputy Howard and said, "I never saw anything burned this bad."

"I can tell you, Detective," Howard said, "this vehicle consumed gallons of gasoline and never moved an inch. It was soaked thoroughly to make sure that it burned beyond recognition. The flames were so enormous that both the fire department and the sheriff's department were called out. There's never been anything like it in this area. Those flames towering into that black night sky were beyond belief."

"Whoever did this had to be a real firebug," Linnert said.

Cam Weir hoped that this might be Carla's vehicle, but he forced himself to remain wary. He asked, "Why do you think that this is Carla Larson's Explorer?"

Howard shrugged his shoulders and replied flatly, "It just fits."

The two Orange County detectives listened attentively as Deputy Todd Howard continued. "What we were able to check indicated similarities to the Larson vehicle in your APB. This was a white Ford Explorer." He pointed to the raised hood. "You listed a V-6 engine in your bulletin, which is what this is. Now we'll have to wait for verification of what kind of tires they were. There's only that little bit left on the underside of the wheels, and that's only because that part sank into the sand, so they weren't totally destroyed. We put this all together with the time element of the crime situation, and we had a strong indication that this is your white Ford Explorer."

Deputy Howard paused, then continued. "It seems pretty clear that whoever flamed this car wanted it completely destroyed. And they damn near made it totally ashes. That's why the vehicle ID numbers are burned to invisibility."

Linnert stated, "Whoever did this saw to it that everything burned, interior, exterior, with nothing left inside or out that might be used as evidence."

"That, of course, was the intent of the person who set it," Barnett agreed. "Let me show you how the perpetrator was very careful in the selection of this location."

He waved his arm like a traffic cop, pointing out how the Ford was cunningly hidden away from the view of passing cars and stuck into a large section of high-growing wild brush and trees. To the north of the vehicle, there was a large section of growth, eight to ten feet in height, that easily concealed the vehicle from view. To the south and east, there was a smaller stand of brush that partially concealed the vehicle from that side.

Linnert marveled, "Who would have believed this? This car is just feet from the main highway and yet it's hidden and protected."

Weir noted, "It had to be someone who was familiar with the location, not someone who just stumbled onto it by accident. I think we'd better get State Fire Marshal Charlie LaCorte down here to look at this," he decided. After a moment he added, "We also need to call our department's forensic analyst, Kristen Hayes."

After they made the calls, while they awaited the specialists, the Orange County detectives discussed the incident with the Brevard officers.

"How did you find out about the fire?" Weir asked.

Barnett answered, "We got a call about it. When we got out here, there were two young guys who told us that they were driving by when they spotted something burning with lots of thick smoke. They pulled over to see what it was. When they saw that it was a real fire, they called in the report on their cell phone."

"Could they tell you anything else?" Linnert asked.

"According to what they told me, they saw a strange guy standing quite a distance from the blazing car. His back was toward them. They tried to talk to him but he was totally engrossed watching the fire." Barnett hesitated, trying to recall details of what the two told him. "They thought that there was something weird about the guy. They didn't know what, couldn't put their finger on anything, but they said the way that he acted was strange. It didn't seem natural to them. Here there's one hell of a fire, something that you hardly ever see, so you'd expect a person right on the spot to say something about what's going on. Something like 'Isn't this the worst thing you ever saw?' or 'Did you ever see such a fire as this?' but this guy just stood there, quiet as an Egyptian mummy, and said absolutely nothing."

"Do you suppose," Linnert asked, "that he was the guy who set the fire and was just making sure that everything burned? If, in fact, he was the guy responsible, he certainly had good reason not to be talking about it."

"You've got something there, John," Barnett agreed. "Anyhow, they said that he just turned and walked away."

"Did they give you any idea where he might have gone?" Weir inquired.

"No, not really. The only thing that they could say was that when he left, he just headed south on foot."

"Could they describe him?" Linnert asked.

"Oh, yes. One said he was six feet tall, about two hundred pounds but not muscular, said he was between twenty-five and forty years old and not wearing a shirt. The other said he estimated his age between twenty-seven and thirty-four years, about five-ten to six feet tall, weighing one hundred sixty to seventy pounds, and had brown or black hair. So the two reports sort of conflict."

Weir said, "Typical eyewitness reporting. Two people see the same thing and come up with disagreeing reports on what they just saw."

Linnert nodded. "Makes you wonder just what this guy did look like."

The two young fellows told Barnett that other people came along to see what was causing such huge billows of black smoke. And then the fire department and sheriff's department guys came on the scene.

The Brevard County helicopter conducted a search of the area in hopes of finding someone secreted in the area, but with negative results.

Authorities searched for an unidentified man seen walking south on A1A from the fire scene, but he was not located or identified.

After things settled a bit, the officials searched the adjacent wooded area and talked to the few persons who were about, getting the names and addresses of each.

Bruce Barnett continued the account. "We couldn't come up with anything, couldn't find anyone who saw anything or who might have been the culprit who set the vehicle on fire."

When Fire Marshal LaCorte and forensic analyst of the OCSD Kristen Hayes joined the group at the burned vehicle location, Weir explained the situation.

LaCorte and Hayes fine combed the site with intense interest. "Pretty damn thorough," LaCorte commented as he observed the demolished vehicle.

He pointed to the right front door. "See here? That was left open about eight to ten inches to allow for the continuing flow of air and oxygen to keep the fires going."

He squatted down to observe more closely the door frame. "And here, look at the specks. They show it was painted black over the original white." He moved around to the left side of the vehicle and pointed. "And see here. There's a dent on the back panel behind the rear tire."

The fire marshal also noted, "The heat buckled the roof inward over the front and rear seats. The windows were all down, permitting unrestricted cross winds building blazing flames."

LaCorte and Hayes, along with Detective Ron Weyland, who joined the investigation, sifted through debris that was removed from inside the vehicle, but they found no items of evidentiary value. They took additional debris from the interior of the vehicle to be submitted for laboratory analysis. Kristen Hayes volunteered to take the samples back to the OCSD. "We have the facilities there. We'll examine everything and make a report."

LaCorte had one of his arson K-9 dogs with him to check for the presence of flammable liquids. As the intricate search proceeded, the K-9 detected their presence. LaCorte also took several samples of soil where the burned vehicle settled into the sand.

"Well, Detectives," Fire Marshal LaCorte said, with Hayes joining in agreement, "we can conclude without a doubt that we have a fire that was incendiary in nature, caused by someone pouring flammable liquid throughout the vehicle entirely and then igniting it." He nodded his head, confirming and endorsing his conclusion.

Kristen made a few comments supporting the fire marshal, pointing out specifically what they found.

Cameron Weir, thinking ahead to the investigation, tapped Linnert's arm and said, "John, I think that we should rescue what's left of this mess."

"What do you mean, 'rescue'? It's beyond that."

"Well, it's not exactly an ideal time of day to do much, so I think that the best thing to do is have this heap moved to the Brevard department now, even though it's almost daylight. There it will be protected until we can have it moved to our own station. What do you think?"

Linnert agreed. "But I think that we should clear this with Bruce."

"Oh, that's no problem," Barnett stated. "Only too glad to help. We're just a few miles from here and moving what's left of this car will give you a chance to work out what you want to do with it."

"Thanks, Bruce. We appreciate everything that you and your department are doing for us," Weir said.

Barnett nodded. "I'll call and arrange for a car carrier, with a lift, to get this on its way to the station garage. And I'll let them know that it has to be handled with special care."

A tow truck arrived at the location, with minimum delay, carefully lifting and setting what was left of the burned vehicle onto the truck. The truck transported it to a Brevard County Sheriff's facility and installed it in a sealed garage. The officials dispersed, returning to their own jurisdictions. Weir and Linnert drove off to their home station in Orlando.

The detectives were quiet on their return trip, but their minds were filled with all sorts of speculation. *Why was the car burned in Brevard County? Did the driver, who was probably the carjacker and even more probably Carla Larson's killer, live in this area? Would the charred remains of the vehicle yield any clue as to who he was?*

On the drive back to Orlando, Weir and Linnert discussed what to do next. "We'll have to make arrangements to get that vehicle back to our base, where we can turn our techs loose. Maybe they can dig out something we can use."

Both men separately were convinced that finding the answer to the torching of the Ford could lead to the perpetrator of Carla Larson's murder.

As the vehicle sped along the highway, Linnert stared out the window and remarked, "You know, Cam, there really isn't anything more beautiful than early morning. Just look at that brilliant sunrise."

Weir stole a quick look and responded, "Yeah, but I think that right now I'd rather be home in bed, catching a little sleep."

Hours later, back at the OCSD in a conference with Lieutenant Mike Easton and Detective Ron Weyland, Weir and Linnert explained the situation. Weyland suggested using an enclosed railroad car to transport the vehicle to their garage.

Easton thought about that and said, "I don't think that's such a good idea. It would be a lot more practical if we had a trucking company pick it up and deliver it right to our garage."

All agreed that would be the best. Easton smiled and said, "Okay, truck it is."

"That's fine, Mike," Weir said, "but we want to be sure that it's a closed truck. If you saw what's left of that car, I'm sure you would be concerned with protecting it from everything in its trip back to Orlando. If there's any evidence left in it, we don't want to take a chance of destroying it."

CHAPTER 8

Detectives Weir and Linnert sat at their desks at the OCSD headquarters and contemplated their next moves.

Weir said, "I sure would like to know more about what led to the torching of that vehicle, and why it was in Brevard County." He looked at the stack of reports that he and Linnert had compiled on the case. He sighed, picking up a handful, and said, "Just look at all the digging we've done already, and no end in sight. All these leads, but nothing conclusive. A guy driving a white—maybe—Ford Explorer. He's maybe in his twenties, thirties or even forties. He's dark complexioned, suntanned, or fair with dark brown or sunbleached hair. He's anywhere from five-ten to six-one, weighs one-sixty to two hundred ten pounds. The only thing the witnesses all agree on is that he's a white man. That really doesn't narrow it down. Just shows you how accurate eyewitnesses are."

Linnert turned his attention to Weir. "I know exactly how you feel, and if I were the kind of guy who gets discouraged, our progress so far would do it. But this is just one of those cases that takes everything you've got before the golden gates open." He leaned forward, his bright brown eyes almost sparkling. "But I truly believe we've made some headway. Just think of that SUV. Catching up with it is a hell of a leap forward. If we can determine how it got to Brevard, it could be another step forward. And maybe the techs will get some kind of clue when they go over it in the garage."

Weir smoothed back his hair. "That's true. Or maybe one of the bystanders at the fire saw something. We'll go talk to some of those guys who were there."

"Which one first?"

"Daniel Hamilton, the maintenance fellow at the Four Seasons Condominiums in Cocoa Beach."

"Oh, right. Yeah, his name is on the list of witnesses who were at the fire."

"I sure hope he can tell us something."

"Me too. Let's go find out."

The detectives interviewed Daniel Hamilton in his apartment at the Dolphin Motel, located on South Atlantic Avenue in Cocoa Beach. The tall, dark, nice-looking fellow told them he was eager to talk about the experience.

"I never thought that I'd ever see anything like that fire," he said, shaking his head in wonder. "Iola, my girlfriend, will tell you that, too. She isn't here right now." He leaned back in his easy chair and began. "I was asleep; it was at night and I had been working hard. I was in a really deep sleep when Iola came into the bedroom and said, 'Dan, you gotta get up and see what's going on. There's smoke all over the place—all up and down the beach. Come on, get up.' I didn't know what she was screaming about; I was half asleep. And then suddenly I was wide awake. I could smell the smoke and my first thought was that our place was on fire. I remember rubbing my face to make sure that I wasn't still asleep and dreaming. Iola yelled, 'Don't just stand there. Come out on the balcony and see what I'm telling you.' I followed her out on the balcony and looked up the beach, where I saw the flames from a huge fire, biggest I ever saw in my life."

Hamilton looked at the detectives, shaking his head, and continued. "It was amazing. We had no idea what kind of a fire it was. I thought that it could have been one of those big gasoline tanks, where they store the stuff. But I really couldn't tell."

Detective Linnert asked, "You followed the flames and drove up to the location, right?"

"Yes, we were in a kind of shock and talked about it. We were concerned to know if it was going to spread our way," he explained. "You get some scary thoughts when you're confronted with something like this. I could see us hustling around trying to pack and rescue all of the things that we care about. But I figured I better keep calm and not do anything rash."

He shifted in his chair and continued. "Iola and I decided that I should go and see it firsthand." He explained that he took Iola's mother's car and drove to the fire. "It was right at Thirty-third Street, blazing away. I wondered, with this fire practically out of control burning this car like it was a pack of wood shavings, why there were no firemen trying to put it out." He looked at the two detectives cautiously, knowing his statement was not a complimentary one.

"You mean, there was no one there to stop it?"

"I don't mean to give you the wrong idea or impression, but it was just a shock to see those flames raging. And the firemen were not there yet." He shook his head.

"Well, there was a crowd that gathered. I don't mean a big crowd, but there were some curious guys there, especially one that was standing off by himself—all alone." Hamilton stopped to explain. "See, I parked the car at a nearby store and walked over to the location of the fire. There were quite a few watching, but this one guy stood in front of the burning car like he was in a trance, like he was hypnotized. I was curious and wondered what his great fascination was, so I walked up to him and asked, 'What's going on here?' " Dan smiled. "I don't know if he thought I was some stupid bastard or what. It certainly was obvious that we had a hell of a fire in front of us and I sure didn't need anyone to tell me what was going on. I just was trying to talk to the guy and maybe get some explanation of what happened, how the fire started or something. But he just ignored me He didn't bother to answer me or to even acknowledge that I existed."

Detective Weir asked, "Can you describe this fellow?"

"Sure. He was six feet tall or maybe a little above that, a well-built guy who weighed at least one-sixty or one sixty-five. What struck me was his hair. It was funny. It was curly in a tangled sort of way, an off-color brown that looked like it was out in the sun too long. It fell down over his ears, behind the back and over his collar. He sure as hell was not an ad for any magazine."

"Do you remember what he was wearing, how he was dressed?" Linnert questioned.

Hamilton nodded with an assured expression. "I remember that he was wearing a white T-shirt and blue shorts, and I wondered if the bugs were biting him like they were me. But he was puffing away on a cigarette, totally wrapped up in that fire."

"What did you do after the guy ignored you?" Weir asked.

"I wasn't exactly thrilled with that, so I just walked away. I left him standing there by himself. I walked over by the river so I could see the fire from the other side."

"What happened after you walked away?"

"I watched the fire from this other spot and was there, I'd say, about fifteen minutes, maybe a little more. You know how easy it is to get mesmerized by a fire. So I may have been there twenty minutes; then I walked back to my original spot. He was gone and I never saw that guy again.

"By this time, I was getting all bit up by mosquitoes and other bugs, since I was wearing shorts and a short-sleeved T-shirt. I wanted to get back to my place and change clothes. But before I left, a guy drove up in a four-wheel-drive vehicle. He told me that he saw some suspicious individual, a white man, running away from the fire. He also told me that the burning automobile looked like the Ford Explorer that the police were looking for. We exchanged some thoughts and wondered if the guy he saw running away might have been the same man I saw staring at the fire, the guy I spoke to but never got an answer from.

"Anyway, I left and went home to change clothes. I put on a pair of long pants, a pair of shoes and a long-sleeved shirt. And then I went back to the fire. Before long, the firemen were there on the job and they began dousing and running in all directions, and it wasn't too long before they had things under control. By this time there were sheriff's men, officers, detectives, all kinds of investigators and specialists joining in."

"That was a pretty exciting experience for you," Cam Weir commented.

"It sure was. But I don't think that I want to see something like that again."

Expressing appreciation, the detectives thanked Hamilton for his cooperation. Handing the subject his card, Cameron said, "If you think of anything else, please give us a call."

"I sure will."

Later that afternoon, the two detectives met with Hamilton's girlfriend, Iola, after she returned to their apartment at the Dolphin Motel.

She verified Hamilton's account of the events just as he related it to them earlier. The detectives thanked Iola for her time and cooperation and departed.

Weir and Linnert conscientiously interviewed the other witnesses on the list who were at the scene of the fire, including the two young fellows who originally reported the fire, but they learned nothing more. Each gave a similar account of the horrific blaze and the smoke and the general excitement. No one else was able to recall the strange fellow who was so mesmerized by the fire, making such an impression on Daniel Hamilton and the two young fellows who first reported the flaming vehicle.

CHAPTER 9

Early Saturday morning, June 28, Tom McCann sat in a window seat on the plane whisking him to Washington, D.C. There he would officially represent the Orange County, Florida, Sheriff's Department in the presentation of the immensely popular television program *America's Most Wanted*. McCann stared out at the clouds and sky, not quite feeling the impact of his situation, that he was on his way to be part of a drama that so many millions of people devotedly watched each Saturday night on their TV sets.

His thoughts turned to the seriousness of his mission. *What if . . . ,* he considered, *What if this program is effective in this case and results in some good leads? Wouldn't that be terrific?* He stopped himself, knowing that crimes were solved by building strong cases through meticulous investigation, not on "what ifs."

Upon landing, longtime friends of McCann's ushered him to their waiting automobile and drove him to their home, where he would spend the night following the broadcast.

After an old-time reunion and catching-up session, his friends drove him to the studio where the program was in preparations for the broadcast that evening.

Eagerly, McCann looked over the impressive studio. It was buzzing with people readying the program for airing in just a few hours. As he moved about, he was impressed with the efficiency of this staff's precision work. He watched for John Walsh, the program's narrator, but didn't see him. When he asked about Walsh, he found out that the man would not be on deck for several hours.

McCann was also impressed by the number of persons equipped with telephone-answering equipment to take the many calls that would come as response to the broadcast.

The dramatic TV presentation of the Carla Larson case gave a national audience of millions the facts relating to the vanishing and murder of the lovely young engineer.

The program faithfully detailed the crime, showed pictures of Carla, the areas involved in the case, her Ford Explorer, described the kidnapping, the search and finally the discovery of the body. The show asked anyone who saw or knew anything about the case to call in with the information.

During the show McCann took calls directly from people responding with tips that they thought could be important in solving the case.

Pleased to talk to the callers, he was hopeful there would be some good leads. But on the whole, what he received was of little or no value.

After the airing some of the personnel of the program asked, "Did you learn anything new? Were any of the callers helpful?"

McCann shook his head in disappointment and responded, "I'm afraid not."

One of the show's producers consoled McCann. "We'll get more calls. We always do for several days after the airing, and we'll pass them on to you," he promised.

Tom McCann cordially thanked him and left.

The Orange County Sheriff's Department personnel were overwhelmed with the impact of the show. It was well presented and reenacted and gave a true picture of what happened. They were sure something positive would come from it.

Detective Weir kept his opinions and hopes for the program to himself. In an exchange with John Linnert, he said, "Everyone seems to think that program is going to solve the mystery of this killing."

Linnert responded, "Well, we can't blame anyone for hoping."

"Oh, don't get me wrong. I'm every bit as anxious as everyone else, but I think that it's kind of like hoping for a miracle. You know, somebody calling the program or calling our headquarters with information on 'whodunit' or with some tip that could be important enough to lead to the solution of this crime," Weir commented glumly. "I'm not against something coming from it, or coming from any other source, for that matter, if it can help us with the investigation. And I don't want to throw a pall on anyone's enthusiasm, but it's always been my experience that the only way we solve our crimes is by digging out the leads and chasing down everything with some connection to the task at hand."

"I know and I agree with you. But we don't want to close any doors. There could be something unexpected, something that we're not necessarily looking for that pops up. Well, we may find out something when Tom gets back."

As the two detectives continued their discussion, Weir received a phone call shortly before midnight.

"Detective Weir, this is Lieutenant Douglas Scragg of the Brevard County Sheriff's Department. I hope you don't mind my calling so late."

"Not at all, Lieutenant," Weir replied. "What's on your mind?"

The lieutenant said, "Something came up over here that might be of interest to you. One of the bouncers at the Illusions Lounge, that's one of those adult-entertainment emporiums, it's located just a short distance from the burned vehicle you were here to see. Anyway, he found a suspicious-looking bag in the Dumpster outside the place."

Weir asked, "Do you think that there's some connection to our investigation?"

"Well, you never know. We wondered if it could have come out of that burned car."

"I guess it makes sense for us to check it out," Weir said. "My partner and I were just talking about something like that when you called, Lieutenant. You know, the unexpected happens and we never know where the next lead will come from. Tell me, how did the bouncer happen to discover the bag?"

"From what I understand, the fellow, the bouncer, was taking out the normal trash to the Dumpster and, when he opened up the cover, the bag caught his attention. It was an unexpected place for a bag like this to be. So he retrieved it, took it inside and gave it to his boss." The lieutenant laughed. "They told me that there was quite a bit of excitement in the place with the discovery. Everybody wanted to see it and find out what was inside."

Lieutenant Scragg said that all kinds of theories were tossed around about the bag. Maybe it was from the burned Ford and maybe linked to the murder. "That's when the manager of the lounge contacted me and asked that I take possession of it, since they were all convinced that it was connected somehow to the murder you are investigating."

The lieutenant said he accepted the bag as possible evidence and placed it into the case file under the number 97105963, describing it as a tan/gray bag. A check of its contents found it contained a blue bedsheet, two empty boxes of Kirkland color print film, a bottle of Banana Boat suntan oil and a bottle of Bausch & Lomb ReNu eye care solution.

The BCSD's case number listing matched the case number used to document the discovery of the burned Ford vehicle and the collection of evidence from the fire scene.

When Weir concluded his conversation, he told Linnert about the bag.

"What do you think?" Linnert asked.

"Well, I think it's just another puzzle in the list of questions we need answered, but we'll collect it and show it to Jim Larson. Let him look at all of it and tell us if he recognizes any of it as belonging to Carla Larson."

"That sounds right to me, Cam."

After the detectives retrieved the bag on Sunday, June 29, they drove to the College Park home of Larson.

Linnert said, "We'll soon know our way around College Park as well as we know how to drive to headquarters."

"At least it's a nice day and there's not much traffic."

Larson greeted the detectives at the door and invited them into the dining room.

Weir explained the reason for this visit.

Larson was surprised. "Do you think there is some connection with this bag?" he asked hesitantly.

"We really don't know much about it," Weir answered.

John Linnert explained how "the bouncer at the Illusions Lounge found the thing in the Dumpster behind the club."

Jim Larson was curious. "How does any of this fit with our situation?"

Weir said, "That lounge is just a short distance from the site of the fire, where your Ford Explorer was destroyed. There's a possibility that someone could have taken this bag from the car and tossed it into the Dumpster."

Jim Larson sat silent, considering the explanation.

"We need to know whether this bag or its contents belonged to you or to your wife," Weir continued.

After a moment Weir pushed the bag across the table to Larson. "Will you take a look and tell us what you think?"

"I'll look at the stuff inside, but I can tell you right now, this bag is not at all familiar to me. So I doubt that whatever is inside would be something that we owned."

Jim Larson opened the tan/gray bag, examined the contents and shook his head. He remained silent.

John Linnert rose and retrieved the bag. Extending his hand to Larson, he thanked him and apologized for taking his time. "I hope that we haven't imposed upon you."

Larson shook Linnert's hand, smiled grimly and said, "I know that you're just doing your job and I'm grateful."

On the drive back to department headquarters, Weir shook his head. "Just another dead end."

* * *

Detective Tom McCann met with Detectives Weir and Linnert with his report of the results of the *America's Most Wanted* TV presentation.

"It's a great program," he reported to the investigators, "and I think they did a terrific job presenting our case. I made notes of conversations I had with those who called." He shook his head in disappointment. "Not one of them really had anything worth telling you about." His frustration showed on his face. "I really thought with this massive audience we'd get some callers who might have something of importance to pass on to us. But there was nothing . . . absolutely nothing."

He paused, then added brightly, "But there still might be some hope. The producers told me that they get calls for several days following the broadcast, so there might still be something that will come in."

The following day, *America's Most Wanted* received a call, which would later have significance, from a Melbourne, Florida, woman who identified herself as Angel Huggins.

CHAPTER 10

Cameron Weir studied the calendar on the wall facing him.

Time sure does fly; no truer words were ever spoken, he thought, realizing that it was now July. *How long is this ordeal going to drag on? How long is it going to take us to catch that killer and give that family some closure?* He was disappointed that of the many calls that were flooding his and Linnert's desk, motivated by the *America's Most Wanted* broadcast, there were no substantive leads. *Surely there should be one call that will lead to something.*

The phone interrupted Weir's thoughts and projections.

"Weir," he answered.

"You have a call and the man says it's important."

"Who's the call from?"

"A Detective Brian Cutcher of the Osceola County Sheriff's Department. I don't know what it's about, but from the sound of his voice, it certainly must be important."

"Put him through, please."

Weir greeted the caller from the neighboring county, "Detective Cutcher, what can I do for you?"

"Hello, Detective Weir," Cutcher answered. "Something

occurred here that could be of interest to you, relative to the Carla Larson case."

Suddenly Weir was totally interested in this caller. "I'm all ears. Tell me what you have."

"Okay. Bear with me because this is strange, to say the least. A woman called the department. She wanted to know if she could come and see me. I was kind of wary because I don't like to have just anyone off the street call and get an authorization to come in to the department for some unknown or unspecified reason."

"I certainly agree with that," Weir said.

"But yet you don't want to be too quick to write someone off as a crackpot or a crank."

"I know what you're saying," Weir agreed.

"Anyway, after listening for several moments on the phone, she had me curious and I felt that I should see her. She came into headquarters, a tall, attractive woman, I'd guess in her thirties, maybe late thirties, and she spoke confidently.

"She referred to her friend and assured me her disclosure was one hundred percent reliable. At first I thought she was talking about herself, you know how they hide behind a 'friend.' Then she asked me if I was familiar with the business of the white vehicle. Right away she had me hooked. I asked her, 'Which white vehicle?' And she said, 'The car that the man was driving out of the woods at Disney World.' Boy, did that get my interest! I couldn't wait for her to tell me more."

Cutcher chuckled and continued. "She said her friend in Melbourne, Angel Huggins, knows all about that white vehicle and could give you or the authorities information that would knock your socks off, and someone should talk to her. So I figured I'd better call you fellows."

The Osceola detective said that she gave him the name, address and telephone number of Angel Huggins, her friend in Melbourne. Cutcher also indicated to Weir that the woman assured him that Angel was eager to talk to the detectives and authorities who were investigating the Carla Larson murder case.

"I'll tell you, Weir, there was something very credible about this woman. She sure sounded like she knew what she was talking about. She made a believer out of me."

Cam Weir's thoughts leaped ahead. *Could this be the break that we were hoping for to spark our investigation, or just another dead end like all the rest? Still, Melbourne isn't far from Cocoa Beach and the burned vehicle,* he rationalized to himself.

He brought his thoughts back to Cutcher, who was still on the line. He told the Osceola detective that he was grateful for his call and the information that he passed on, and they would certainly pursue it.

After he hung up the telephone, Weir discussed Detective Cutcher's phone call with Linnert.

"There are more unexpected developments in this case than I ever thought possible," Weir commented. "According to Cutcher, this woman in Melbourne knows something about the Ford Explorer and is apparently more than willing to talk to authorities. Not as eager as I am to talk with her," he said dryly. "And how far is Melbourne from Cocoa Beach, where the vehicle was burned up—five miles or ten? For some reason, call it a gut feeling, I think that this sounds more promising than anything we've had so far. Cutcher sure seemed convinced."

"Sounds good. I hope your hunch proves out. Let's not waste any time seeing her."

"Should we drive to Melbourne now?" Weir looked at his watch. "It's after two o'clock. It's about sixty-five miles, so it should be about four-thirty when we get there and find her house."

"No time like the present," John answered, "and we really can't put off anything that even suggests information that we could use."

Weir sighed. "I know you're right." He brightened up. "The trip is actually a nice ride and we can use the break."

In the official car, as the two detectives drove toward Melbourne, located on the east coast about twenty-five miles

south of Cocoa Beach, Weir recounted some other things
that Detective Cutcher told him in their phone conversation.

"Cutcher was emphatic that this woman who gave him
the story focused on the abuse that Angel put up with from
her husband."

"What does that mean? Domestic violence?"

Weir answered, "This is very complicated, what with
third parties involved. Let me see if I got it straight. This
woman we're going to see, Angel Huggins, told her friend,
who told Cutcher, that her husband had a violent history—
domestic violence with his first wife."

Linnert commented, "You're right. It is complicated. Is
she still married to him?"

"Yes, still married. They are separated but haven't divorced. According to what our Osceola detective was able to
pick up, Angel Huggins apparently filed for divorce in 1995
based on issues of domestic violence. I understood from
Cutcher that she didn't go through with it as yet because of
financial problems. Evidently, she has been having money
troubles.

"But getting back to her husband, Cutcher was told that
after their marriage on February 14, 1994, Valentine's Day, no
less, her husband was arrested and has been in and out of jail
ever since. I'll bet he has a lulu of a rap sheet. But what
caught Cutcher's and my attention is that the informant mentioned something about the white Ford seen in the Disney
World area."

"That's what we're interested in," Linnert remarked.
"That would make this a most worthwhile trip. But I sure
don't want to get our hopes up, in case it fizzles out."

"True. And I agree. However, I can't help feeling optimistic."

Arriving in Melbourne, the two detectives soon were at
the residence of Angel Huggins. Automatically, as police officers do, they made a quick visual survey and appraisal of
the house and the neighborhood. It was a modest home on a
tree-lined street of similar residences. The shrubs surround-

ing the building were neat and well kept. They noticed a shed to the rear of the property.

At the door of the home, after the lawmen introduced themselves, Angel Huggins invited them inside.

"I'm glad to see you, Detectives," Mrs. Huggins greeted. "Please come in," she urged. As she led the men into a tidy living room, with comfortable chairs and a sofa, both officers were struck with how attractive she was. Her honey-colored hair complemented her bright blue eyes and lovely oval-shaped face. She was tall, in her thirties, with a slender figure and a warm, friendly smile.

She seems to be handling this situation with composure, Weir thought in his initial study of her.

Mrs. Huggins invited them to "please be seated."

When they were comfortably settled, Weir said, "Ma'am, I guess you understand that we're here through a roundabout message that you might have some information relative to a case that we're working on."

Mrs. Huggins nodded. "I suppose," she began slowly in an uncomfortable tone, "you were not expecting to hear from me, either directly or indirectly." She seemed reluctant to continue, as though she were trying to decide how much she should tell the detectives.

"Mrs. Huggins," Detective Linnert said, "in our work we get all kinds of leads, tips, information that take us in all sorts of directions to all kinds of places. Our policy is just to collect the facts. We don't assume anything or make any judgments." He paused, then picked up. "Detective Cutcher of the Osceola County Sheriff's Department told Detective Weir that a close friend of yours said that you would be willing to talk to investigators in the Carla Larson case."

Angel Huggins nodded her head several times. "That's right," she answered hesitantly after Linnert's explanation. "I just felt that it was time for me to let the police or the sheriff's department hear what I could tell them."

"Well, Mrs. Huggins, here we are." It was the detective's turn to nod his head.

"First of all, I want to thank you for coming to see me. I know that you drove over from Orlando and I appreciate that. I just have to tell you that I never in my entire life thought I would ever be caught up in an ordeal the likes of which I am still going through."

Weir looked at the woman sympathetically and steered the conversation. "I understand you know something about the white Ford Explorer we're interested in. You might like to start there."

"That vehicle"—Angel tossed her head, shrugging impatiently—"didn't come into the story at the beginning. There's a lot more to what happened before the white Ford came into the picture."

The detective team watched quietly, waiting expectantly, wondering what Mrs. Huggins would say.

"I think I should go back to that date that is so important to everything that happened since. June tenth. See, John— my husband, John Huggins—we're actually separated and I'm staying here at my mother's house with my two kids. To get back, he came over and wanted to take the kids and me to Gatorland in Orlando. He was on some kind of a bend to make up to me and the kids for his lousy treatment of us for a long time, too long."

Weir and Linnert were impatient for her to get on to something of relevance to their case, but they could see Angel was going to tell it her way in her own time. They settled back to listen.

"John really fits the category of a 'bad boy'—not just for one or two things but for a long, consistent history of everyday things," she continued. "But this time there was something that he was trying to do. I didn't understand it then and I don't understand it now. He explained that he wanted to get all of us together, the kids, me and him, so we could spend some time together. I was taken in by the idea and agreed to go along with his plans.

"John got his kids and, with mine, brought us all to Orlando to go to Gatorland and have a great time. He had it all set and we arrived on June ninth and checked into the Days Inn in Kissimmee. Apparently, everything was hunky-dory. We all went to Gatorland and had a good time; the day was just great. Afterward, everyone went back to the suite of rooms at the Days Inn."

Angel paused, seeming uncertain or maybe somewhat embarrassed, but continued. "I probably should have known better, but John and I got into an argument over past problems. And a lot of it had to do with his former wife. That's when I got into bed with my clothes on, and all hell broke loose."

Angel stared past the detectives, recalling that evening. "As the hours wore on, John decided that he would like to make love to me. I let him know that I didn't feel up to it. But that did not go down very well with him. At first he turned on his best charm and tried to persuade me. The more he tried, the more disinterested I became. I turned my back on him. He got really persistent, and I got just as obstinate as he was. I was determined not to be persuaded. He became infuriated, and no longer was he the kindly lover. He began tearing off my clothes. I pushed him away. The more I tried to fend him off, the more physical he became. He grabbed me and threw me on the bed. Now he wasn't interested in sex anymore, only in showing me that he was still the boss. He's still my husband, and I am his slave."

She said at this point that John was enraged, but she managed to move over to the couch. "But he picked me up and pushed me back over the arm of the couch. Then he choked me, trying to strangle me. He was determined to kill me. I was literally scared to death. He had his hands on my neck and he was choking me with all his might. His big body—he's over six feet—was crushing me and I started to black out. But I refused to let him destroy my life. I twisted and turned and finally struck him in the head with my fist. Then, through some kind of miracle, I broke loose and ran into the bathroom and locked the door."

At this point of reliving her harrowing experience, Angel stopped, breathless.

Weir soothed her. "Calm down. Just relax."

Angel sat breathing hard, trying to gather herself to continue.

"Can I get you something? Would you like a glass of water?" John Linnert asked anxiously.

"No, no, I'm all right. It's just when I remember what happened, it all comes rushing back."

"It's okay," Weir said. "Whenever you're ready."

"I'm ready," she began. "Well, I just sat in the bathroom for an interminable time. I was afraid that he would smash down the door and drag me out. But for some unexplained reason, nothing happened. I just sat inside that bathroom, terrified. Hours crept by, until I finally got up enough courage to unlock the bathroom door and peek out to see if he was still there."

He was gone and Angel said that she didn't know what to think. Since she was exhausted from the terrible ordeal, she went into the children's bedroom and got into bed with them. John Huggins apparently left the motel. It was morning, June 10.

Angel continued to reveal her life with Huggins. She told the detectives that in his series of missteps with the law, he was in and out of jail constantly. "We have not been living together, but I did see him off and on, from time to time. My two girls and I are currently living here with my mother in Melbourne."

She said, "I have a son, Austin Junior, who lives with his father in Maryland. John has two children from his previous marriage. They live with John's mother up near Bushnell, Florida."

"Your family seems to be a bit scattered," Linnert observed.

Angel nodded. "A lot more than you think." She smiled. She explained that John was previously married to Marianne. "She was killed in an automobile accident."

Angel said, "Earlier this summer, my son, Austin Junior, came to town from Maryland to visit me. At the same time

John was spending time with his two children. That's when he decided that we should get the family together for a vacation. That was the trip to Gatorland."

Angel continued her account. "After John disappeared, sometime on the morning of June tenth, he was gone for hours. During this period of his absence, the maids and then later the manager came into the suite and wanted to know if we were checking out. I really couldn't tell them until I knew something from John. Finally, about two-thirty or three that afternoon, he came into the suite. He was wearing an army-green T-shirt.

"He had a red bruised blemish on his forehead. He was sweaty, looked like a truck driver who had been on an all-night run. He acted peculiarly, went straight into the bathroom and closed the door, shutting himself off from me." Angel shook her head in despair. "I tried to talk to him through the bathroom door. For the longest minutes, you could hear the silence. I tried again, telling him that they wanted to know if we were staying or not. Then suddenly he yelled through the door, asking if I was going home."

Once again Angel sat quietly, recalling the stress of that day.

She picked up the thread of her story. "He finally eased out of the bathroom. There was something that was different about him. Something odd that I never saw before. I looked at him and wondered where he had been, what he was up to. But I sure wouldn't ask him anything. Asking him anything is a no-no."

Angel said she was puzzled when he again asked if she was going home. She told him she thought she should, but wasn't sure about the directions or the roads.

She said he became very solicitous and explained the routing and the best way to go. "He was very helpful with his directions. When he finished, he told me, 'Take the kids with you.' "

The detectives listened to Angel's story attentively, totally attuned to the developing details she was relating.

"I went about packing all of the belongings of the kids and myself," Angel continued. "I had no idea where John was or if he took off again. I carried bags out to the car and looked around for him, but I didn't see him anywhere. I asked his son, Jonathon, to go out and look for his father. But there was no sign of him."

Angel said that she didn't know what to do, and she was worried about being unfamiliar with the road and the driving, but she had no choice. "I got the kids into my car, my white Geo Storm—it's a tiny car and with all the kids and our belongings we were packed in like sardines. Anyway, I followed John's directions and we headed for Melbourne. I think that we arrived home about four or four-thirty," she said.

"The big surprise lay ahead," Angel stated. "It was so unexpected. About fifteen minutes after we were home, John appeared. I was amazed to see him so soon. We looked for him in Orlando and were unable to locate him. Also now he was driving a beautiful white Ford Explorer I never saw before."

Angel stopped and stared at the detectives, whose interest instantly perked up with the mention of the vehicle.

"I don't need to tell you, I was shocked with the sight of that vehicle. It was a very good-looking automobile. I asked John, 'Where did you get that car?' And just as calm as could be, he said, 'I rented it.' I looked at him and saw something in his eyes that told me that wasn't true.

"Seeing my skeptical look, John gave one of his sly smiles and changed his story. This time he said that the vehicle belonged to his girlfriend." Angel smiled and shook her head. "You never know what that man will come up with."

She told the detectives, "The girlfriend he was referring to is Gracia Hill. She lives in Rockledge. I've got her address and telephone number, if you want them."

"Yes, we certainly do," Weir said.

Angel thought a moment and then said, "I didn't really know, but I thought there might be some truth to John's story about it belonging to Gracia. The kids told me the other day that Gracia had some kind of a truck."

Angel told the detectives that her mother, Faye Elms, arrived home from work at about that time and saw the vehicle parked out front. Surprised, she entered the house and asked her daughter to whom it belonged.

Angel said that she was not sure. "I can tell you what John told me, but I can't tell you if you can believe that story."

While she and her mother talked, she said, John gathered up his children, loaded them into the Explorer and took off.

Later that evening, Angel said she received a phone call from John Huggins. He said he was sorry for what happened last night at the motel and wanted to make it up to her. He apologized for his attack on her and suggested taking the group to Sea World.

Angel said she was hesitant. She was still upset over what happened yesterday, but John persuaded her that they would have a good time and the children would love it. Reluctantly she agreed to John's plans.

She said he asked her to pick him and his kids up at his friend Kevin's house.

Angel explained that his friend was Kevin Smith and he lived in Cocoa Beach. "As I look back, I can't remember seeing that white Ford when I arrived to pick up my passengers. I didn't even think of it.

"We drove to the Holiday Inn in Melbourne and spent the night. The next day, we headed into Orlando and registered at the Holiday Inn on International Drive. Then on Father's Day, John kept his word and took us to Sea World."

Angel stopped. "Would you gentlemen like a cold drink or anything?" Both men declined. "I'm just going to get a glass of water. Be right back."

While she was gone, the two detectives exchanged glances, somewhat surprised by the story she was telling, trying to glean some connection to their case out of all the details she was relating.

Angel returned with the glass of water, set it on the small table beside her chair and picked up her story.

"We took in all of the attractions, which made a big hit with everyone. While we strolled about, John's son, Jonathon, came up and told me, 'Dad had a real cool, cool truck.' He had a big smile and went on, 'It has a radar detector, and wow! It has air-conditioning all the way in the farthest backseat. And it has a radio and you can tune it even from the backseat, and it has an alarm. How about that? It's such a really neat truck.' "

According to Angel, the group returned home to Melbourne, to a lot of excitement. Angel's sister, Nancy Parkinson, and her children, along with Melanie Cramden, a friend of hers, arrived at the house from Greenwood, Delaware.

With the family activities in full swing, Angel's mother invited John and his children to spend the night in her home.

Angel said that on the morning of June 21, she arose and looked for her sister, Nancy, who was nowhere to be found. Her children and her traveling companion, Melanie Cramden, were also gone.

Angel said she and her mother discussed that and decided that the group must have gone to Walt Disney World. They knew Nancy and Melanie were very eager to go and were planning it. Faye suggested that maybe they left early and didn't want to disturb the household. But they were both surprised that she didn't say anything the night before about going today.

Angel continued her seemingly unending story to the detectives. "Later that same morning, John came to me and wanted to borrow my car. I turned him down flat, and he just walked away with no reaction, which is not like him at all."

A short while later, Angel discovered that her automobile, her estranged husband and his children were, like Nancy and Melanie, gone.

Angel was furious and she complained to her mother that they should not have invited John to the hospitality of their home. For the remainder of the day Angel Huggins raged.

Faye found it difficult to calm her daughter. About eleven o'clock that night, John Huggins called Angel.

She demanded to know where her car was. Huggins calmly told Angel the car was safe, that he had needed to borrow it for a little trip. He said it was parked at the Econo Lodge in Rockledge, where she could pick it up. He gave no explanation for taking the car or for leaving it at the motel. Then he was gone.

Angel said that a few days later, on June 27, Nancy came back to the residence of Faye Elms. She returned to pick up Angel's son, Austin Junior, and drive him back to his father's home in Maryland.

Disturbed and upset by Nancy's action, Angel allowed an unpleasant exchange to ensue between them. Angel wanted to know where Nancy had disappeared with Melanie. Nancy said that she was in St. Augustine and she objected to Angel's interrogation.

A raging argument occurred between the sisters when Angel informed Nancy of some facts she had learned. Through many phone calls over several days and thorough checking, Angel traced her sister and her estranged husband, John, to the Royal Mansions Condominiums in Cape Canaveral.

Angel described John Huggins and Nancy Parkinson to the management of the Royal Mansions, receiving the response, "Oh, yes, they are registered here."

This situation infuriated Angel. She could not believe that her sister was so deceptive.

When she confronted Nancy with the information that her sleuthing uncovered, Nancy exploded.

Furious, Nancy collected Austin Junior, and along with her own children and her friend Melanie Cramden, departed, presumably for her home in Delaware.

"I was stunned, absolutely stunned, with this whole thing," Angel explained to the officers.

"These things happen," Detective Weir calmly assured her. He wondered just where all this was leading. His interest was in the Ford and its connections, if any, to this whole long narrative about Angel's marriage difficulties.

He and Linnert continued to listen quietly, albeit impatiently, as Angel leaned back in her chair and continued. "On the evening of June twenty-eighth, I was taking it easy, trying to get over the unhappy past few days, when I got a phone call. It was from Tom Victor. Tom Victor," she explained, "is my sister Nancy's boyfriend." Her face showed her surprise. "I wondered why Tom was calling me." She took a deep breath and went on. "It didn't take long for him to tell me that he saw Nancy and her friend Melanie Cramden in Easton, Maryland. The shock was that John was with them. I still get upset when I think about it." She stopped, waiting for the detectives' reaction.

Linnert looked at her, thinking, *Your domestic life is pretty complicated, and I'm sure it's very interesting, but that's not why we're here. Get back to the Ford, that's what we want to hear about.* He sighed under his breath.

Angel Huggins continued, telling about a telephone call she received from Kevin Smith's live-in girlfriend, Kimberly "Kim" Allred, who told her about all the commotion going on around their home and about a car that burned near there. Kim described in detail the helicopter search and the explosion of activities in the area. She also told Angel that the burned vehicle was involved with a murdered woman from Orlando and that the case was going to be featured on the *America's Most Wanted* television show later that evening.

Angel told the detectives that when she watched *America's Most Wanted*, she recognized the Ford Explorer as the one John Huggins was driving on June 10.

She said her friend Kim called her after the show and they discussed the vehicle. Kim also was positive that was the same SUV she saw John Huggins driving.

Angel said she became very suspicious of Huggins. She decided to do some checking and phoned the Days Inn in Kissimmee to verify the dates they stayed there. She also determined that the location of the motel was across the street from the Publix market where Carla was last seen. Angel shook her head as she recalled the situation. She stated that she then called *America's Most Wanted* and reported her suspicions.

She also told the detectives about a situation that developed when Nancy did not return her son, Austin Junior, to his father on time. The man went into a tirade and called the police for assistance to get his boy back.

Angel also recalled that during one of her telephone calls with Huggins he told her, "Don't be surprised if I call you and tell you there's something in your house." She said she thought Huggins had planted a bug on her telephone and said as much to him. He told her that it was not a bug, it was jewelry.

The two detectives, who had been sitting quietly listening to Angel's narrative, were instantly alert. The word "jewelry" was a red flag flashing at them.

The woman said she and her mother searched the house but did not find any jewelry.

She continued telling the detectives the woes of her marriage, with more details of conversations, phone calls and events that took place after that fateful week in June.

At the conclusion of the interview, with their curiosity piqued, the detectives asked and received permission from Angel and her mother to search the home. However, they found nothing evidentiary during this search.

At the conclusion Weir and Linnert interviewed Angel's ten-year-old daughter, Tiffany. Angel was present during the session.

The child happily recalled the trip to Gatorland and staying at the Days Inn suites in Orlando. She remembered her mother and John having an argument but she could not tell what it was about. "They sounded like they were very mad." She said John Huggins left the motel the next morning and she didn't see him until late afternoon. "When he came back, he was all sweaty. Yuck!" She heard Huggins tell her mother to take the kids home. "Then he left again." She said everybody else rode home with her mother.

Whitney stated that after they arrived home, Huggins showed up driving a white "Jeep." Jonathon told her that it was really neat and that his dad had rented it.

CHAPTER 11

When the interviews and the search were concluded, Weir and Linnert walked slowly to their automobile. They were worn out, but elated with the information they learned.

"I never thought this buggy would look so good to me." Linnert laughed.

As he unlocked the doors, Weir said, "What a staggering report. It boggles the mind. I can't say that I'm not grateful, but I didn't think Mrs. Huggins's saga would ever end. It had so many twists and turns, it was hard to follow. Lucky we took notes."

"Ain't that the truth," Linnert agreed. "My mind is reeling. But if the information she gave us checks out and is true, this could be our major break. Thanks to *America's Most Wanted*. Her account fits the time frame, and it explains why the car was in Brevard County."

The detectives clearly felt they were finally making progress in the investigation.

On the drive back to Orlando, Weir commented, "Mrs. Huggins sure gave us a starting point." He nodded his head, obviously pleased with the information from Angel. "But there are a number of things that she told us that we should discuss and try to sort out."

"Sure. Where do you want to start?"

"Mrs. Huggins put it all together in a nice package, checking the dates when they stayed at the motel and also sorting out its location across from the Publix."

"She sure did," agreed Linnert. "Hope it holds up when we check it out."

"I'm interested in that curious phone conversation she had with Huggins," Weir said.

"Me too. She got my attention with his statement about 'finding something in your house.' When she said he admitted he meant jewelry, I had a tough time keeping a poker face."

"Yeah, my ears perked up with that word, too. But her search and now ours didn't turn up anything. There must be some significance to Huggins's remark about jewelry. We'll have to check that out further, but I'll bet that jewelry is somewhere in that house."

The detectives kicked that discussion around, knowing that the jewelry was a key issue.

"With all the other information she gave us that we have to follow up, we've got our work cut out for us," Weir stated.

"I can't wait to see Huggins's rap sheet. I'll bet it's a doozy," Linnert remarked. He stared off into space, projecting what he might find out about John Huggins.

Back at their desks, Weir leaned back in his chair. "Been a busy day." He checked his watch; it was 8:42 P.M. He wondered aloud, "Is it too late to call him?"

"What are you mumbling about?" Linnert asked.

"I'm thinking about calling Jim Larson."

"What about?"

"I want to ask him about the Ford Explorer's interior, the way it was set up. Remember Angel said Huggins's son made such a point about the air-conditioning going all the way into the back with separate controls? And how the controls for it and the radio were mounted in the end of the front center console between the seats. Larson could tell us about that."

"Sure, call him. It's not that late."

In response to the call, Larson gave Weir a full explanation about the A/C controls, which matched their description. Larson also told him that a radar detector was mounted below the overhead console and wired into the electrical system of the Explorer.

When the call concluded, Weir turned to Linnert. "Larson confirmed all the information we got. Everything was just like the Huggins kid said it was."

"That's terrific." Linnert smiled.

"The unfortunate thing about it," Weir said, "is that all of it was destroyed in the fire." He shook his head sadly. He thought over the details of the information Angel gave them. For the first time in this case, he felt they had a direction, which made him more optimistic.

"I'm bushed. How about you, John?"

"Yeah, me too. Let's call it a day. Let's go home and see if our wives still recognize us."

Early the next morning, back at their desks, the detectives were eager to start following the new promising leads. John Linnert suggested, "Cam, let's discuss that Gracia Hill."

"What about her?"

"According to Angel, she is Huggins's girlfriend and he said that the white vehicle he was driving belonged to her, that he just borrowed it. I think that we should go talk to Ms. Hill and get a look at whatever she is driving."

"Right. We don't want to leave any stone unturned," Weir concurred.

Angel Huggins had provided the detectives with Gracia Hill's address. They drove to her home in Rockledge, several miles north of Melbourne on Florida's east coast.

The woman who answered the door was surprised to see detectives on her doorstep, but she invited them into her home, which was small but obviously well cared for. The detectives observed an attractive woman in her early thirties, about medium height, with blond hair and a nice figure. She led them into a cozy living room, and after they were seated, she looked at them expectantly. "How can I help you, Detectives?"

Weir said, "Ms. Hill, we understand that you are a friend of John Huggins's. Is that correct?"

"Well . . ." She hesitated. "I'm not sure how to describe 'friend' in this case. What is this about?"

"We're checking into a situation that involves Mr. Huggins," Detective Weir explained. "Would you mind telling us how you met him and something about him?" He looked at her encouragingly and smiled.

She said, "I met him when he was a patient at the Wuesthoff Hospital in Cocoa Beach." She looked at the officers somewhat defensively and went on, "He asked for my telephone number. One evening, after he was discharged from the hospital, he called me."

"Have you talked to him lately?" Linnert asked.

Gracia Hill thought for a few moments and recalled, "I think about a month, or month and a half ago."

"What else can you tell us?" Linnert pressed.

"I went with him once when he drove over to return a car to his mother's residence near Bushnell." She stopped, frowning in concentration, then offered, "This was around June first or second." Again she paused to recall and continued. "He was staying at the Econo Lodge in Cocoa with his children. I remember meeting him there one night and swimming in the pool with him and the kids."

"Do you know what kind of a car he was driving at the time?" Weir prodded.

"It was a blue Taurus, which was what he left at his mother's home."

"What kind of car do you have, Ms. Hill?" Weir inquired.

"A green Ford Ranger pickup truck."

The men thanked Gracia Hill and left.

As they drove off, Linnert grumbled, "Just another bit of nothing."

"On the contrary, John. We know that the story Huggins

told his wife about borrowing the white Explorer from Ms. Hill was a lie," Weir stated positively.

Slowly John Huggins was emerging as a viable suspect.

Weir checked his notes. "The next one on our list is Kimberly Allred. She's the friend of Angel's who saw the *America's Most Wanted* program and recognized the Ford. She lives in Cocoa Beach with her boyfriend, so it's right up the road."

They arrived at the location and scanned the surrounds. The home was an average-size duplex, on a peculiarly shaped lot, narrowing at the back toward the river.

Kim Allred met the detectives at the door, not entirely surprised to see them. "Come in," she invited, showing them into the living room.

"What can I do for you?" the slender woman asked.

"We're investigating the murder of Carla Larson, the woman killed at Walt Disney World last month," Weir began. "I understand you saw the *America's Most Wanted* TV show and we'd like to ask you about some details."

"Sure." She smiled. "What do you want to know?"

"It's our understanding you recognized the white Ford Explorer shown on that show. Is that correct?" Linnert asked.

"Certainly is," she stated positively. "When I saw that TV show, it struck me like a flash of lightning that the white Ford Explorer they showed looked exactly like the vehicle that John Huggins parked in back of our house." She described it in precise detail as white with a tan strip around the bottom.

"Do you remember the date it was parked at your home?" Weir inquired.

She stared at the ceiling. "I think it was June twelfth."

Weir filed that date in his mind for future reference.

"It stayed on our property for two to three days," Allred volunteered.

"What can you tell us about Mr. Huggins? How do you know him?" Linnert asked.

"I guess you know I live here with Kevin Smith," she said.

Weir nodded.

"That doesn't explain much, but this should help. Kevin and John Huggins are friends. They met when they were in the Sharpes jail together. And after they were released, they stayed in contact with each other." Her expression clearly showed her disapproval of that friendship. Rather defensively she explained, "Recently Huggins contacted Kevin and asked him to help him buy some marijuana." She gritted her teeth and added, "When Kevin had the pot, he called Huggins on the phone and arranged for him to come over and pick it up.

"When he came, he was driving this beautiful white SUV. After they finished their business, he asked Kevin if he could leave the car here for a while. Kevin thought he meant for a few hours, but it turned out to be two and a half days.

"I probably wouldn't have cared, but John parked it in my way," Allred explained. "See, the way the lot narrows in back, I couldn't get into our back door easily. When I came home from the market, for example, with two bags of groceries, it was so inconvenient to get into the house. I'm glad that you weren't around to hear what I said under my breath when I tried to get in with the stuff." She laughed. "It's funny now. It wasn't then."

Detective Weir nodded sympathetically as she continued. "And then I ran into the darn thing late one night. Kevin and I were out and we were pretty much at each other's throats arguing about everything. By the time I pulled onto our property where the grass was wet and the ground slippery, I skidded right into the back end of the Explorer. I hit the back panel on the left side behind the rear tire. When I got out and looked, I could see that the Ford was dented from the impact, and I scraped some red paint off it from my car."

Shaking her head ruefully, she recalled that Smith was even more upset than he had been all evening. "He said, 'Now you did it.' I didn't answer. We didn't report the accident to our insurance company or to any law enforcement agency," Allred explained. "The right front turn signal on my truck was already damaged from an earlier accident, which was also not reported.

"Kevin couldn't wait to tell John Huggins that I crashed into his car. Surprisingly, it was a big joke to John. I don't know how he was figuring, but he told Kevin that he had a five-hundred-dollar deductible insurance policy, so it made no sense to me that he thought it was funny."

Kim Allred said that Huggins told Kevin Smith that the white Ford was a rental. "But I couldn't keep up with all of the stories that came out of John Huggins."

"So you were extremely annoyed with Huggins about this car?" Linnert asked.

"That's putting it mildly. I wondered when the hell he was going to take this damn car away. Anyway, we were having a barbecue on Sunday, the fifteenth for Father's Day, and when I came home, the white Ford was gone."

Allred said that Angel stopped by during the barbecue, and she told Angel that she ran into John's vehicle. Later, when she told Kevin about it, Smith said that Angel was not supposed to know about it.

"When I saw that Ford Explorer on *America's Most Wanted,* I was stunned. I couldn't wait to call Angel."

Kim Allred recounted her phone conversation with Angel Huggins. "When I told her that the vehicle they showed looked just like the one John Huggins left here a few weeks ago, Angel asked, 'Do you really think so?'

"I told Angel that I'd bet my life that it was the same car."

Linnert asked, "What did Mrs. Huggins say about that? What was her reaction?"

"At first I thought that she didn't believe what I was telling her, but as we talked, it became obvious that she believed anything about her estranged husband. She wanted to know everything I could tell her about it."

When asked, Allred said that on Thursday, June 26, the night of the burning of the vehicle, she was home alone with

Smith. She could not remember anybody showing up at their home. She recalled all the commotion surrounding the burned vehicle, which happened less than a mile from their place, and she remembered the helicopter circling the area.

At the conclusion of the interview, Detective Weir asked permission to inspect her truck, to photograph it and collect possible evidence as necessary.

"I have no objections," Allred stated.

At Detective Weir's request to the Brevard County Sheriff's Department, Deputy Criminalist Virginia Casey arrived at the Cocoa Beach residence to examine Kim Allred's vehicle. She was joined by Florida Highway Patrol officer Corporal Steve Ashburn, as well as Sharon Ballou, crime laboratory analyst of the Florida Department of Law Enforcement.

The three photographed the right front quarter panel of Allred's red 1988 Nissan pickup truck. Ballou made sketches and examined the panel of the truck for microanalysis evidence. They also took paint scrapings from the damaged area to try to match up with the Ford Explorer.

The detectives were unable to meet with Kevin Smith at this time. Kim Allred explained, "We argued earlier and he left in a huff."

Later, Detectives Weir and Linnert received a phone call from Kevin Smith. They arranged a meeting at Smith's home for 4:30 that afternoon.

After the arrival of the detectives, Weir explained to Smith the reason for the interview, and he agreed to help in any way he could.

Smith, a tall, lean man with sharp brown eyes and long shoulder-length rusty brown hair, told them, "I'm sure that you know by now that John showed up here on June twelfth, big as life in that fancy white Ford Explorer. It had a bug guard on the front, luggage rack and lightly tinted windows. I took one look at that automobile and thought, 'Wow! What a car.' I wondered where John came by it. I really admired it, even sat in it. It had grayish cream-color leather interior. I noticed the radar detector suction-cupped to the windshield." Smith leaned back in his chair and explained that "I was surprised because it was hardwired directly into the electrical circuit, instead of being plugged into the cigarette lighter, which is normal."

He continued, "I asked him where he got the car. He said it was a rental, but I was skeptical because I know rental cars don't come with radar detectors hardwired into the electrical system.

"John asked if he could leave the car parked behind my house for a bit while he went next door to the lounge." He gestured in the direction of the Illusions Lounge. "I said, 'Sure,' thinking he'd be back in a couple of hours. Instead, it was a couple of days. He finally took it away on the fifteenth."

Smith hesitated a moment, then continued. "Several days after John drove the Explorer away, I was doing some tidying up in the back of my house. I found several items on top of our hot-water heater that didn't belong to us and one was the radar detector, sitting there along with other stuff. I thought I was seeing things. But I knew positively that it was the detector from the Ford. It had the same style suction cup attachment hanger system as the one in the Explorer." He said that the power cord was cut.

"What happened then, Mr. Smith?" Linnert inquired.

"Well, I'm hesitant to say." He looked at the lawmen, reluctant to reveal more, but he knew he would have to talk.

"Just tell us. There won't be any problem," Weir assured him.

"Okay. I was afraid of what would happen if it was found here, so I got rid of it."

"Where?" Linnert asked.

"I threw it in some bushes a few blocks from here."

"Can you take us there?" Weir asked.

"Sure."

Smith silently led the two detectives to a spot on South Atlantic Avenue, east of A1A, where he directed the officers to a thicket of bushes. He leaned down and retrieved a black instrument, which he held up, stating, "This is it. I threw it into the bushes here this morning."

Weir and Linnert glanced at each other, thinking, *Was it before or after he knew of our visit to his home?*

"Why did you discard it?" Weir asked.

"I was upset; I just didn't know what to do," Smith answered frankly. He laced his fingers together and went on. "Kim told me about your investigation and I just got concerned. I didn't want to get involved in any way. I was worried about that detector and I just wanted to get rid of it and everything connected with it, so I threw it away." He hesitated and added, "This morning."

"Did you see John Huggins any time after he retrieved the Ford?" Weir inquired.

"I got a call from him about a week later, asking me to get some marijuana for him, which I did. When he came by to pick it up, he had a nice-looking woman with him. I was surprised and asked him who she was. He told me it was Angel's sister. I asked no more questions." He paused. "Angel is a friend of Kim's."

At the wrap-up of the interview, Weir summoned Deputy Criminalist Virginia Casey of BCSD, who photographed for evidence records the detector, where it was found and the top of the water heater area, where Kevin Smith said he found it.

CHAPTER 12

The investigation broadened, moving forward slowly but inexorably, with the detectives following up meticulously on every bit of information that they learned about John Huggins.

Weir verified that John Huggins checked in the Holiday Inn on June 10. "He stayed through June eleventh," the inn clerk told Weir. He also said that Huggins used a passport for identification. *That's strange,* Weir thought. *Why would he have his passport with him? Why not use a driver's license?*

In answer to questions that Detective Weir asked, the clerk said that Huggins paid cash for his room. But when the detective asked about the vehicle that John Huggins was driving, he was told that they didn't have any surveillance cameras overlooking the parking area.

Weir relayed the information to Linnert. "I'm just sorry we couldn't establish what vehicle Huggins was driving when he checked into that Holiday Inn," he said gloomily.

"Yeah, it would have been helpful," Linnert responded. Adding a positive note, he said, "But we know that he was driving around on June tenth, and we have good indications that it was in Carla Larson's Ford Explorer."

Weir nodded in agreement.

The detectives checked out the Huggins clan's visit to Orlando. "We need to establish their being here when these events occurred." Weir checked the notes on his pad.

When the motel confirmed the Hugginses' visit on the dates Angel told the detectives, they were satisfied that she was truthful.

Linnert gloated. "Finally things are beginning to fall into place. So far everything she told us has checked out. I have a good feeling that the rest of her story will, too."

"Yeah, I like a girl who tells the truth." Weir smiled at his partner's enthusiasm. "Now let's get back to the radar detector Kevin Smith gave us."

"Let's check with Jim Larson and find out if it came from the Explorer."

"Right. If it was theirs, he should be able to give us the full background on it."

When the detectives arrived at the Larson home in College Park, Jim greeted them with a friendly smile. "Good to see you."

Weir noticed that the man seemed thinner, and the detective wondered how Larson was coping with his situation.

"We've been going over some things and need to talk to you about something," Weir explained.

"Sure. I'm glad to help you in any way I can. What's up?"

"The radar detector."

"What about it?" Larson asked, a puzzled expression on his face.

"We know that your wife had one in her vehicle and one was found behind a residence in Cocoa Beach. We feel very strongly that it came out of the Explorer."

"Really?" Larson asked. "How can I help?"

"First of all, we need to know when you acquired it," Weir continued.

"We had two," Larson responded. "One in the Honda and one in the Explorer. I bought both of them by mail order. I should have the paperwork on them."

Jim excused himself and went into another room, where

he found the purchase order and serial number of the radar detector mounted in his Honda.

"I know that we bought the detector for the Explorer in 1995, but I haven't been able to find the purchase order," he explained as he handed Detective Weir the document with a serial number. "This is the one for the Honda, but I don't know what I did with the receipt for the one in the Ford."

Larson left the room again and returned with files filled with papers and receipts. The two detectives, along with Jim Larson, sat at the dining-room table and tediously searched through all of the papers.

Finally they found a sales receipt from Cincinnati Microwave, showing the purchase of a Passport 4500 Radar Detector by Carla Larson on August 31, 1995. "This is good," Weir commented, "but, unfortunately, it does not list the serial number."

There was also an item on the Larsons' Discover credit card corresponding statement, which listed the purchase.

The detectives took the paperwork for their evidence file, then returned to their office, where Linnert contacted the Cincinnati Microwave company to try to determine the serial number of the Larsons' radar detector to compare with the recovered instrument.

Linnert spoke with Jennie Girdler of the company, who apologized when she informed the detective that the serial number could not be traced because the company changed its computer systems and was no longer keeping detailed records of its sales.

Over coffee the detective team reviewed their efforts and the progress they were making.

Linnert reflected, "I keep coming back to Angel Huggins's phone call from her husband and his mention of jewelry."

"Yeah, me too. It's time that we look into that again," Weir said. "If we can find that jewelry and it turns out to be Carla Larson's, we will have one really strong link to John Huggins."

"Absolutely," Linnert agreed.

"We need to get permission from Angel Huggins and her mother," Weir continued, "to search through their property again. We've been missing the boat in the search. Let's get some techs and really dig in."

Angel and her mother, while somewhat puzzled, gave permission for the search, and both signed consent. This time the detectives made arrangements for a team of department personnel to assist them in this project, which would take place on Tuesday, July 8.

The group included Detective Ron Weyland, Detective Russ Girgenti, Deputy John Philbin and Detective Sue Coleman.

Weir told the group, "I am convinced that jewelry is here somewhere. So let's give it our best shot."

The search went into operation, the department officers and specialists combing through the entire residence. Detectives Weir and Linnert moved separately through the house, room to room, working with one officer and then another.

After more than two hours of looking through drawers, under beds, into overhanging lights, into vents, under carpets and rugs, into corner wastebaskets, through cupboards, closets and even into shoes and slippers, Weir called his team together.

"I don't know where we're missing the boat, but we are. That jewelry is here, I just know it. Anyhow, Linnert and I agree that we should abandon the effort at this time. Maybe we'll get better information and come back."

The group of techs filed out of the residence and drove back to OCSD headquarters, somewhat dejected.

Disappointed with the unproductive search, Linnert said, "We haven't talked to Faye Elms yet. She apparently had a great deal of contact with John Huggins, maybe we can learn something from her."

"I was thinking that," Weir answered. "She certainly seems friendly and cooperative. Anyway, we've got nothing to lose."

"Ma'am," Weir said, approaching her. "Detective Linnert and I would like to talk to you about John Huggins."

"He's my son-in-law."

"Yes, ma'am, we're aware of that. We're also aware that he is your 'estranged' son-in-law," Weir responded pleasantly.

"What do you want to know?" she asked, mildly suspicious.

Detective Weir answered, "We've spent a good bit of time with your daughter, and she was entirely cooperative with us. We hope that you can be also."

"Okay. I'm sure that we can get along."

Detective Linnert asked, "How long have you known John Huggins?"

"We, I'm including my daughter Angel, have known him since 1992. We were living in Oviedo back then in a rented trailer." (Oviedo is a small town bordering Orlando to the east.) She wrinkled her forehead, remembering. "In the Black Hammock reserve. Things changed there for us and we moved to the Wickham Village in Melbourne, which didn't work out. Then we found this place and it fit our needs and our likes much better, so we moved in."

Elms explained, "John Huggins, along with his wife, my daughter Angel, were with us from time to time."

"How did you feel about him generally?" Linnert pursued.

"I was never really comfortable with John Huggins. I just thought that there was something about him in a shadow of doubt."

"What do you mean by that?" Weir asked.

"It wasn't long before I knew that John Huggins was in and out of step with the law. After his release from prison this past February, he came and went frequently to my home. I pretty well accepted that. Then on June tenth, I got home from work and found a strange vehicle parked out front. I wondered about it. I thought that it was a neat white truck and I tried to figure out whose car it was. I went inside and looked around for the owner. It never occurred to me that it was John, and I didn't see him inside the house. But John's kids, Ruth Anne and Jonathon, were here. I stopped Jonathon and asked him whose car that was. He just beamed and told me, 'It's Dad's. He rented it.' "

The woman said she left to attend a college class at 5:30 P.M. "When I got back around nine o'clock, the white vehicle was gone."

She told the detectives when she went inside, she learned that John Huggins and his children were gone. "I never saw that automobile again."

"You have another daughter, Nancy?" Weir asked.

"Yes."

"We understand from Angel that she visited down here."

"Yes, that's right. She's Nancy Parkinson. She arrived on, let me see, June fourteenth. She brought her kids and also her neighbor Melanie Cramden."

The woman smiled as she recalled that with Nancy's arrival and all the others: "We had a great family gathering."

"When did you last see John Huggins?" Linnert asked.

Faye thought a few minutes and answered, "On June seventeenth, when the whole family, including John Huggins and his children, joined in a gathering at the Wekiwa Springs in Sanford, Florida."

"Thank you, ma'am," Weir said. "You've been very helpful. Now we need to talk to your daughter."

"Fine. I'll get her."

When Angel came into the room and sat down, Detective Weir told her, "We just need to check some dates and other details."

"Good. Because I was thinking a lot after our last meeting and I worked on an outline. It's sixteen pages, some of the things I told you and things I thought of later." She explained, "I've got the dates of significant conversations and observations I made and where we stayed together. I remembered that I saw that white Ford again on the eleventh of June."

Since Angel was under the impression that it belonged to John's girlfriend, she said she did not want it parked on her property. "John asked me to follow him as he drove it to the Courtyard on the Green apartment complex. He just left it there, although he didn't know anyone who lived there. He backed it into a parking spot on the south side of the complex, with the rear against a tall hedge."

Angel said that in one of her conversations with Huggins, he told her he stole the vehicle to use in a robbery.

On the morning of June 12, she drove Huggins back to the vehicle. He told her he needed it to take care of some business with his friend Kevin Smith.

Angel said that later that day Huggins called, asking her to pick him up at Smith's, which she did. She recalled that she parked in the front of Kevin's residence, and Huggins walked out from the rear of the home to meet her. She explained that from where she waited, she did not see the Ford Explorer, reportedly parked in back where Kim and Kevin normally parked.

She recalled staying at the Holiday Inn in Melbourne on June 13. She said John accused her of seeing another man. She responded by stating that he was driving another woman's truck and John replied, "It's not my girlfriend's truck. I told you I stole it, and I plan to use it in one of my robberies."

The detectives exchanged glances but made no comment.

Angel said that in her outline she also detailed the history of John Huggins's physical abuse of her over a period of years.

In a surprising revelation she added that she had seen footage of a bank robbery on television news one night. When the surveillance tape was shown, she recognized her husband, John Huggins. "I'd know him anywhere."

Linnert asked, "Do you know where John Huggins is now?" He waited, hoping she had an answer.

"No. The last I heard about him he was up in Delaware or Maryland somewhere."

"Thank you, Ms. Huggins." Weir assured her that "you will be hearing from us."

Weir and Linnert were pleased to see that Angel's second statement was consistent with her first, and when combined, it put the events surrounding John and Angel's travels in good chronological order. It would not be difficult to follow through with checking everything out.

Weir also notified Detective Joe Jenkins of the OCSD robbery division, apprising him of Angel Huggins's statement about John Huggins and the bank robberies.

Jenkins interviewed Angel and subsequently pursued her helpful information in that investigation.

Although worn from the intense sleuthing, Weir and Linnert were both satisfied that all was moving ahead. They finally had a suspect and all their attention was focused on John Huggins.

"Things have certainly turned around," Linnert remarked.

"Yes, indeed," Weir agreed, stretching his arms wide. "What do you say if we knock off for today?" He took a deep breath and added, "I'm bushed."

Linnert looked at his watch: it was almost six o'clock. "That's the best idea you've had today," he responded.

The phone broke in. "I knew it," Linnert groaned. "An early evening. Too good to be true."

Weir answered the call. "No! Well, I'll be. Wait till I tell John." With the phone still at his ear, Weir faced his partner and shook his head unbelievingly, totally surprised with the news he just heard.

"It was Tom McCann," Weir identified as he hung up.

Linnert waited expectantly. "Don't keep me in suspense."

"It's Huggins. Huggins is in Maryland. Arrested."

"Holy jeez. What's the story?"

"This is one for the books," Weir answered, his eyes lighting up. "Tom McCann got word from detectives in Salisbury, Maryland, that Huggins is in custody in that state. He was arrested on June thirtieth on a Seminole County warrant.

And the Seminole Sheriff's Department placed a no-bond hold on him."

"No kidding! Wonder what the charge is. Maybe we should notify Angel about it," Linnert happily offered.

"Yeah. I think so." Weir shook his head. "The surprises with this guy Huggins have no end."

"A warrant from Seminole County? And they arrested him in Maryland? Huggins used to live in Seminole County, didn't he?"

"I think so," Weir answered. "We should talk with Sheriff Don Eslinger and get the scoop from him on the warrant."

"Great idea. We'll call him tomorrow. I sure like the way things are going now."

CHAPTER 13

Wednesday morning, July 9, was hot, normal for that month; and when Cam Weir arrived at headquarters, the temperature was already in the upper eighties. *What did we do before air conditioning?* he mused as he walked the short distance from the parking lot to the door of the sheriff's department. He thought briefly but longingly of tree-lined mountains and cool breezes and sighed.

"Good morning, John," he greeted Linnert, already at his desk.

"Morning, Cam. You look bright and fresh so early in the day."

"Yeah, the key word is early. Wait until later."

They laughed and settled down to work.

"First on the agenda, I'm going to call Sheriff Don Eslinger over in Seminole County," Weir said, "and see what he can tell us on the Huggins arrest."

"Right. I sure am curious what the charge was," Linnert responded.

"We'll soon find out," Weir confirmed as he placed the call.

"Sheriff," he began after he reached his target, "this is Cameron Weir with the Orange County Sheriff's Department."

"Hello, Cam, it's been quite a while since we've talked. How are you?"

"Great, but busy. How are you, Don?"

"I'm fine, too, but going at top speed is a bit wearing. What can I do for you, Cam?"

"I heard some interesting news and I want to ask you a couple of questions."

"Sure. Shoot."

"Our detective Tom McCann received word yesterday that John Huggins was arrested and jailed in Salisbury, Maryland."

"That's interesting. When was he arrested?"

"I understand from McCann that he was busted on June thirtieth. Today is July ninth, so I guess we could say a week ago. The interesting thing about it, Don, is that he was arrested on a Seminole County warrant. And that's the reason for my call. I'd like to know about that warrant. Huggins is a suspect in the Carla Ann Larson murder case here in Orange County."

"Oh, yes," Sheriff Eslinger said. "She was that engineer working on a project at Walt Disney World, right?"

"That's right, Sheriff."

"I'll get that information on the warrant for you. Glad to do it."

"There's something else, Don."

"Just ask."

"I'd appreciate it if we could also have Huggins's arrest record."

"Certainly. No problem. I'll be glad to get that for you. That guy has been a guest in our little bed-and-breakfast here from time to time over the years." He chuckled. "And I've heard him described as a 'bad guy.' I'll take care of this for you."

"Thanks, Sheriff."

"Glad to be of help."

Later in the day, the detectives drove to the residence of John Huggins's mother, Joanne Hackett, in Lake Panasoffkee, Florida (about fifty-five miles northwest of Orlando near

Bushnell). She was the guardian of John Huggins's two children, who lived with her.

The tall, older woman met the officers at her door, her straight black hair tied in a ponytail.

Although the woman was courteous, it was clear that she was not pleased with the appearance of two detectives at her home.

After the officers introduced themselves and showed their official ID cards, she asked stiffly, "What can I do for you?"

"Mrs. Hackett, we would like to talk with you about a car that your son, John, rented," Weir explained.

The woman glared suspiciously at them before answering. "Is it against the law to rent a car?" she asked in a sardonic tone.

"No, ma'am," Linnert answered in a calm soothing voice. He began the story the two detectives concocted as a ruse to be able to talk to Huggins's son. "We're not here to upset or offend you. We're just trying to determine what happened to a rental car that was not returned. And we have some information that John's son, Jonathon, was a passenger in this particular vehicle and might be able to tell us something about it. We would like very much to talk to the boy."

"What's going on here?" Her husband came to the door, a scowl on his face.

"They want to know about some automobile that John is supposed to have rented, which was not returned," she told her husband.

"Who are these men?" he demanded, staring at the officers, obviously annoyed with this intrusion.

"They are detectives with the Orange County Sheriff's Department and they want to talk to Jonathon."

"I'll be damned," he blustered. "He's a kid; he's only ten years old."

"We're not going to upset the boy," Weir stated soothingly. "We only want to ask him a few questions."

"What if we refuse to let you see or talk to him?" the man asked belligerently, moving defiantly closer to the detectives.

"I just hope you won't do that," Weir responded pleasantly but firmly. His statement was conveyed in an ominous tone.

The husband glared at the two detectives. Weir stated in an official tone, "Sir, we can and will take the necessary steps to talk with Jonathon, if that's what we have to do—"

"No, no," Mrs. Hackett interrupted, taking command of the situation that was going out of control. "That won't be necessary. Come in. I'll get Jonathon and you can talk with him," she said.

Moments after she seated the detectives in her living room, she brought her grandson into the room and introduced him to the officers. "Jonathon, these men are detectives and they want to talk with you about the car that you were in with your daddy."

The boy smiled and said, "That was a cool car that Dad had."

Weir and Linnert smiled warmly at the boy. Weir explained, "We just want to ask you some questions about that car."

As the detectives proceeded, the boy's grandmother quietly motioned her husband to a couch, where they were seated and could oversee the interview.

"Jonathon, what kind of a car was your father driving when you were over in the Melbourne area?" Linnert questioned the boy quietly.

"It was a rental car," he answered. He raised his head and looked directly at the detectives. "It was parked down the street from the house." Apparently desirous to help, Jonathon continued, "We used the car to go to the store and get things."

After the friendly opening with the young boy, Linnert asked, "Who drove the vehicle?"

"Dad would go get it and my mother, not really my mother, Angel, would go with him to get the car from its parking place."

"We understand that you really liked that car," Weir remarked companionably, encouraging Jonathon to go on.

"Oh, yeah. I was at Angel's when Dad drove up with that cool car. I thought it was great and I wanted to get in it. And

I did. It had a thing that told the temperature and it told the direction that you were going." He stopped to look at his grandmother for reassurance. She smiled at him and he picked up. "We went to different places in that car. Boy, it was fun."

"Jonathon," Weir directed the friendly discussion, "tell us about the vehicle. What did it look like? What color was it? What was it like on the inside? Just tell us everything about it that you can."

"It was a black car." He stopped and then thought about that. "Maybe it was green, dark green. It had those shiny steel wheels." He waited for encouragement and Weir nodded to him. "It had four doors and it was big and roomy. Inside the leather, you know, the seats and all were gray. It sure looked nice." Jonathon was excited to recount his experience in the classy car.

Again he paused to recall and then went on, "It had a shiny metal roof rack. The seats were really good. They had air cushions that changed and you could set them as soft as you like. They were so comfortable to sit on." He remembered that there was a spare tire inside the van. "And there was this cool control thing that you could adjust the air-conditioning and the radio volume in both the front and the back."

The two detectives listened attentively as the boy described the controls as being in the rear of the center console that separated the front seats. "It also acted as an armrest," he stated. He wound up with his observation that the key for the vehicle had a button that locked or unlocked the car. He looked at the officers with his big blue eyes glowing enthusiastically as he described all the details.

Weir thanked Jonathon, and Linnert complimented him. "You did a fine job, Jonathon, and we're proud of you." The boy smiled happily.

Cam Weir turned to the boy's grandmother and expressed appreciation for her cooperation and departed.

The following day, July 10, Inspector Dan Nazarchuk, a long-experienced officer with the OCSD, and Detective William

Hinkey, who partnered with him for many years in the department, were called in. Their assignment was to look into the check-ins and stays of Angel Huggins, John Huggins and Nancy Parkinson at the various hotels and motels in the central Florida area in the immediate period of the vanishing and murder of Carla Larson.

"Check on their stories," Cam explained to the two veteran officers. "We have to know where they stayed and when—just anything that you fellows can find out about them."

"Gotcha," Dan Nazarchuk answered.

Nazarchuk and Hinkey lost no time in their pursuit. They found that Angel Huggins was a guest at the Bugetel Inns in Melbourne, Florida, on June 15, 16 and 17 in 1997. They obtained the hotel registration cards.

Tracking Angel's travels, they found she stayed at the Days Inn in Titusville, Florida, on June 17, and checked out on June 18, at 11:50 A.M. The hotel records indicated that rooms 116 and 118 were rented to her.

The officers requested and were given the registration card and the record of telephone calls made from the two rooms.

The two lawmen drove to the Econo Lodge Motel on North Cocoa Beach, Florida, where they found records indicating that Nancy Parkinson, Angel's sister, rented one room on June 27. She checked out of the room on the same date at 10:46 P.M.

The officers secured the registration card. No phone calls were made from the room during the rental period. "She rented the room just for the day. Wonder if she was alone," Nazarchuk speculated.

Hinkey laughed. "Good question."

The investigators then checked the Royal Mansions Condominiums at Cape Canaveral, where they learned that Nancy Parkinson registered on June 22 and remained there until June 27. The officers obtained copies of the registration and telephone tolls.

Nazarchuk looked at records of the phone calls and told

Bill Hinkey, "We'll have to check these calls when we get back to headquarters."

Hinkey nodded. "Yeah, they might be important."

In the continuing investigation, Cam Weir and John Linnert learned that the Brevard County Sheriff's Department had some information for them. It came by chance to the Florida Highway Patrol, then passed on to the BCSD.

When Weir got the call from BCSD, he straightened up in his chair and told Linnert, "Listen to this."

Linnert looked up from his paperwork. "It better be good."

"It is. Or maybe could be," Weir said. "A man named John August in Melbourne reportedly saw Carla Larson's Explorer on June twenty-fourth or twenty-fifth."

"Well, let's have that checked out. Sounds promising, but let's get some more details."

Weir assigned Nazarchuk and Hinkey to meet with August and get his story.

The two officers met with the man in Melbourne.

After introductions Nazarchuk said, "We understand that you saw the Ford Explorer that is involved in a case that we're investigating. Would you tell us about it, the date, the description and whatever you can remember?"

August answered, "Yes, of course. It was June twenty-fourth or twenty-fifth. I saw it on the Eau Gallie Causeway, going east headed for A1A."

"Did you get a look at the driver?" Bill Hinkey asked. "And can you describe that person?"

"I drove right alongside him and got a good look at him." He seemed very positive. "He was a white man and, I guess, he was thirty-five to thirty-seven years old. His hair was dark, dark brown, I'd say, and it was collar length. I think it would be a safe bet to guess his weight at just about two hundred. From the way he was sitting behind the wheel, he had to be five-eleven or six feet tall."

Nazarchuk encouraged the witness. "What else can you remember about him? Anything that you can tell us could be important."

"It wasn't so much when I saw him that it struck me." August paused for a moment, organizing his thoughts. "It was when I watched the news on television."

"What did that tell you?" Dan Nazarchuk asked.

"They said on the news that the white Explorer had been poorly spray-painted black. That's what struck me. I thought about it and thought about it. I couldn't get that vehicle out of my mind. And then when I saw the drawings, the composite of the supposed wanted man, I knew right then and there that those drawings did not resemble the man I saw driving that black Explorer."

The investigators showed John August a photographic lineup of six different possible suspects, including one of John Huggins. August studied the pictures and selected one. It was not John Huggins. August told the officers that he was confident that he could correctly identify the driver he saw at the wheel of the black Ford Explorer, if he could see him in person.

Later, Nazarchuk lamented to his partner, "It sounds like just another dead end."

Hinkey agreed. "Well, you can't win them all."

Cam Weir and John Linnert reviewed what they assembled in their investigation so far. Weir, who is generally not given to a great deal of optimism, pushed his desk phone aside and said, "You know, John, I think we're moving ahead, going in the right direction. I just wish it could be a bit speedier—"

The phone interrupted him.

"Detective Weir," a strong, clear voice greeted him. "This is John Thorpe from the Seminole County Sheriff's Department. It's been a while since we talked."

"Yes, it has, Lieutenant, but I'm glad to hear from you."

"Sheriff Eslinger asked me to give you a call. He said that you were interested in the warrant that was issued, arresting John Huggins in Maryland."

"That's right."

"I have that information. The charge against Huggins is his failure to appear on stolen property charges," Lieutenant Thorpe stated. "We're drawing up extradition papers to return Huggins to Florida to our jurisdiction. I'll be glad to send you a copy of that, along with John Huggins's arrest record, if you would like."

"I'd be very grateful. Thanks, Lieutenant, this is the best call I've had today."

With a king-size smile, Weir turned to his partner and said simply, "We got it."

"Well, men, how's the case going?" Sheriff Kevin Beary paused as he was passing the desks of Weir and Linnert.

"Coming along, Sheriff," Weir answered.

The two detectives discussed their progress and then brought up their plans to fly north that afternoon to interview Melanie Cramden and Nancy Parkinson. They also had a faint hope of interviewing John Huggins in jail.

"Fine, fine," encouraged the sheriff. "Keep up the good work."

The flight to Washington, D.C., was uneventful, and before long the two detectives arrived in their rental car at the home of Melanie Cramden in Greenwood, Delaware.

John Linnert rang the doorbell of the residence and waited. He looked at the setting sun. "It's been a nice day," he observed.

Weir asked impatiently, "What's the delay here?"

"Maybe she's not home," Linnert replied.

"Do you think that she is deliberately not answering, wondering who we are and why we're at her door?"

"Now, now, Cam, don't be so suspicious."

As he spoke, the door opened, revealing a small, pleasant-faced woman, probably in her late thirties or early forties. After introductions Melanie Cramden invited the officers inside.

Weir began sociably: "Did you have a nice trip to Florida?"

She smiled. "I'd say it was a nice trip overall, but it had a lot of unexpected things that we never figured on."

"How's that?" Linnert asked.

"My whole idea or desire was to make this trip with my neighbor Nancy Parkinson, to visit Walt Disney World." She reached over to an end table and picked up a brochure of the entertainment complex, which she brought back with her, and held it up for the detectives to see. "I'd heard so much about this place for years that I wanted more than anything to see it, especially Cinderella's Castle. And when Nancy asked me to go along with her and the kids as company on her trip to Melbourne, I just thought that was a gift from heaven."

"That must have been an exciting experience for you." Weir nodded.

"It was great. You know, the realization of a dream. I could have spent days there. But we didn't have the time. And I was disappointed that we were constantly going around with no real plan or organization.

"We drove down in Nancy's minivan. It's a nice-size vehicle, but with Nancy, her three kids and me packed into it, we did not have a luxurious setup. It wasn't bad, though."

Continuing, Cramden said, "The first week we were in Melbourne, all of us stayed with her mother and her sister, Angel Huggins, at their home. On June twenty-first Nancy and I, with Nancy's kids, went to Disney World. I didn't know it but I was in for a big surprise. We met John Huggins there. He had his two children with him."

Melanie Cramden squirmed in her chair, clearly uncomfortable at telling this. "I didn't realize it at the time, but it became clear to me that the meeting of Nancy and John Huggins was not by chance. They, without a doubt, planned and arranged it.

"Anyway, after spending the day at Disney World, we all went to the Sheraton World Resort Hotel in the Orlando area."

She looked at her Disney World brochure again. "Everything about this part of central Florida is wonderful, spectacular. First the weather is great, and then there are all those fabulous resorts beginning, of course, with Walt Disney World, all the marvelous hotels and motels and the great restaurants. It was a paradise on earth."

Linnert smiled at her enthusiasm. "Maybe our chamber of commerce should hire you to promote tourism."

"That sounds good to me, Detective Linnert. Then I could live in paradise all the time."

They laughed; then John Linnert asked, "What did you do after your visit to Disney World?"

"We only stayed at the Sheraton one night. The next day, June twenty-second, we helped John Huggins drop off his wife Angel's car at a motel." A sly look crossed her face as she said, "None of us was staying there." She giggled. "It was just a place to abandon the vehicle, as John was going to spend time with us, with Nancy, that is."

"What then?" Weir asked.

"We all drove together to the Royal Mansions in Cape Canaveral. Rental condos. We had two rooms."

The detectives waited patiently as Melanie Cramden continued. "I was a little surprised but pleased to learn that John Huggins paid for the rooms. My curiosity got the best of me and I asked him how he made his money, but he didn't answer me." She had a puzzled expression on her face.

"I guess that you were having quite a time of it," Weir encouraged her.

"Yes, indeed. For example, on—let me think—yes, it was June twenty-sixth, I was moving some things from the room into Nancy's van, and while I was straightening it up, I found a gun under the driver's seat." She stopped and looked at the lawmen. "I wasn't thrilled with that. I don't like guns."

Detective Weir asked, "Can you describe the gun?"

Cramden slowly recalled it. "I don't know much about guns. This one was black, maybe it was silver—dark. It's the kind that you push a clip of bullets into."

"Do you know whose gun it was, who owned it?" Weir asked.

"When I first asked about that, no one answered me. Later, I was with Nancy alone, and I asked her about the gun. She admitted to me that it belonged to John Huggins."

Linnert prompted, "Did anything else happen that day, the twenty-sixth?"

"Nancy, her kids, John and I went to Cocoa Beach to the pier, where we had lunch. And Nancy had several drinks, too many drinks. She got drunk. We returned to the hotel room, and Nancy passed out in the bedroom."

Melanie Cramden closed her eyes, wondering if she should have disclosed Nancy's excessive drinking. She paused and the detectives encouraged her to go on.

"Sometime in the evening—"

Linnert interrupted, "On the same day, the twenty-sixth?"

"Yes, the same day. It was about seven o'clock when John picked up the keys to Nancy's van and he took off."

"Do you know where John went?" Linnert asked.

"No, I don't have any idea and I sure wouldn't ask him, because you don't ask John Huggins questions at any time." She rubbed her hands together nervously.

"When did you see him again?"

"He was gone for about two hours. And he didn't say anything to me when he got back. The kids were watching a TV show when he came in, and he just walked into Nancy's room."

"What happened after that?" Weir asked.

"Pretty soon Nancy came out of the bedroom and asked me to go with her to pick up some food for the kids, since they hadn't eaten any dinner yet."

"Is that what you did, went out to get some food?"

Cramden nodded and said, "I was ready to get out for a little fresh air and I was glad that Nancy asked me to go with her. As we were driving along in her van, that gun slid out from under the seat. I picked it up and handed it to Nancy. She smiled casually and put it into her bag. We drove around looking for a place to buy something for the kids, but most of the restaurants were closed. She finally stopped at a Dunkin' Donuts and got some doughnuts. We also got some sand-wiches at a 7-Eleven."

Linnert asked, "What happened next?"

Cramden said, "The next day, the twenty-seventh, we checked out of the Royal Mansions. We all stood around for a while and then we went into the snack bar for coffee. At this time we talked about John and discussed the possibility of him riding back with us to Greenwood, Delaware. After that was decided, the talk centered on John again, and in that conversation it came out that he was wanted for DUI."

Melanie stated that she didn't really know what John and Nancy's game plan was about the DUI. "But it seemed logi-cal that he wanted to get out of the jurisdiction of that charge, and going to Delaware offered him an out."

Also at this point, she said, it was decided that John's kids would be dropped off with John's mother. "While at his mother's, Nancy pointed out a blue Taurus and said that it was John's car.

"From there we drove back toward Melbourne and checked into a motel. Nancy and John left and came back after a while and he was beaming with pride, like he'd hit the jack-pot. I guess he had. He had a stash of marijuana that he picked up somewhere." Melanie seemed somewhat embar-rassed to tell them that information, but she continued. "I stayed with some of the kids, while Nancy took her youngest and drove to her mother's home to pick up Angel's son for the trip back to Maryland, where he lived with his father.

"John was in a hurry to check out. He explained that Angel found out that he was with Nancy at the Royal Mansions and he was afraid that she was going to show up here."

The detectives were hard put to keep up with the activi-ties of the group.

Cramden went on with her tale. "Later that same day, we left for Delaware. Our party now included Nancy and her children, me, John and Angel's son. He was to be returned to his father in Easton, which is close to Greenwood, Delaware, our destination."

"Your simple trip to Orlando to see Disney World certainly became a complicated travelogue," Detective Weir commented.

"It certainly became involved," she agreed. "But as I look back, I can tell you that seeing Walt Disney World made it worthwhile. We drove straight through, with no stops, other than for gas and the bathroom. We went to Salisbury first, rather than to Easton to drop off Austin Junior. We wanted to get John Huggins settled in a hotel room."

She paused. "All the while we were together, Nancy and John Huggins were getting tighter." She stopped and added, "And then there was Tom."

Cramden quickly explained that Tom is Nancy's live-in boyfriend.

"Somehow Tom learned that Nancy was back in town. Meanwhile, it was John and Nancy's intention to hide John in Salisbury, so Tom wouldn't find him."

Melanie Cramden seemed to be enjoying the attention the detectives were giving her, as they were hanging on her every word.

She seemed a little embarrassed as she went on. "And after they got John his room, Nancy and he spent time together alone in that room, as they had on other occasions in Florida." In a very quiet voice, Cramden told the detectives, "I just patiently waited for Nancy, reading in the lobby of the motel."

Melanie said, "Nancy came back into the lobby in a happy mood and said, 'Let's go back to Greenwood.' I just went along with her."

She talked on and on more and more freely with Weir and Linnert and got to the point where she related a conversation that she had with a local police officer in Delaware, who was involved in the return of Angel's son. While Nancy was sidetracked making arrangements for John Huggins's accommodations, Austin Junior's father became worried by the delay of his son's return and reported that to the Delaware police.

"I've got to tell you this," Cramden concluded, "along with the information that I gave to the officer about Austin Junior, I told him that John Huggins, who had traveled with us, was wanted in Florida."

The detectives thanked Melanie Cramden for her information and cooperation and departed.

When they were outside, heading to their vehicle, Weir asked, "What did you think of her?"

"I felt like you can't tell the players without a program." Linnert laughed. "A lot of what she said we already heard, but there were a couple of points that were interesting, like Huggins disappearing for a couple of hours on the twenty-sixth. Could that be when he torched the Explorer?"

"Yeah, I thought about that, too. We'll have to check everything."

When they arrived at Nancy Parkinson's door, she seemed open and friendly, willing to answer their questions and help them.

After the initial greetings Detective Weir asked about Nancy's purpose for her trip to Florida.

"I drove down to Florida to pick up my nephew and bring him back to Maryland." She explained that they made the trip in her Lumina minivan. "My neighbor Melanie Cramden made the trip with me. She came just to keep me company, but she also wanted to go to Walt Disney World while in Orlando."

"Is that everyone who made the trip?" Linnert inquired.

"Oh, no. My three kids were with us. I wouldn't leave them here while I took off for Florida. Besides, I knew they would have a great time on the trip, and they would get to visit their grandmother.

"We drove straight through, arriving at Mother's house in Melbourne on June fifteenth. I was pleased to see my sister, Angel, there with her children."

Parkinson rambled on, explaining that Angel's husband,

John Huggins, arrived on June 17. At this point, with the mention of John Huggins, her facial expression changed. She made a point of stating, "I didn't know the status of things between Angel and John at this time. I mean, the status of their marriage." She said, "I was aware that there was some kind of a situation between Angel and John, but I didn't know if their problems were serious."

In her careful account of their comings and goings, Parkinson stated, "The entire family took a trip to Wekiwa Springs and spent the night at a motel. While at the motel, John got alone with me for about fifteen minutes. He told me that he wanted to get to know me better." Nancy smiled as she continued. "He said that he wanted to spend some time with me during the next week."

Parkinson, looking smug, stopped to light a cigarette, then went on. "A little while later, John took me aside again and talked about spending time together at Cocoa Beach."

Detective Weir, surprised by Nancy Parkinson's frankness, bluntly asked, "Didn't you have any compunction about that with your sister's husband?"

Parkinson stared at the detective, puffed her cigarette and made no reply.

"Did you meet with John Huggins in Cocoa Beach?" Detective Linnert asked.

Parkinson overlooked that question as well and stated, "On Saturday, June twenty-first, Melanie and I planned to go to Walt Disney World. That was the big thing in Melanie's mind and I didn't want to disappoint her and the kids, who were also looking forward to it."

Nancy explained that it all just fell into place. "John also arranged to meet us at Disney." She laughed. "He was supposed to meet us at one P.M. I waited around for him, constantly looking at my watch, wondering if he was going to make it or not. He made it. But it was three o'clock when he showed up."

"Were you upset with that?" Weir asked.

"I wasn't exactly upset, but I wasn't happy, either. John

walked up with his two kids and it just was not the time for me to show any displeasure. I just thought that he must have had a bit of a problem getting away, but here he was, kids and all."

There was an indication of something in the tone of Parkinson's voice, and Weir asked, "Did you have a problem with John Huggins's arrival with the kids?"

"No, it wasn't anything about the kids. I was a bit startled when he told me that he came in Angel's car." She hesitated. "I couldn't understand that he was cozying up to me and giving me indications that things with him and my sister were not going so well. I wondered, if that's the case, why is he driving Angel's car?"

"Are you sure that she gave him permission to take it?" Linnert asked.

"You've got something there." Parkinson brushed her hair back, puffing quietly on her cigarette. "Much as I know about John Steven Huggins, I can tell you that the unexpected goes hand in hand with him. In other words, I wouldn't bet my last buck that Angel gave John the go-ahead to use her car." She laughed.

"What else went on between you and John Huggins?" Linnert asked, wanting to get a firsthand report.

Nancy evaded. "There is really so much about John and there were so many things, that it takes a little doing to get it all into order." She paused, took a last drag on her cigarette, stubbed it out, then said thoughtfully, "One thing that stands out in my mind is his talking about a ring."

That statement instantly caught the attention of the detectives. Any mention of jewelry set their minds spinning.

"What about a ring?" Linnert asked eagerly.

Nancy Parkinson continued. "While we were together at Disney World, John admired my engagement ring." She lifted her hand so the officers could get a look at it. "I didn't understand his interest, but then he told me that he had a ring similar to mine, but bigger. He was kind of like bragging, like a little kid saying, 'My dad can whip your dad.' "

The detectives smiled. They sat impassively, but their hearts were racing.

"Then he said something that puzzled me," Nancy continued. "He told me that the ring was at my mother's. That just bewildered me. He said that my sister was sitting right on top of it, and she didn't even know it. Then he burst into laughter. He just thought that was so funny."

Weir asked, "Did you pursue the subject?"

"Yes, of course. I wanted to know what he was talking about and I asked him point-blank to tell me about the ring and where he got it.

"He looked at me with those big green eyes and told me confidentially, 'I bought the jewelry as protection. Someone could steal your cash, but having jewelry hidden in a safe place is not that easy for someone to rip off.' "

"That's a good story," Detective Weir acknowledged. "Did he say specifically what pieces of jewelry he had locked away somewhere?"

"No, Detective. John Huggins is never specific about anything. He did indicate that the jewelry was at my mother's, but he didn't say where at my mother's."

"What else can you tell us about him?" Weir asked.

"Stories about John Huggins never end. But you might like to hear about his kindness."

"Yes, we would like to hear that," Linnert said.

"I was having some serious car trouble." Her head dropped as she explained. "I just didn't know where I was going to get the money to have the car repaired. Somehow John found out about my car trouble, and he also learned that I was short of money."

Parkinson waited for the detectives' reaction as she lit up another cigarette.

"He gave you the money to have your car repaired," John Linnert suggested.

"Not exactly."

"Okay, don't keep us in suspense," Weir urged.

"When I saw John, he asked me a peculiar question.

'Have you looked under your floor mat lately?' I would have laughed, but the way he said it, there was nothing funny about it."

Parkinson leaned back in her chair and said, "I thought, no, I never looked under my floor mat. He didn't explain anything further, but I got into my car and I looked under the floor mat. And guess what?"

"You found a round-trip ticket to Hawaii," Linnert joked.

"No, but in this case it was something better. I found a hundred-dollar bill with a note that said, 'Fix your car.' I was overwhelmed."

"I would think so," Linnert commented.

Softly Nancy Parkinson told the detectives, "That's not the first time he gave me a hundred bucks." She did not elaborate, but the detectives freely imagined the occasions of this kind of generosity.

Weir and Linnert listened attentively as Parkinson confirmed what they already heard from her friend Melanie Cramden about their stays in the different motels in Orlando, Titusville, Cocoa Beach and Melbourne.

Nancy said that she told her mother they were going to St. Augustine to sightsee, but she said she really met with John Huggins. They followed Huggins to the Econo Lodge, where they left Angel's car, then stayed at the Royal Mansions in Cape Canaveral. She said they checked in under her name, because John Huggins was wanted, and they got one room for the eight of them. However, during their stay they changed rooms.

The detectives' interest was piqued when Parkinson recalled a trip she made with Huggins on Tuesday, June 24.

"We drove my van to this kind of isolated spot in Cocoa Beach and pulled up to a peculiar house. It looked like a trailer that had been added onto with wood from discarded crates. There were high bushes surrounding the place, apparently to provide some privacy for whatever activities took place there.

"After parking, John got out of the car and went into the

house while I waited in my van. I looked around the area and counted twelve motorcycles parked on the open land near the house.

"In about fifteen or twenty minutes, John reappeared, accompanied by a tall, bearded guy who looked like he might be on a wanted poster."

According to Nancy, he and John seemed to have a special rapport. In short order they parted and Huggins got back into the van. She said she asked him how it went and he answered, "Fine. I got some good stuff that we can enjoy later."

Parkinson said Huggins told her that money was tight and that he worked out a deal with his friend to set up another pot dealer for him to heist. He laughed and said, "I'll walk away with about ten thousand dollars for my efforts."

"That certainly was an interesting trip," Weir remarked.

"That's right, but there's more." Parkinson nodded, waving her cigarette. "As we rolled along, I was just thinking that I'd be glad to be finished with this junket. Then John said, 'I've been thinking about our talk about the ring. I'd like to get my ring and the rest of my stuff from the house and from the shed.' He asked me if I would help him retrieve all of his personal belongings. I agreed, but we never actually got into that. Nor was John ever able to pick up his things."

"What happened?" Weir asked.

"We were getting ready to leave for Maryland and Delaware, and I had to drive over to Mother's house to pick up Angel's son, to take him back to his father in Maryland. Well, when I got to the house, I met Angel and all hell broke loose. She found out that John and I spent the past week together and she was fit to be tied. We had a real battle royal. There wasn't much I could do but get out of there, which I did. I picked up Austin and made a beeline to collect the others and then we headed for the nearest route to Maryland."

"Probably a wise thing to do," Cam Weir commented dryly.

CHAPTER 14

John Linnert hummed "Maryland, My Maryland" as he and Cameron Weir drove to the Salisbury Police Department.

"You feel pretty cheerful, John?" Weir asked.

"Yeah. I think the net is getting tighter and tighter around Huggins. More and more, he's looking like our prime suspect. I'm really looking forward to catching up with that bastard."

Weir shook his finger at Linnert and censured, "Now, now, we mustn't speak that way about our arrested subjects."

They both laughed heartily.

At the Salisbury Police Department, the Florida detectives met Sergeant Mark Tyler.

"We certainly appreciate your cooperation," Detective Weir said.

"Glad to help. This guy is something else," Tyler stated. "I have these records and things that I'm sure you'll want." He handed Weir the hotel registration for the Salisbury Inn, where Huggins was a guest at the time of his apprehension. The records showed that room 234 was registered to Melanie Cramden.

Linnert said, "Guess that was to conceal his ID, since he was wanted."

"I'm sure that this will interest you, too," Tyler told them. "The next guest who checked into the room that Huggins occupied at the inn found a toy gun and turned it in to the front desk."

"Well, that is strange. I'd be interested in seeing that," Weir stated.

"I was sure you would, so I arranged a meeting for you with the manager of the inn."

"Oh, that's great. We sure appreciate that," Linnert said.

The sergeant also gave Weir a copy of the phone calls that John Huggins made while staying at the motel in Salisbury.

At the conclusion of the briefing with Sergeant Tyler, while John Huggins was being transferred to an interview room, Detectives Weir and Linnert drove to the Salisbury Inn and met with Marjorie Bush, general manager.

The attractive, well-dressed woman welcomed the detectives. "How may I help you gentlemen?"

Cordially Detective Linnert explained that they were in Salisbury on a case in Florida, and asked to see the toy gun from room 234 that was turned in to the desk.

"Of course," she agreed. "Let me get it for you."

As Weir accepted the plastic gun, he noted that it bore a serial number 96656230. Turning to Linnert, he said, "This looks exactly like a large-frame semiautomatic handgun." Weir passed it to him.

"This thing shoots BBs or pellets," Linnert remarked. "I wonder what Mr. Huggins was doing with it."

"Let your imagination run wild," Weir answered.

Returning the plastic piece to Ms. Bush, Weir thanked her for her cooperation and told her that she would be hearing from Sergeant Tyler of the Salisbury Police Department. Weir intended to make an official request for the plastic weapon.

Back at police headquarters, Detective Weir gave the sergeant an account of their visit with Ms. Bush. The sergeant assured the detectives that he would arrange for the plastic gun to be collected and sent to the Orange County Sheriff's Department.

* * *

When the detectives had interviewed Nancy Parkinson, they noticed that she was a heavy smoker. They asked her if John Huggins also smoked. She assured them that he did and his favorite brand was Marlboro. On the way back to the jail for their interview, the two detectives stopped to buy a pack of cigarettes. Their purpose was to get DNA samples from the ones Huggins smoked.

Since neither of the detectives smoked, they tossed a coin and Linnert lost, so he had to smoke with Huggins during the interview. "There's no limit to what I'll do to solve a crime," Linnert joked.

The two detectives waited in the private conference room for John Huggins to be brought into the room for the interrogation.

The detectives placed disposable ashtrays on either end of the table so Huggins's butts would be totally separate from Linnert's.

The door opened and John Steven Huggins, shackled at the wrists and ankles, was escorted into the room. He sat at a table opposite the Florida detectives, who came many hundreds of miles for this special moment.

Introductions were made by Sergeant Tyler, with little acknowledgment by the men, only curt nods. The 6' John Huggins casually gazed around the large room with his hazel green eyes, basically ignoring the detectives. He seemed totally disinterested in the surroundings and the men. It was clearly evident that he was not happy to be in this meeting.

The detectives studied John Huggins's appearance. They were somewhat shocked at the sight of him. He was an unsightly man, excessively overweight, with long, unkempt brown hair swept into an ugly ponytail cascading down the back of his shoulders. He had a bearded face, cold, hard eyes, and was dressed in a discolored T-shirt and pants. But what struck both of the investigators forcibly was that there was little if any resemblance to the composite drawings made of the suspect from the eyewitness accounts.

Linnert pulled the pack of cigarettes from his pocket and started to light one. Immediately Huggins asked, "Could I have one?"

"Have all you like," Linnert invited.

Bringing the purpose of the meeting into focus, Detective Weir began. "Mr. Huggins, our purpose in making the trip from Florida to be here was already explained to you. We would like to ask you some questions. But first I want to advise you that you have certain constitutional rights that I am about to read to you."

Weir also explained to Huggins that they set up a tape recorder to make a record of this session. (There was also a hidden camera filming the meeting.)

Detective Weir then read John Huggins his constitutional rights from an official form.

"Do you have any questions, Mr. Huggins?" Weir formally asked.

"No. No questions. I am waiving my rights and am willing to answer your questions," he responded quietly.

"Fine," Weir answered. "For the record, Detective Linnert and I are investigating a crime that occurred in Orlando, Florida, on June tenth of this year."

Huggins nodded his head and said, "I know that."

Weir stated, "It concerns the disappearance and death of Carla Larson."

The detective paused, letting the name Carla Larson sink into Huggins's mind. The homicide detective continued. "We know that at the time of Carla Larson's disappearance, you were in the area where she was shopping at the grocery."

Calmly Weir told Huggins, "In a video surveillance from the Publix supermarket parking lot, you, Mr. Huggins, were seen." He stopped again, his deep brown eyes focused on the hostile eyes of John Huggins. "You were in that parking lot at the time of Carla Larson's abduction."

In an unexpected reaction Huggins rose. "I was in Kissimmee during that time. I was with my wife, Angel."

Detective Linnert said, "Please sit down, Mr. Huggins.

Now explain to us where you were, exactly, on the afternoon of June tenth."

Huggins panned from one detective to the other before answering. "I did leave the hotel room that day. I went to a strip mall shopping center to meet a guy. I met him and completed a drug deal with him. As part of that transaction, I had to drive a vehicle back to Melbourne."

"Who was the man you met?" Linnert asked.

"Detective, you know better. If I were to give up this guy's identity, I'd be killed in quick order."

Detective Weir followed up, asking, "What kind of a car were you to drive to Melbourne?"

"It was just a brown Jeep." He glared at Weir.

Detective Linnert questioned him next. "Mr. Huggins, your wife, Angel, and others told us that they saw you driving a white Ford Explorer. The kind of car that Carla Ann Larson was driving. How do you explain that?"

"That's easy to explain," Huggins retorted. "You wouldn't know this, but my wife is a bitch." Huggins lit up another cigarette and took a few puffs before continuing. "My wife was just being vindictive toward me for being with her sister. That's all there is to that."

Detective Weir turned to a new subject. "How about drugs? How deep are you into them?"

Huggins pulled on his wrist cuffs. "I don't have any problems like that, even with the medications that I take."

"We would like to have a saliva sample from you, Mr. Huggins," Detective Weir explained. "The purpose of the saliva is for its use in DNA evidence comparison with what was found on Carla Larson."

"You'll get no damn saliva sample from me. I don't have to comply with that and I sure as hell am not going to," Huggins answered in a firm, unshakable voice.

Detective Linnert leaned closer to Huggins and asked, "Do you know that a radar detector was found at your friend Kevin Smith's place, and it was determined that it was from the white Ford Explorer that you reportedly were seen driving? Tell us about that, Mr. Huggins."

"I don't know anything about any radar detector." He stiffened and said, "I never had no Ford Explorer at Kevin's home or anyplace else."

Losing some of his cool facade, Huggins went on. "Kevin was just telling those stories. He wanted to get me out of the way." He rubbed his head, hampered by the handcuffs laced on his wrists, and added, "He had his eye on Angel. He wanted her."

Linnert looked at Huggins and asked, "Tell us about you going to Kevin's home with Nancy Parkinson, you know, when you went to buy some marijuana."

John Huggins did not acknowledge the question. He sat and stared at the detectives defiantly.

Weir tried another approach. "Mr. Huggins, we have it on good authority that you left the Ford Explorer at Kevin's home."

"I don't know what you're talking about. I did not leave a vehicle behind Kevin's house."

The interview went on, and for every question the investigators asked, John Huggins gave a fanciful or vague answer.

Reversing the procedure, John Huggins pushed his head forward, with his green eyes blazing, and demanded to know it if was true that "you two detectives questioned my son, Jonathon?" As he delivered his question to the detectives, his face reddened with anger.

"Yes," Weir answered positively. "We talked at length with Jonathon." He smiled, further annoying Huggins. "He's a nice boy."

"You had no damn business talking to him, a ten-year-old boy."

"Mr. Huggins, let me point out to you," Detective Weir corrected. "No one can tell us who we can or cannot talk to, and that goes especially for you."

Huggins sat sullen. Detective Weir continued. "Your boy, Jonathon, said that you were driving a sport utility vehicle with a radar detector and other features similar to that of the Larson vehicle."

The experienced detective pressed the upset father. "Would you say that your son, Jonathon, was a liar?"

Shaking in fury, with the handcuffs clinking, John Huggins stated flatly, "Jonathon would not lie."

Weir, not surprised with the reaction from Huggins, turned to Linnert, "I don't see any purpose of wasting any more time with this man, do you?"

"Not at all."

The detectives summoned Sergeant Tyler and returned Huggins to Maryland custody.

The interrogation was over. It ran approximately two hours and ten minutes.

The gleeful detectives gathered the separate disposable ashtray they provided for Huggins. There were three cigarette butts that the suspect smoked during the interview. They were collected as evidence, and later used as a comparison source of DNA testing.

Both Orange County detectives thanked Mark Tyler and extended a warm wish for a Florida visit. "We'll be glad to see you in the Sunshine State."

CHAPTER 15

That evening just before eight, Detectives Weir and Linnert drove to Trappe, Maryland, to meet with Angel Huggins's former husband and seven-year-old son at their residence.

The father, in a good mood now that his son was returned, indicated his willingness for the officers to talk with the boy.

"Austin, we would like to ask you a few questions," Detective Weir began in a friendly approach.

Looking to his father for approval and support, the little boy had a puzzled expression on his face. "It's all right," his parent assured him.

"We're going to talk to you about your visit with your mother in Florida," Weir said.

A smile crossed the boy's face with the mention of his mother, and he nodded slightly.

"You remember that your daddy drove you to Florida and left you with your mother for a visit?"

"Yes," the boy answered. "I remember. We had a nice ride to Florida."

"Do you remember seeing Mr. John Huggins, who is now your mother's husband, when you got to Florida?"

Austin nodded. "Yes, I remember."

Weir described the time that the boy saw John Huggins with

the group of his step-and half brothers and sisters when they stayed at the Holiday Inn and then the Days Inn suites, which Austin recalled. But when he asked the boy if his mother argued with John Huggins while they stayed at the Days Inn, Austin said that he did not see or hear any arguments between his mother and Huggins.

In answer to a final question from Detective Linnert, the boy told the detective that he did not see John Huggins driving any car other than his mother's.

The questioning of Angel's son was concluded.

As they drove away from the residence, Weir sighed. "I guess that was a no-score."

"You don't catch a fish with every cast," Linnert philosophized. "But that doesn't mean that we have to stop fishing."

On Saturday, July 12, Weir and Linnert discussed the progress of their investigation. They decided to talk to Nancy Parkinson again before they returned to Florida.

Linnert suggested, "She's had time to do some thinking about our visit. Maybe she remembered something more. What do you think?"

"My mother used to say, 'It couldn't hurt.' Let's try."

At Nancy Parkinson's residence, the two Florida detectives held a second interview with her.

"It's nice to see you again," Nancy greeted skeptically.

Linnert smiled. "We'll try to make this painless for you."

"Oh, you don't have to be so concerned. I know that you're just doing your job."

"I'm glad you understand," Weir said.

"How can I help you this time?" Parkinson inquired.

"First of all, Ms. Parkinson," Weir began, "we would appreciate your making this a sworn statement for the record. Is that all right with you?"

Nancy Parkinson agreed to have her statement sworn and tape-recorded. When they began, she told the detectives she had done a lot of thinking since they last talked to her about the time she spent with John Huggins, and she recalled more details.

She said she wanted to tell the detectives about being with

John Huggins and her friend Melanie Cramden at the Cocoa Beach pier on June 26.

"Sure, tell us about that," Weir agreed.

"We were having a good time and I was looking at some jewelry in a display case when John asked me why I wasn't wearing earrings." Nancy reached up and felt the lobe on her right ear, as if to check for an earring. "I thought that was an odd question for a man to ask. I didn't think that men paid much attention to earrings. I never heard a man say, 'Did you notice the pretty ruby earrings Jane was wearing?' "

Nancy watched the detectives for their reaction, then continued. "I told John that I left my earrings at home and that I really didn't have much jewelry anyway.

"He looked at me like he felt sorry for me. And I was sorry that I said what I did, about not having much jewelry. He told me that he had a pair of diamond earrings. He just looked at me then, as if he was expecting me to say something, maybe ask him for them. But I didn't say anything at all. Then out of the blue, he asked me if I would like to have them. I thought about that and, naturally, I told him, 'Yes, I would like to have them.' There was no more conversation about them and I never saw any diamond earrings from John Huggins. The issue was never discussed again."

"That's interesting," Detective Linnert commented, thinking about Carla Larson's missing diamond earrings.

"What else?" prompted Cameron Weir.

"John called me from jail. Collect," she added with a tinge of asperity. "He asked me to come and see him. I knew from his serious voice that it had to be important. I agreed to go to the jail."

Parkinson paused to light a cigarette. "When I met him at the jail, sitting on the opposite side of a separator, he was in a happy mood. He pushed as close to me as possible so he wouldn't be overheard, and kind of stage-whispered, 'I want you to do something.' I stared at him; I had no idea of what was coming next. Evidently, the jail authorities gave him permission, because he passed me a check.

"I saw that it was made out to me, in the amount of thirty-five hundred dollars. I asked what it was for. He explained that three thousand was for his mother. I was to pass it on to her. He told me the other five hundred was for me. Not to buy my silence, he said, it was just to help me with my expenses. He emphasized that."

"I guess even a bad apple has some good portions to it," Detective Linnert remarked.

"What else can you tell us about your friend Huggins?" Weir prodded.

"I imagine you'll want to hear about this. I spoke with John by phone the day before you two interviewed him. He was in a good mood, and I thought that he might be willing to talk freely with me, tell me things.

"There are times when he is as silent as that big Rock of Gibraltar, and there are times he flows out with everything like the Mississippi River. But you never know which channel he's into. I just figured that I would ask him some of the things that were in the back of my mind. The worst he could do is answer no. So that night I asked John if he blew up that car in Cocoa Beach." She stubbed out her cigarette.

Detective Linnert straightened in his chair as he and Weir waited expectantly.

"What did he say?" Linnert asked.

Parkinson said calmly, "He just laughed."

She said that he explained, "Angel was just trying to get revenge."

"Did you ever ask John if he murdered the woman at Walt Disney World, in Orlando?"

"I never asked him that," she said flatly. She lit another cigarette to give herself a break.

The detectives sat silently, waiting for her to continue.

Parkinson picked up her conversation. "I didn't want to ask John too many questions. I didn't want him to get mad at me."

"Did he know that we talked with you?" Linnert asked Parkinson.

Carla Thomas,
grade school photo.
(Courtesy of James Larson)

Carla Thomas's high school
yearbook photo from
Pompano Beach, Florida.
(Courtesy of James Larson)

The future
Mrs. James Larson in
her wedding picture on
December 1, 1990.
(Courtesy of James Larson)

Blissfully happy, Carla and Jim Larson in Orlando, Florida. (Courtesy of James Larson)

Jim Larson, his daughter Jessica, and his stepmother Ada Larson. (Courtesy of James Larson)

Deputy Tom Woodard of the Orange County Sheriff's Department was the first officer responding to the report of the disappearance of Carla Larson.
(Courtesy of Orange County Sheriff's Dept.)

The Publix grocery market in Kissimmee, Florida, the last known location where Carla Larson was seen.
(Author's photo)

Detective Cameron Weir, co-lead Orange County Sheriff's Department Homicide Detective in the Huggins case. *(Author's photo)*

Detective John Linnert, co-lead Orange County Sheriff's Department investigator in the Huggins case. *(Author's photo)*

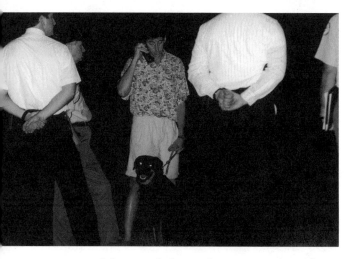

Jim Larson joined the search for Carla Larson with Carla's Rottweiler. (The Orlando Sentinel, *June 13, 1997*)

Portion of the vast area searched where Carla Larson's body was discovered. (Courtesy of Orange County Sheriff's Dept.)

Carla Larson's leg extending from beneath a large palmetto bush, as discovered by searchers.
(Courtesy of Orange County Sheriff's Dept.)

Detective Tom McCann, who represented Orange County Sheriff's Department in the *America's Most Wanted* telecast.
(Author's photo)

Side view of victim Carla Larson's burned Ford Explorer.
(Courtesy of Orange County Sheriff's Dept.)

Riverfront site of Carla Larson's burned Ford Explorer.
(Courtesy of Orange County Sheriff's Dept.)

Larson's Ford Explorer at the Orange County Sheriff's Department garage where technicians examined it. *(Courtesy of Orange County Sheriff's Dept.)*

Interior of gutted Ford Explorer. *(Courtesy of Orange County Sheriff's Dept.)*

Seminole County Sheriff Don Eslinger cooperated in the investigation of the Huggins case. *(Courtesy of Seminole County Sheriff's Dept.)*

Lt. John Thorpe of the Seminole County Sheriff's department worked with the investigators in the Huggins case.
(Author's photo)

John Huggins was arrested as a suspect in the murder of Carla Larson. *(Courtesy of Seminole County Sheriff's Dept.)*

John Huggins in the Seminole County Sheriff's Department jail. *(Courtesy of Seminole County Sheriff's Dept.)*

The electrical wall box in the shed behind Huggins's mother-in-law's house where Carla Larson's jewelry was found. *(Courtesy of Orange County Sheriff's Dept.)*

The Centex Rooney pendant Carla Larson always wore. *(Courtesy of Orange County Sheriff's Dept.)*

The motel in Kissimmee, Florida, where the Huggins family stayed on June 10, 1997. *(Author's photo)*

Gatorland, a tourist attraction visited by the Huggins family in June 1997. *(Author's photo)*

Public Defender Bob Wesley, who represented John Huggins. *(Courtesy of Bob Wesley)*

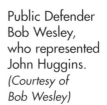

Assistant State Attorney Jeff Ashton prosecuting John Huggins in his second trial. *(The Orlando Sentinel, July 26, 2002)*

Angel Huggins, estranged wife of accused killer
John Huggins. (The Orlando Sentinel, *January 27, 1999*)

Chief Judge Belvin Perry presided over
the John Huggins trials. (*Author's photo*)

Carla Larson's parents, Mert Thomas and Phyllis Thomas,
seated with Ada Larson and Jim Larson
at the second Huggins trial in Tampa, Florida.
(The Orlando Sentinel, *July 24, 2002*)

John Huggins being escorted into the Orange County
courtroom for his sentencing.
(The Orlando Sentinel, *September 20, 2002*)

Phyllis Thomas, mother of murder victim Carla Larson, hugs prosecutor Jeff Ashton after the jury recommended that John Huggins be executed.
(The Orlando Sentinel, *July 27, 2002*)

"Oh, yes, I told him that. And he told me that I didn't have to talk to you officers." She laughed. "And then he said that I should not talk to you anymore.

"Before we finished our conversation, John said he wanted me to do something." She said he explained that he was going to be transferred and he wanted her to come to the jail before that occurred. He wanted her to pick up his belongings and ship them home for him.

Parkinson said that Huggins asked her to look into his suitcase and carefully go through all of his personal belongings for what looked like a gun or weapon and get rid of it. Linnert thought, *Did Huggins forget that he left that plastic gun in the Maryland inn? Or did he have another one?*

She said, "I was stunned with this request. I thought of the ramifications of finding some kind of weapon, which would then sure as hell implicate me. I didn't know if he was joking, but I decided not to get John's belongings as he requested."

"How often did you see him in jail?" Linnert inquired.

"I saw him twice, that's all."

"What about telephoning?" Weir asked.

"I talked with him on the telephone numerous times."

"Ms. Parkinson, Detective Linnert and I are grateful for your help in this investigation."

"Thank you for that. I do want to be of assistance to you. I think that's the right thing to do."

"Along those lines, we hope that you might do something else with us."

"What's that, Detective?"

"We'd like you to talk with John Huggins on the telephone at the Wicomico County Detention Center, where he is incarcerated. And we would like to record the conversation. Maybe you can get him to say something incriminating about the murder. Would you be willing to do that?"

"Yes, of course."

Detectives Weir and Linnert met with Sergeant Richard

Ashley of the Maryland State Police Troop 5 and explained their plan to record a telephone call to an inmate, unknown to the inmate.

"The second party, who would initiate the call, is consenting to the recording of the conversation," Weir explained to Sergeant Ashley.

"You've got no problem, Detective Weir," Ashley told the Florida detective. "In Maryland it is legal to record a telephone conversation if one of the two parties to the call consents to the recording."

With the program effected, the detectives placed a recording device on Nancy Parkinson's telephone.

The institution personnel took John Huggins to the telephone to receive Nancy Parkinson's call, which was recorded.

"Hello, John," Parkinson greeted Huggins in an affable tone.

"I didn't expect this," he answered, surprised at hearing from her.

"I just had to talk to you. I told them it was a family emergency."

"Okay, Nancy, what's your problem?"

"Are you sure you want to know?"

"You called me, didn't you? So tell me what's going on, okay?"

"The detectives just left here, and they scared the hell out of me."

"What do you mean? How? What did they tell you?"

"They said that I might get arrested for conspiracy. I'm scared. I don't know what I did to give them something to arrest me for. I don't want to be in trouble, John. What should I do?"

"Calm down. Don't be scared. You don't know anything. I spent the entire afternoon with them. Those pigs came after you to work you because they weren't able to get anything out of me. Now they're mad at me."

"Tell me, John, with all this going on, are any of the

things concerning the murdered woman true? Did you do it, John? Did you do it?"

Parkinson waited for Huggins's answer, but he remained silent, and after a moment he told her, "No." He then added, "I didn't have anything to do with it."

John Huggins explained to Nancy Parkinson that if the detectives had proof of his involvement, the "pigs" wouldn't need to talk to her.

Huggins also told Parkinson that the detectives told him that she passed out the night before they all left Florida. Huggins said they claimed that when she passed out, he left the condominium.

Huggins told Parkinson on this call that he told the detectives that she didn't pass out and he did not leave the room. He said that he told them that they stayed together.

Parkinson then asked Huggins about the jewelry.

He answered, "The pigs were asking about the jewelry because they didn't have anything to pin on me." Huggins paused and then said, "Angel got the whole thing started."

Parkinson asked about the jewelry again. "You know, the police searched my mother's home for hours. They didn't find anything."

Huggins was silent, and Parkinson asked, "Did you get everything out of the house?"

Huggins answered, "Honey, there's . . . Nancy, listen, baby, listen. You're getting confused now. Okay?"

Parkinson replied, "All right."

Huggins continued, "You've never been told anything about that. You've never seen anything like that—"

Nancy Parkinson interrupted him, "I've got to go. My boyfriend is coming in the house."

The conversation concluded. It was clear from the recording that the plan failed and the detectives learned nothing. Evidently, John Huggins trusted and confided in no one.

CHAPTER 16

Cam Weir buckled his seat belt on the plane and turned to John Linnert, smiling. "Wasn't there a great song 'Going Home' that someone wrote?"

"I think there was, but I can't tell you who wrote it. Whoever it was had the right idea. And I've got one, too."

"What's that?"

"How about taking the wives out to dinner tonight?"

"That's the best idea you've had this week, John. I hope they're still speaking to us." Weir laughed heartily.

The two detectives arrived in Orlando, exhausted and glad to be back in the Sunshine State.

They followed the plan and took their wives out for a relaxed, leisurely dinner. The women glowed with the attention that they had missed since the two officers became entangled with this murder case.

Both men awoke the next morning refreshed and energized, ready to go on with the case.

"Look at this stack!" Weir exclaimed as he grasped a handful of envelopes, mail and reports on his desk. "What a way to greet us. And I was going to say it's good to be back." He chuckled.

"What have you got there?" Linnert asked.

"I'm not sure what most of it is, but there's Huggins's arrest report we requested from Orange County. And there's an envelope from the Seminole County Sheriff's Department." He opened the large manila packet and studied the pages enclosed. "It's the stuff on Huggins sent over by Lieutenant Thorpe."

Grinning, John said, "That's just what we need after our trip to Maryland. Huggins certainly has become an important part of our lives." He shook his head.

"Boy, there's a lot here. That John Thorpe is really on the ball."

Leafing through the stack, Cam Weir said, "These seem to be reports made to the OCSD and the SCSD over a period of years. We'd better split the pile. Let's find out what Huggins was up to in the past."

The two took their copies to their desks and started reading.

The Orange County records showed only an arrest for marijuana possession.

After a short time Linnert said, "Cam, look at this." He held up a stack of papers. "Pages and pages of allegations, complaints, charges and countercharges—all domestic violence, going back to 1986. Huggins beat up on his first wife, Marianne, so many times over the years. In this report she found and destroyed a bag of John's marijuana, so he beat and choked her. Then he told her he knew someone who would take care of his problem by killing her. Another time he threw her into a pond adjacent to their residence. What a bastard."

Weir agreed. "It sounds like he's got a violent temper."

"Makes you wonder why she continued to stay married to him," Linnert remarked. "I never understood why women take these severe beatings and don't leave."

Weir looked up from a report he was reading. "Yeah, they even stay when their kids are in danger. In February 1989 Marianne Huggins said Huggins choked her and threatened to choke her daughter. She reported that she was beaten and hospitalized with broken ribs in the past. She said she feared for the lives of herself and her daughter."

Weir continued reading. "Here's a new angle. Marianne stated that about two years ago she caught her husband watching her daughter and a girlfriend showering. Marianne said that John went to the extreme of boring a hole in the wall adjoining the bathroom. She found him hiding in the bushes under the bathroom, where he was watching her daughter showering. Marianne told the investigator that when John was confronted, all he would say was that he would never touch her daughter and that it would never happen again."

"Yeah—sure. 'Trust me. I didn't do it and I'll never do it again,' " Linnert said sardonically.

Reading further, Weir said, "Well, she did try to get rid of him. It says that Marianne asked John to leave, but he refused. Two days later, he still refused to leave. She called his mother, at which time John got very violent. According to the report, he grabbed Marianne by the throat and told her that he was going to snap her neck. He said that if she told anyone what happened, he would kill her."

Linnert read that Marianne told the investigators that in the past she was hospitalized three times due to John's severe beatings.

"Man, he really is a nasty guy," Linnert commented.

"Jeez, besides all the domestic violence complaints," Weir stated, "there's a constant record of burglaries and robbery charges."

"I'm not surprised. I'm reading a different kind of report involving Huggins. This goes back to September in 1991." Linnert read the papers. "A woman requested the authorities to investigate numerous credit card and loan accounts that may have been established through fraudulent use of her father's identity."

Linnert paused. "The father was John Walter Lee Huggins, the father of the complainant. Also the father of John Steven Huggins. John's sister advised the authorities that her father, who disliked charge or credit cards, died on June 6, 1991, after which she discovered that many accounts were opened in his name, and the account addresses listed were those of John and Marianne Huggins."

Linnert asked Weir, "How do you like that?"

Weir shook his head wordlessly. "He seems to have a finger in so many different pies, I'm beginning to feel like nothing about John Steven Huggins surprises me."

There were more reports of violence between the Huggins couple, and the police noted in the complaints that John threatened Marianne's son, "to have him taken care of."

"More threats of killing," Weir remarked.

Detective Linnert, reading from a report, got Weir's attention. "You gotta hear this, Cam. Deputy Hare responded to a call and met with Angel. This was before she married Huggins. She told Hare that she was dating Huggins but said, 'I broke up with him. His wife, Marianne, threatened to kill me.' She said, 'Both the Hugginses have been harassing me.' "

Angel claimed that Marianne had some mental problems.

"It sounds to me like maybe more than one of them had mental problems," Weir replied dryly.

"Here's the same old scenario," Linnert stated. "In May of 1995 John Huggins, now married to Angel, was doing replays of what he did with Marianne, threatening to do her bodily harm, also threatening to take her child away from her, and doing a plethora of other unpleasant things to her."

"No end with this guy," Weir said. "Incredible."

"You said it. Now here's a twist. This is dated May 3, 1995. John Huggins called the Sanford Police Department to have his wife, Angel, arrested to prevent her from testifying against him during a child custody hearing involving his children from a previous marriage. Huggins also called the Seminole County Sheriff's Department Communications Center and requested a deputy. He said that his wife, Angel, was in violation of a restraining order, and that she was violent."

Linnert looked up from reading. "Huggins said *she* was violent?"

Then he continued the recap. "Deputy B. Brady responded to the location. Deputy Brady checked the presented paperwork and found them invalid, as were allegations that the state attorney's office had pending prosecution cases against Angel Huggins. Upon checking, it was learned that there were two felony cases and arrests, but—get this—John Huggins was the defendant."

"What an operator." Weir shook his head. "He beats up on these women unmercifully over a period of years, and here he's using the law to try and have his wife arrested? Talk about gall."

"He sure has that." Linnert stared at the roster of Huggins's activities. "Did he ever work? These reports all list him as unemployed. How did he live? Where did his money come from?"

"Good question. Maybe from his robberies," Weir replied facetiously, and focused on a report he was reading. "Listen to this. On June 22, 1993, there was a report made regarding a fire to the John Huggins residence in Oviedo. This fire was believed to have started in the kitchen and it completely destroyed that place. Well, now, this naturally raises a question in my mind about any fire that in any way might involve John Huggins. I'm thinking, of course, of the burned Ford Explorer."

"A natural speculation," Linnert remarked. "Here's a change. In November 1995 he was stopped by Melbourne police and charged with driving without a license, and possession of a concealed 9mm pistol. So he had a real gun as well as the plastic toy one."

"What has emerged from all this mountain of complaints and reports," Weir concluded, "is a continuing history of violence. There are burglary and fraud charges, a fire at his home, and his wife, Marianne, who complained she was in fear for her life, died in a shadowy automobile accident. His criminal activities stretch from childhood with a juvenile record to allegations of bank robberies."

"The only thing I can say, Cam, is that Sheriff Eslinger was right when he said Huggins was a bad guy. And that's putting it mildly."

When they finished reading about Huggins's criminal activities, Weir said, "For my money, he's our guy. But we don't have enough for an arrest. We have eyewitnesses who give conflicting descriptions, some who saw him in the Ford Explorer, which was white, black or dark green. He was in the area where Carla Larson was snatched, but no one saw him there. And although his friend Kevin Smith's home, where he allegedly parked the Explorer, is only two-tenths of a mile from where the vehicle was burned, no one saw him set the fire. And we haven't been able to find the missing jewelry. So unless the DNA can tie him to the body, our hands are tied."

"I know," Linnert commiserated. "There just has to be some evidence somewhere that links him to the murder, that proves he's the one. We'll just have to keep plugging to find it, no matter how long it takes. I just hope we're not applying for our pensions by then," he added gloomily.

The two men reviewed their interview with Nancy Parkinson and her talks with John Huggins on the subject of jewelry.

"Descriptions of the jewelry were distributed to every jewelry store and pawnshop in the entire central Florida area, but nothing has surfaced," Linnert said glumly.

"That stuff just has to be in Faye Elms's house," Weir insisted. "Huggins meant something when he boasted that Angel was sitting on the jewelry. But what? If we could solve that, we might have a shot at finding it. Should we search her house again? What do you think?"

"Well, I don't know where else to look. But we searched

her place so thoroughly the last time. I can't imagine where it could be hidden."

"I know, but it's about our only lead."

"Okay." Linnert sighed. "Let's do it."

On Wednesday, July 16, the two detectives, along with Investigators Weyland and Spahn, and Postal Inspector Ed Moffit, went to Elms's residence to proceed with another search.

Inspector Moffit and Detective Larry Spahn, using a portable X-ray machine, examined piece after piece of furniture. Careful not to overlook even the slightest possibility, Weir asked that Angel's car seats be X-rayed, ever mindful of Huggins's boast that "Angel was sitting on the jewelry."

While the search was going on, Angel showed Cam Weir a letter that she received from John Huggins. Weir smiled in amazement as he read the return address, " 'Maryland Jail, Just for You.' "

Weir read on, " 'God Bless you, One day we will all stand in front of god and be judged for our sins. May he have mercy on Me and You. I will always love Sarah. Good Bye John.' " (The identity of Sarah remains one of the many mysteries of John Huggins. The mis-capitalizations are all Huggins's.)

The detectives were disappointed but not surprised with the negative results of this latest search of Faye Elms's house.

"We'll just keep trying," Weir promised. "My gut tells me it's there."

On the morning of Thursday, July 17, Detective Weir spoke with officials at the Wicomico County Detention Center and learned that prisoner John Huggins was picked up on July 14 by Transcor, a private prisoner transport company, and transported to the Seminole County, Florida, Jail.

"Good," Detective Linnert remarked when told of that development. "Now we can proceed with that guy."

Weir agreed. "At least he's back in our territory."

Late in the afternoon, Weir received a phone call and his face lit up in a huge grin. When he replaced the receiver, he boomed, "Bingo!" and shot his fist up in a victory sign.

"What?" Linnert asked eagerly.

"That call was from Faye Elms," he burst out. "She found the missing jewelry! She found it! I told you it was going to turn up at her place."

"Wow! You were right after all. Where was it? How did we all miss it?" John exulted.

"She didn't go into any of the details, so let's go to her place now."

"Right." Then Linnert suggested, "Let's have Sergeant Head and Deputy Cawn make the trip with us. This is really up their alley."

The two detectives arranged for the crime scene specialists to follow them in a separate vehicle to Melbourne. Carl Head and Sandy Cawn would document the items, photograph them and collect them as evidence.

As the official vehicles pulled into her driveway, Faye Elms, in eager anticipation, met them and flashed a warm smile of welcome.

The two detectives' attention was caught by Faye Elms waving a wadded-up paper towel fiercely clutched in her hand.

Elms handed the wrapped package to Deputy Sandy Cawn and said, "I'm sure that you'll want to examine this." Cawn placed the package on the hood of her vehicle and began carefully unwrapping the paper towel, with the other officers and Elms watching.

"There it is," Weir almost whispered.

Spread on the hood of the sheriff's vehicle lay a pair of diamond stud earrings, a pear-shaped diamond solitaire ring and a gold chain. The chain was laced through the ring.

Deputy Cawn shot picture after picture of the jewelry, including the paper towel. She photographed the pieces separately and also grouped together.

Weir, with Linnert beside him, questioned Faye Elms about her discovery.

"How did you find this stuff?" the detective asked. "We

searched for hours on two different occasions and with sophisticated equipment, and found nothing."

Elms pointed to a shed at the rear of her property and stated happily, "In there."

"I'll be damned," Detective Linnert exclaimed. "We searched in there. Where was it?"

"Come into the shed. I'll show you exactly where this stuff was hidden."

Weir turned to Cawn. "I want you and Carl to come along. We'll need pictures of that, too."

Inside the shed Faye pointed to an electrical wall box with the cover off. She told them the jewels were jammed inside. The electrical box was situated about one foot above the floor, on the east wall of the shed, near a sink. As the investigators examined the whole setup, Elms handed them a metal cover that belonged to the wall box.

"The big question in my mind," Detective Linnert said, "are there any other pieces of jewelry stashed somewhere else in this shed? Maybe the Centex Rooney pendant or the garnet one."

"Good question, John," Weir answered. "We'll comb through the whole place again. Let's see if there is anything else that we might have overlooked."

For the next forty to fifty minutes, the sheriff's people checked through and looked over, into and under everything, every nook of the Elms shed, but they found nothing additional.

Deputy Sandy Cawn and Sergeant Carl Head continued taking pictures inside the shed, and then endless shots outside, including the general surrounding property, for future reference and evidence. Upon completion of their work, the crime scene specialists took the packaged jewelry and returned to OCSD headquarters, where they turned it in to the evidence department and wrote up their report.

Still at the Elmses' property, Detectives Weir and Linnert took a detailed statement from Faye Elms.

"I got home about five-thirty," she began. "I cooked dinner and Angel, the kids and I ate. After dinner I put up some laundry, and since it was still light, thanks to daylight saving time, I did a little yard work.

"You know, you can never get caught up with everything around a house. I went into the storage shed and I noticed a screwdriver lying on the floor. I didn't think much about that at first, but then I began to wonder how it was left on the floor. For some reason I looked at that wall box and noticed there were only two of the four screws holding the cover on it. Then I looked at the screwdriver again, and it hit me that something was wrong with the wall box. So I took out the two screws that were holding the cover in place."

Elms shook her head. "I couldn't believe what I saw. There was a paper towel wadded up in there. I pulled it out of the wall box and then I just couldn't believe my eyes. Sparkling jewelry, diamonds, a ring, a gold chain."

Faye Elms recalled that shocking moment. "I didn't know what to think. I was scared. Then I thought, 'How in the world could that valuable stuff get into that box?' And what scared the hell out of me, was that this was in the storage shed on my property. I sure didn't want to have the police coming to my place, finding this stuff and taking me to jail as a robbery suspect. I figured that the best thing that I could do was call the sheriff's department and tell that I found this jewelry. And that's when I called you."

"What do you know about this jewelry?" Detective Linnert asked Elms.

"I told you everything, just as it happened. I don't know a thing about these pieces of jewelry. I never saw them before."

"You're sure?" Linnert pushed, wanting positive assurance about the pieces.

"Of course I'm sure. Does it make any sense to you that I would call you to report this stuff if it was mine?"

"Does it belong to your daughter Angel? She lives here

with you," Linnert persisted. He wanted there to be no question of the ownership of the jewelry.

"Detective, get this straight," she snapped. "This jewelry does not belong in this residence to anyone who lives here. Not to me," she insisted, "not to my daughter Angel, nor anyone that I know of."

Detective Linnert pushed further. "Who do you think might have been in this shed recently? Do you recall anyone?"

Faye Elms stared at the detective and her eyes seemed to glaze.

"What are you thinking, Ms. Elms?" he persisted.

"I don't know if I should even talk about this, because I don't really know anything. I don't want to mislead you, and I don't want to be a mis-informer." She paused, thinking deeply.

"Well, tell us what you're thinking," Detective Linnert prodded.

"I really don't know that this means anything. I don't know that there is any relationship to the jewelry, but the last few times that my son-in-law was here, he seemed to be in and out of this shed many times." She hesitated. Now that she had pointed a finger, she seemed to have qualms about whether she should have said anything.

"Your son-in-law, you mean John Huggins?" Detective Linnert asked calmly, suppressing the elation he felt.

"Yes."

"What did John Huggins do in this shed?"

"I don't really know. I didn't pay that much attention to John. None of us ever pays any attention to John. He's always working on something that he never talks about."

"All right, Ms. Elms. Thank you for your cooperation. We'll be in touch."

Faye Elms was glad that this was over, but she worried about having implicated her son-in-law.

On Friday morning, July 18, Cam Weir and John Linnert met in the parking area at the sheriff's department at the

Thirty-third Street, Orlando, location, and walked into the building together.

"It's going to be another hot one," Weir remarked.

"Yeah, we sure could use some rain. It might cool things off a bit. Whatever happened to those nice, gentle afternoon showers that we used to have?"

"Guess the weather patterns have changed. Well, maybe we'll get an early hurricane. Isn't that something to look forward to?" he asked, joking.

They were at their desks when Jim Larson arrived at the invitation of the detective team. They needed his identification of the jewelry.

"Thank you for coming in, Jim," Cameron Weir welcomed.

"What's up, fellows?" Larson asked the officers, with whom he was now friendly. He was surprised to see Detective Ron Weyland of the crime scene unit, Sergeant Carl Head and Lieutenant Mike Easton of the major case division all present in this conference room. "It looks like something important is in the wind."

"It is," Weir answered.

Cameron Weir produced a tray, which he placed on the large oval-shaped table in front of Jim Larson.

When Larson saw the jewelry spread out on the tray, he was speechless.

"These were found in a shed on the property of Mrs. Faye Elms," Detective Weir informed Larson.

The name Faye Elms meant nothing to Jim Larson, who continued to stare at the tray of jewelry as though mesmerized.

After Larson's long study of the items in front of him, Weir asked, "Jim, do any of these pieces look familiar to you? Do you recognize any of them?"

Larson nodded and somberly answered, "This looks like the same jewelry that Carla wore." His eyes softened.

Linnert and the other officers looked at each other, knowing that the investigation had just moved a gigantic stride ahead.

"Are you sure? Look again," Weir asked, not wanting to lead him.

"That ring," Jim responded. "I recognize it from the size and the shape. It's Carla's." His head moved closer to the tray of jewelry, his eyes welling with unshed tears. Choking back his emotions, Larson stated, "It appears to be the one I gave Carla." His voice faded into silence. In a while he added, "When we were engaged to be married."

Larson picked up the pair of diamond earrings from the tray. He looked closely at the separate stones that made up the pair, and a faint smile appeared. "These, I know, I gave to Carla." His eyes blinked as he recalled. "I selected the diamonds for these earrings from a flat of loose stones. After I made the choice, I discovered that there was a difference between the two diamonds. I thought about it but decided that it didn't matter, that no one would be holding the two earrings together, checking the size of them against each other."

He looked around at the several officers and noticed that they were smiling at his explanation.

Returning to the tray, he picked up the gold chain and said softly, "This looks like the chain that Carla was wearing when she disappeared." He rubbed his palm over his face at the reminder of what happened to his beloved wife.

Cam Weir and John Linnert were elated. Finally they had the tie they needed to link John Huggins to Carla Larson, a giant step forward in the murder investigation, making him the prime suspect at last. Following the trail finally paid off. Now they could narrow the investigation and proceed to collect the evidence needed to make their case.

CHAPTER 17

"This is great country," Weir declared, scanning the picturesque setting of the North Carolina wooded area through which he and Linnert were traveling.

"No argument there. It's nice to see mountains. And this cool weather is certainly a welcome change," Linnert replied. "But here we are far from home, still pursuing the details of our case. It's already July twenty-third and I don't see us anywhere near the end of our investigation." He sighed. "It just gets more and more complicated. It's like the Mississippi, it just keeps rolling along. I guess it goes with the territory." He laughed. "But I think it would be a little easier if the territory were not so darn big."

"Agreed."

The Florida detectives arrived at the Lab Corp Center for Molecular Biology and Pathology, where employee Anita Matthews greeted them.

As he had earlier outlined over the telephone, Detective Weir laid out and explained the packet of jewelry that he and Linnert brought to the lab for their study. The work of the lab, it was hoped, would develop DNA evidence that the Florida department could use or pass on to the state attorney's office, possibly to be used in trial.

Ms. Matthews took the items of jewelry, and very carefully and thoroughly swabbed each item separately and completely with a special sterile fluid for the possible removal of any DNA materials that might be present on the jewelry.

Weir and Linnert watched each step of the operation. Matthews informed them confidently, "Detectives, if there is any DNA present on these pieces of jewelry, you can be sure that we'll turn it up for you." She added, "Just wait a minute and I'll package your items and return them to you."

The officers thanked her for her cooperation, and when she gave the package back, they drove off to lunch.

At the restaurant Weir said, "John, I'm going to call in to Sergeant Corlew and check on the doings back in our bailiwick."

"Good, I'll get us a table," Linnert replied. When Cam Weir returned to the table, Linnert asked, "What's wrong? You look like you just dropped five grand in the market."

Weir hesitated, then pushed the menu away, no longer interested in food. "I can't say you won't believe this, because you certainly will." He paused, Linnert avidly awaiting his news.

"The damned press learned about us taking this trip."

"No," Linnert replied.

"Ron Corlew told me that somehow the press found out about our trip up here to North Carolina and that it was related to the fact that there was a possible suspect in our case."

"I'll be damned," Linnert swore.

"It certainly upset everything at headquarters, and after meetings and discussions," Weir continued, "they made the decision to announce to the media that Huggins was a suspect."

"That's really going to put the pressure on us," Linnert said.

Weir nodded. "One good thing," he added, "no information concerning evidence was released to the news media at that time."

"Thank God for small favors."

When the news broke that the Orange County investigators were focused on John Huggins as a suspect in the murder of Carla Larson, the media personnel barraged the Seminole County Sheriff's Department, where he was incarcerated, demanding information, interviews or whatever scraps they could get. But Huggins steadfastly refused to see any of them.

In a totally unexpected and surprising move, word came to Sheriff Don Eslinger that suspect John Huggins wanted to talk, to be interviewed—but only by reporter Steve Olson of WFTV, Channel 9, in Orlando. Sheriff Eslinger was surprised, but he agreed. He spoke with Olson, advising him that he had authorized permission for the interview.

The tall, well-built sheriff, in his normal friendly manner, reached across his wide, highly polished desk and shook hands with the popular TV broadcaster, whom he invited into his office to discuss the upcoming interview.

Sheriff Eslinger explained, "Mr. Huggins asked for you specifically. He won't talk to any other media people."

"I'm pleased to hear that, of course. But I wonder why he chose me," Olson replied.

"I don't know, but whatever his reason, Steve, it's my hope that you can make your interview with him something truly productive."

"Yeah, it would be nice if he decided to confess." Both men chuckled at the thought.

Weir and Linnert continued following up on every facet in their investigation. They contacted Daniel Hamilton in Cocoa Beach. He was the man at the site of the burning automobile who saw an "odd" man there. The detectives showed him a photographic lineup they prepared of six pictures, one of which was John Huggins, Number 2.

"Mr. Hamilton," Weir requested, "would you please look

at these photos and see if you recognize the man you saw at the automobile fire?"

"Sure, no problem." Hamilton looked over the lineup very carefully. Finally he picked Number 5. "This looks like him in the face and the hair."

"Are you sure?" Linnert asked.

"Well, that's the best I can do."

The detectives thanked him and left.

"That was sure disappointing," Linnert said.

Weir shook his head regretfully. "Well, it was a long shot at best."

On July 21 Detectives Weir and Linnert measured the distance from the car fire in Cocoa Beach to Kevin Smith's residence, which was two-tenths of a mile away.

They met with Kevin Smith again at his residence to clarify issues surrounding his discovery of the radar detector. He stated positively that he did not remove it from the Ford Explorer that John Huggins left on his property. Weir encouraged Smith to explain.

"I don't know how it got on my water heater, but I assumed that John left it there." He reluctantly admitted, "I wiped it off with my shirt before I discarded it in the bushes."

Linnert asked, "Do you remember where you were on June tenth?"

"Yes, of course. I was at work."

"Where do you work?"

"I work for Mike's Lawn Service. My supervisor is Mike Varcadipane, the owner of the company." He gave the detectives the information on how to reach his boss.

Weir and Linnert arranged to meet with Varcadipane at a Burger King in Melbourne. When asked about Kevin Smith's schedule on June 10, he verified that Smith worked that day from 7:30 A.M. until 5:00 P.M.

After the meeting Weir said to Linnert, "Well, I guess that sheds a little favorable light on Kevin Smith."

Following up on Angel Huggins's information about John Huggins abandoning the Ford Explorer at the Courtyard on

he Green in Melbourne, the detectives met with the man-
ger of the complex and the maintenance supervisor. The of-
icers learned that because of a recent change in management,
hey only recently started to track abandoned cars found on
he property. That tracking only began on June 19, 1997, so
here was no record of an abandoned Ford Explorer found at
he complex.

The next day, Weir and Linnert took their photo lineup to
how to Milton Johnson. He was one of the first to see the
nan in the Ford Explorer coming out of the woods on June
0. Johnson scrutinized the photos of the six men but was
inable to identify the man he saw in the vehicle.

As they drove away, Weir commented, "Sometimes eye-
vitnesses are not the best evidence in a case."

Linnert nodded in agreement.

TV broadcaster Steve Olson went to the Seminole
County Jail on July 25 and entered the room provided for the
nterview. It was a small, bare room with stark white walls,
urnished with only a table and several chairs. There were two
leputies present with Olson. With all the equipment set up,
Huggins was brought into the room in handcuffs, wearing
he jailhouse navy blue jumpsuit.

Olson later described the scene. "When he came in, he
was dressed in a Seminole County Jailhouse coverall and his
hair looked like a bad case of sleeping on a jail bunk." He
was overweight and had a ruddy, jowly face, Olson observed, and his eyes were wary. He was unshaven and his
complexion was dotted with tiny blackheads.

As they spoke, Olson felt that Huggins was pumping him
to find out more about the case against him as strongly as
Olson was hoping for a confession.

Huggins was soft-spoken, sitting quietly, seemingly calm.
Steve Olson stated flatly, "He never did confess."

Huggins appeared to be relaxed, at ease. As he answered
questions from Steve Olson, as well as the two deputies, his

answers, though seeming candid, skillfully evaded the question of whether he killed Carla Larson.

Huggins said, "I know how Jim Larson feels, losing a loved one. I lost my first wife in an auto accident."

The statement shocked the observers in the room. How could this man compare the two situations? He was accused of murdering Carla Larson, of causing Jim Larson's loss. *What chutzpah,* thought one.

When asked about his participation in the murder, Huggins responded that he really didn't know, but he didn't think he killed her. "I'm not that kind of a guy," he protested mildly.

He stressed that he was subject to blackouts due to the medication he was taking, Coumadin, a blood thinner, coupled with his abuse of alcohol and marijuana.

Huggins stated flatly that he felt he had no future. He said that he had no fear of the electric chair, and stressed that he saw no light at the end of the tunnel.

Unemotionally he said, "With my health, even if I got a twenty-year sentence, I wouldn't ever walk out of prison."

He admitted that he was guilty of other crimes, but he was sure he was not guilty of murder.

Huggins was almost indignant when he stated, "They say my motive for the killing was for her vehicle. I rob banks—if I wanted a vehicle, I would just go buy it."

He also stated that he did not recall driving a white Ford Explorer like Carla Larson's.

In his self-appraisal Huggins said, "I don't think I did anything to anybody. I'm not that kind of person."

Olson asked how Huggins felt about the police and how he had been treated by them.

"Unfairly," was Huggins's response, his voice raised and greenish eyes flashing.

In the only change from his soft-spoken demeanor, he told Olson that he did not like one Seminole County investigator in particular. He claimed that she tried to pin the traffic death of his first wife, Marianne, on him.

After a pause Huggins continued, referring back to the Larson murder. In his soft monotone, unemotionally, he said, "Inside myself I feel I didn't kill her. If someone can prove I did, I don't know what to say about that."

The interview concluded, with no new or helpful information for the police.

Steve Olson said, "A couple of days after the jailhouse interview, Huggins called our Channel 9 live truck, collect. He asked me something to the effect, 'Do you know why I chose to do an interview with you?' I didn't know how to answer. I thought maybe because I was a good reporter." He laughed heartily.

Olson said that Huggins went on to tell him that "it was because I had the same last name of a friend he made in the Seminole Jail in the late '80s or early '90s, when Huggins was there apparently on another charge. He said his friend's name was Joey Olson.

"I was crushed. Joey Olson was a guy who murdered his parents while on a drug binge. He then got into a standoff in traffic on SR 434 with the Altamonte Springs Police Department. Olson was arrested, tried and sent away on the murder rap, but while in jail Olson apparently engaged in sexual relations with a nurse at the jail. It was quite a sensational story. My name tied into this? My, my, my." He chuckled.

For the two weeks following July 30, Detectives Cameron Weir and John Linnert went through an intensive period of verifying items for evidence. They checked the purchase and appraisals of Carla Ann Larson's earrings and diamond ring with several jewelry stores and dealers.

Weir and Linnert followed up by thoroughly checking the telephone calls made from the various hotels, motels and inns where John Steven Huggins and/or his relatives had registered and stayed. They were also able to contact the guests who stayed at the Salisbury Inn and found the plastic gun in the room vacated by John Huggins, to verify their discovery.

They measured the distance from the Days Inn suites to the Publix market in the Xentury City Plaza. The detectives noted that the two are located almost directly across the street from each other, with a distance of four-tenths of one mile between their parking lots.

"Roll that over in your mind," Weir said to Linnert.

CHAPTER 18

In their ongoing investigation, Cam Weir and John Linnert learned of an interview on the TV station WFTV, Channel 9, that reporter Rucks Russel held with a woman, Annette Moore.

The point of interest to the detectives was her address.

Weir told Linnert, "That's right across the street from Angel and her mother's house."

Linnert replied, "We gotta talk to this Annette Moore."

The two detectives met with Annette Moore on August 14. After a few introductory remarks, Moore readily agreed to be sworn in and to provide a statement of what she saw.

"Ms. Moore, will you please tell us what you know about a vehicle you saw here in this neighborhood?"

"Yes. It was all very strange. It was June eleventh. I know because that was my son Roger's birthday." She stopped to explain. "Because it was his birthday, I remember distinctly that was when I saw the white Ford parked at Faye Elms's house. I think that they call that particular Ford, the Explorer."

"Yes, ma'am," Linnert said, "that's right. And they are very popular."

"It had gold trim around the bottom, and I think there were roof racks on the top of it."

"Did you notice anything else?" Weir asked.

She hesitated, then added, "It looked like a new car, you know, like one that wasn't driven around very much, and the windows weren't tinted."

"What was there about this vehicle that got your attention?" Detective Linnert inquired.

"Maybe this isn't much, but it did catch my eye. When I first spotted the car, it was parked on the grass, just off the driveway to the left. I looked at that and thought that it was odd. I still don't know why it was parked that way."

"Is there something more, ma'am?" Linnert asked.

"I just wanted to say that I thought I saw that same vehicle parked at Angel's twice. I'm not exactly sure, but I think I saw it there on two different occasions." She thought for a moment, then clarified, "I think it was on June tenth that I first saw the Ford Explorer."

The June 10 date raised the detectives' investigative antenna.

"I didn't do anything about it," she continued, "but then I saw the incident mentioned on the television, about the woman being murdered in Orlando, and the disappearance of her vehicle."

The detectives asked Annette Moore a barrage of follow-up questions, but she stated that she never saw a driver or anyone in that Ford Explorer. She could not make any other positive statements that the officers found helpful.

However, Moore said that her live-in boyfriend, Derek Hilliard, probably also saw the white Ford parked at the Elms house.

In the subsequent interview with Hilliard, he confirmed that he saw the vehicle. "I was on my way home from work at about four-thirty in the afternoon when I saw that white Ford Explorer."

"Do you remember the date?" Linnert asked.

"I'm pretty sure it was on the eleventh, because that's Roger's birthday."

"Is there anything else you can tell us?" Linnert inquired.

"I just remember that it was a plain white Ford Explorer with windows that weren't tinted." He paused. "There's something else, but I'm not sure about it."

"It's okay. Just tell us what's on your mind," Weir encouraged.

"A couple days after I first saw that Explorer, I thought I saw the same vehicle parked at the same residence. Only now it was black. Spray-painted black. It was a lousy paint job, with streaks and bands of uneven paint across the body."

The July 29 edition of the *Orlando Sentinel* printed an article entitled HUGGINS ARREST SHOCKS PASTOR.

The writer stated, "A group of Christian missionaries is shocked that a volunteer they know is the prime suspect in the killing of an Orlando woman.

"John Steven Huggins is remembered for making at least 5 missionary trips to Haiti in the past 10 years to help run clinics and build churches and schools. 'I've been beside John Huggins and seen the tears running down his cheeks in compassion for the children we were working with. I cannot imagine him hurting someone intentionally,' said Pastor Sandy Stafford of Northwind Ministries on State Road A1A."

The article also stated that John Huggins had an alcohol problem at one time, but Stafford thought he had put it behind him. He considered himself a born-again Christian.

Preparations began at the Orange County Sheriff's Department for the collecting and gathering of the diverse materials and enormous evidence that the detectives and their associates had compiled over the past several months. The compilation would be delivered to the state attorney's office, which would present it to the grand jury.

On Wednesday, August 20, 1997, the Orange County grand jury indicted John Steven Huggins for the murder of Carla Ann Larson.

Thirty-five-year-old Huggins, whose entire life was devoted to a continuing career of robbery, burglary, wife beating and a variety of criminal activities, was indicted on charges of first-degree murder, kidnapping, carjacking and robbery.

Speaking to the national and local representatives of radio, television and press, Orange County/Osceola County State Attorney Lawson Lamar stated unequivocally that the state would seek the death penalty for John Huggins.

In his quiet, unemotional manner, Lamar said flatly, "Anytime someone as innocent as this lady is strangled to death, you have an excellent case for the penalty phase. Strangulation is a means of death which affords the killer a chance to stop. In this case he obviously didn't stop."

In the eager deluge of questions from the reporters, the dominant theme was whether the victim was sexually molested. The cautious state attorney carefully stated that it was not certain whether John Huggins would be charged with sexual battery.

On Monday, September 22, after being delivered to the Orange County Jail from incarceration in Sanford, John Steven Huggins made his first appearance in the court. He was charged with the first-degree murder of Carla Ann Larson, as well as the associated crimes of kidnapping, carjacking and robbery. He requested bail, which was summarily denied, and he was remanded to the Orange County Jail.

The criminal career of John Huggins continued to unfold like an old-time serial movie that linked one perilous adventure to another and another.

Cameron Weir entered the sheriff's headquarters on Friday morning, September 26, and greeted John Linnert, who was already at his desk.

"Morning, John." He seated himself at his own desk and asked, "Did you read the morning paper?"

"Not yet. Anything interesting in it?"

"Yeah." Weir smiled. "There was a story that Huggins is now being linked with two robberies in Brevard County."

"No fooling?" Linnert asked incredulously.

"No fooling," Weir replied. "A Cocoa Beach police-woman, Kim Smith, said that Huggins is charged with two separate robberies at the Space Coast Credit Union. One on February twenty-third and one on June twelfth."

Weir stopped, a grim expression crossing his face. "June twelfth," he reminded his partner, "that's the day Carla Larson's body was discovered here in Orange County."

"That's right," Linnert said thoughtfully. "He didn't wait long after the murder. Guess he was short of money." After a pause he asked, "You say he robbed the same bank twice?" Linnert was amazed at the audacity.

"That's what the paper said. The story said that they suspected that the two felonies were committed by the same person, because in each case the man entered the credit union in the early afternoon, approached a teller and showed her a semiautomatic handgun and demanded money." Weir paused, shook his head and said, "Wonder if it was a real gun or if it was the same plastic handgun discovered at the Salisbury Inn in Maryland. Anyhow, the robber was described as a six-foot-tall, two-hundred-pound man. Ironically, the witnesses to the bank robbery subsequently ID'd Huggins from his pictures shown when he was named a suspect in the Carla Larson murder."

Linnert shook his head in amazement. "That guy is a never-ending surprise."

The saga continued. On November 27, 1997, in Sanford, Florida, John Huggins was tried for possessing $5,000 worth of tools, stolen from a former neighbor in Oviedo. He pleaded no contest in February but asked to withdraw the plea, saying his judgment was impaired at the time of the plea. He said that at his birthday party, the day before the hearing, he used alcohol and methamphetamines.

Judge Seymour Benson, unmoved and unconvinced, rejected that excuse and sentenced him to fifteen months in prison.

Assistant State Attorney (ASA) Jeff Ashton felt complex emotions as he stared at the wall of his office in the new extravagant Orange County Courthouse in downtown Orlando. Moments ago Ashton had accepted an offer to assist the prosecutor of one of the most compelling, most publicized, most talked about cases of murder in his memory.

A pleasant man with incisive brown eyes, and slightly wavy grayish brown hair, Jeff's tall, trim figure of 185 pounds packaged a personable fellow with an amiable smile.

As he sat at his desk, Ashton recalled the more than seventy murder trials that he had prosecuted in Orange County, Florida, and he concluded that none compared with the intensity, the interest or the challenge of this case.

A native of Florida from St. Petersburg, a graduate of the University of Florida and that institution's law school, Class of 1980, Ashton was a 100 percent Sunshine State product.

His thoughts drifted back to the meeting with his good friend and fellow assistant state attorney Ted Culhan, who would prosecute the Huggins case.

Culhan had come into his office, and after he was seated, he faced Ashton with a serious expression. "I'd like you on this case with me, Jeff."

Startled by the statement, Ashton had sat silent for a long moment looking at him questioningly.

Culhan, a stocky, 5'9", brown-eyed, gray-bearded attorney, with a warm smile, then began to explain why he wanted to bring another attorney onto his case.

Ashton worked with Culhan for many years and knew the lawyer was capable of handling a big case alone, even one as important as this.

"Jeff," he had continued, "I'm having some health problems, and at this point I don't know how serious, but I would like you to work the case with me. How about it? Are you interested?"

Ashton, facing his friend and associate of two decades, had answered, "Sure, Ted, I'll be glad to work with you."

Jeff Ashton dragged his thoughts back to his desk and focused on the mountain of paperwork and evidence lying before him on this new case with which he would have to familiarize himself.

CHAPTER 19

Ada Larson, who became Jim's mother in a full sense when he was eight years old and she married his father, is a charming, capable woman, with engaging hazel eyes and dark blond hair.

She has somehow acclimated herself to tragedy. Remarkably strong, Ada Larson has experienced and lived with the intrusion of death into her quiet life since August 1990, when her daughter, Sonja, was one of the five victims brutally murdered in the Gainesville mass-killing spree by Danny Rolling.

In a further tragedy her husband, who never recovered from the grief in the loss of their daughter, succumbed to an early death.

Ada's life suddenly veered from its comfortable orbit to focus on the subsequent trial and hearings of Danny Rolling, her daughter's killer, which she attended with religious fervor.

Amazingly, Ada Larson somehow was able to cope with tragedy again, this time the loss of her beloved daughter-in-law. She wrote a column of thankful observations that appeared in the *Orlando Sentinel,* fittingly, on Thanksgiving Day, November 27, 1997.

She wrote:

Orlando can be very proud of the way in which it reached out to our family after the tragedy of Carla Larson's disappearance and killing in June. It has been a wonderful feeling to be the recipients of such an outpouring of sympathy, love and support, which has been showered upon us. The community has really gotten behind our family and has shown us what a caring community can do.

The Larson and Thomas families are thankful for the concern, generosity and thoughtfulness that made our tragedy more bearable. The kindness shown to her husband, Jim, and daughter, Jessica, has indeed been uplifting and of enormous help.

Some examples of help we received during our initial shock after Carla's untimely death: Meals provided by area businesses and many neighbors. Some meals came anonymously. Other meals continue to arrive. Groceries were purchased during our ordeal by neighbors who seemed to know exactly what we needed. Neighbors came to pick up a grocery list; others offered to watch baby Jessica.

Baby supplies, such as diapers, bottles, wipes, clothing, toys, stroller and car seat (Jessica's stroller and car seat were in the Ford Explorer when it was carjacked) were received from numerous neighbors and friends.

Neighbors and friends offered lodging and opened their homes to our out-of-town family members. Several of our neighbors offered much-needed legal assistance and have been advising Jim in this area.

Members of the United Methodist Church in College Park opened their hearts to us and took care of our needs at the memorial service. The Rev. Fred Ball visited, consoled and was available to us. He listened and grieved along with us. Since that time the church has provided much needed child care for Jessica in its Child Development Center, "a lifetime scholarship."

To help in the manhunt, neighbors designed a flier and a printer printed thousands of them, all gratis. Merchants allowed the fliers to be displayed at their businesses. Thanks to the efforts of loving and concerned citizens, many fliers were distributed in other counties and to many sheriff's offices.

Some of the merchants in the College Park section of Orlando, such as Chapters Bookstore and Café, have been collecting donations for the Jessica Trust at Barnett Bank, a fund set up by friends for the well-being of Jessica.

It amazes us that people still remember our tragedy, but the kindness continues. Special people became special friends because they were of such enormous help. They anticipated our needs. They stayed with Jim until family could arrive. The memorial on the cul-de-sac of Princeton Court is only one example of their love. They landscaped the area, planted a tree in honor of Carla and placed a lovely marker there. Another couple added a bench where we can sit and remember Carla.

We have not mentioned all the kind deeds bestowed upon us during the past months. People have helped in so many ways. We are greatly touched by this community. We feel very fortunate to have such good friends and neighbors who have opened their hearts to this family in a way we never could have imagined.

We know from experience that there will be rough times ahead, but the community's actions will have eased our anguish and pain. And for that we are thankful.

CHAPTER 20

The trial of John Steven Huggins neared in the new year of 1998, and the incarcerated suspect still did not have a defense lawyer. Months previous, the court appointed a well-known attorney, Cheney Mason, to represent Huggins, but on Monday, January 12, 1998, in a dispute over legal fees with the county, Mason withdrew from the case.

In his argument over payment, Mason contended that the $50-per-hour rate that the county was paying defense lawyers in death penalty cases like Huggins's was ridiculous.

Judge Belvin Perry, Orange County's chief circuit judge, considered Mason's harsh criticism and ordered the fee paid to attorneys defending the accused in capital cases to be increased to $125 per hour.

Attorney Mason said that the fee was still inadequate.

Judge Perry stated that he made a study of other judicial circuits and the rates of other government agencies, which led him to conclude that $125 per hour was just and proper.

Several lawyers who were asked to take on the Huggins case refused because they believed that the trial was expected to begin as early as late February. The general feeling of the attorneys was that the time was too short to provide an adequate defense for the accused client.

Eventually a defense team composed of Bob Wesley and Tyrone King stepped forward and took the case.

Bob Wesley, a heavyset 6'6" attorney, and Tyrone King, a very bright young lawyer working with him, were disturbed that no one would represent Huggins. When asked why he and King took on this case, Wesley answered, "It looked like nobody would step forward, and so Tyrone and I said, 'Goddamn, the guy's got to have a lawyer. We'll do it.' "

Wesley was born on Kennesaw Mountain, Georgia, but his family moved to Florida when he was a baby. He is a graduate of the University of West Florida in Pensacola, and received a master's degree from Rollins College in Winter Park, Florida. He is a 1981 graduate of the Florida State University Law School.

Huggins would be well represented at his trial.

The two sets of attorneys, prosecution and defense, worked diligently preparing their cases for the John Huggins murder trial now set for January 1999. Meanwhile, another prosecutor worked to prepare a case against Huggins for a bank robbery committed on March 7, 1997, the first of three similar robberies committed in Orlando.

Prosecutor Sandra Deisler appeared in an Orange County courtroom on Friday, October 30, 1998, before a jury of three men and three women, accusing John Steven Huggins of robbing the AmSouth Bank on Michigan Avenue in Orlando.

Huggins confessed to investigators that he robbed the banks, but his attorney Bob Wesley argued to the jury that the confession was bogus.

Huggins also tried to have the robbery cases moved to federal court. He testified that he suffered from blood clots and preferred to serve his sentence in federal prisons because he contended they have better medical facilities.

Prosecutor Deisler presented a powerhouse case. She argued that it was clear from surveillance photos that Huggins used threats and a BB gun (possibly Huggins's same plastic piece that was recovered in Maryland) to make off with $18,300. The jury found Huggins guilty.

In an added comment, Deisler said that Huggins should be labeled a career criminal because of his long record of crime.

"Here we go again." Detective Cameron Weir looked up from the newspaper he was reading.

"What now?" Detective Linnert asked.

"Let me read you an item in this morning's *Orlando Sentinel*. 'Alex Fishback, Sheriff's Agent in Brevard County, reported that arrest warrants were issued on Thursday, January 8, 1998, on John Huggins that accuse him of armed robbery with a deadly weapon and possession of a firearm. The warrant specified that Huggins, a convicted felon, is accused of robbery on November 24, 1995, of a Publix Supermarket in the Suntree development, located near Melbourne.' How do you like that?"

"You know, Cam, we think that we know so much about this guy Huggins and then a whole new chapter opens."

Weir went on to say, "They're also asking for warrants on Huggins for the holdup of a Publix market at the Merritt Square Mall."

"When was that?" Linnert asked.

"That was January 17, 1996."

Weir continued to read and discuss. "Fishback pointed out that several agencies throughout central Florida are looking at John Huggins for nine different Publix robberies that occurred between August 1995 and January 1996."

"He must have an affinity for Publix markets. He snatched Carla Larson at one of them," Linnert recounted.

"Guess you're right." Weir read that Fishback indicated that the series of robberies matched each other, as though they were designed and followed through by the same person.

"This is what's really interesting, John," Weir went on with a grin. "We never know when some unexpected source will come up with a key to an investigation. You'll love this.

The Brevard robbery cases were inactive. And then a cashier of the Publix market was watching TV and saw Huggins when he was arrested. She recognized him as the man who robbed her store. She was surprised; I guess stunned was a better word. She called the Brevard Sheriff's Department and told them what she knew about the robbery of the store where she worked, and then about seeing Huggins on TV."

Weir read that Fishback followed through by taking a photo lineup containing a picture of John Huggins to the Merritt Square Publix market. The cashier witness looked over the photos and, with no hesitation, pointed to the man who robbed her, stating, "That's him—that's him," identifying Huggins.

Alex Fishback said that in the two heists that Huggins pulled in Brevard, he was very calm, very calculating and seemed to know what he was doing.

Shaking his head, Weir commented, "He should. We know that he's had a lot of practice. He just got very good at it. In the fullest sense of the words, John Steven Huggins really is a career criminal. Crime is his profession, and he works hard at it constantly."

"He evidently makes enough work to keep several law enforcement forces busy. How much did he get in those two Publix holdups?" Linnert asked.

"The report is that he came away with a thousand or two thousand, just in Brevard."

"Well, we wondered where he got his money, when he was always listed on his arrest reports as unemployed." Linnert laughed. "Now we know."

CHAPTER 21

The location of John Huggins's trial, although scheduled to be held in Orange County in January 1999, remained undecided.

The defense team of attorneys Bob Wesley and Tyrone King was apprehensive about the massive publicity that the case received, and they thought it would be difficult to select an Orange County jury without preconceived opinions of guilt or innocence.

ASA Jeff Ashton was against moving it out of Orange County and countered, stating that people did not know much about the evidence against the accused Huggins.

Chief Circuit Judge Belvin Perry was concerned with ensuring that the accused receive a fair trial. He was aware of the extraordinary publicity and national attention that was focused on the case, and he, too, questioned whether the case should be tried in Orange County.

It seemed as though everyone had an opinion about the case and it was a popular topic of discussion. One woman was heard to say, "They should hang the bastard for what he did to that lovely young mother. Show him the same mercy he showed her." That seemed to be the popular sentiment.

In an intense meeting on Monday, November 2, 1998, the

two sides presented their arguments before the judge for a change of venue. He finally announced, "All I'm concerned about is that Mr. Huggins get his fair day in court."

He said that he would make his decision within a week whether the trial would be held in Orange County or be moved to another Florida court.

At a subsequent meeting the judge announced his ruling. The defense prevailed and there would be a change of venue. The trial would be moved to the large city of Jacksonville, located in Duval County, 150 miles northeast of Orlando.

Through the long summer, fall and winter, Bob Wesley and his associate Tyrone King planned the defense strategy that they would use in the ensuing trial, scheduled to begin on January 25, 1999.

In their thorough study of the case and Huggins's criminal background, the defense lawyers held meetings and depositions with possible witnesses, as well as other official investigators. Wesley and King worked tirelessly, preparing their defense for what promised to be a difficult trial.

When Wesley was ready to depose Detective John Linnert, he learned that the detective was no longer in Florida. Linnert had resigned from the Orange County Sheriff's Department when his wife was offered an excellent new position in Massachusetts. He told a friend, "This is a great opportunity for my wife, and I don't want to stand in her way. Besides, I think it will be a wonderful change for us to live in the historic Boston area."

As a result, Wesley flew to Boston to question the former Orange County investigator about his work in the Carla Larson murder case.

Linnert later described his Boston meeting with Bob Wesley as a "very stressful deposition." He explained that he "was deposed in the office of a local law firm located on State Street, a short distance from Boston's old State House and the site of the Boston Massacre."

He said, "I left work to meet him, and spent at least one and a half hours or more being questioned."

Stressing the "grilling" that the determined defense attorney put him through, Linnert said, with a restrained smile, "Wesley questioned everything about our investigation, our procedures, all our work on the case, and even asked why I moved to Boston."

He said that Wesley's main questions were centered around the veracity of key witnesses.

In their concluding opinions for the defense, Wesley and King were confident that they could and would show that the prosecution's case lacked actual witnesses and proof to the reported killing, and that their case was ineffective, without evidence. Their premise was that no witness could place the accused John Huggins at the crime scene, and no genetic evidence linked him to the crime. They felt that the evidence was inadequate and therefore did not meet the requirements of "beyond a reasonable doubt" for a guilty verdict.

Speaking to a reporter, defense lawyer Wesley indicated great confidence in his case and said, "We know what we have to do." He emphasized that it was the duty of the prosecution to prove its case with enough evidence to overcome reasonable doubt.

While the defense toiled away preparing for the Huggins trial, ASA Ashton and ASA Culhan also worked unending hours assembling the case they would present to convict John Steven Huggins of murder.

The prosecuting team agreed that Huggins was not only guilty of murder in the first degree, but that his crime was of such a heinous nature that only a death sentence was the proper punishment that fit the crime. Jeff Ashton stated, "This is a man who lived a life of crime, culminating in this terrible murder."

As they did with their other witnesses in preparation of their case, the prosecutors spent a great deal of time with Detective Weir.

Weir walked into the reception room of the Orange County/Osceola County State Attorney's Office at the new courthouse and told the receptionist that ASA Jeff Ashton expected him.

In moments the tall, personable Ashton appeared and warmly greeted him. "Cam, good to see you again."

He ushered the detective into his private quarters and invited, "Have a chair."

When they were comfortably seated, Weir looked around, appraising Ashton's office. "Swanky digs you've got here, Jeff. This whole new building is something. Quite a step up from your old quarters in the bank building."

Ashton grinned in agreement. "Pretty upscale, huh? It's a new stand, but the same old business. So let's get to it."

"Right. Jeff, this is one for the books."

"It sure looks like it. From our interviews and reading the files, I know that you and Linnert worked like a couple of beavers on it."

"Yes, it was pretty much a round-the-clock ordeal for us," Weir told him. "So many times we hit a brick wall; then something would come along and send us on a new track. And we put in some travel time, too."

Weir recounted the long hours that he and Linnert worked, digging out answers to the homicide. He went over the list of witnesses who saw a man driving the white Ford Explorer on the day of the murder. He detailed their following up endless tips and leads.

"But we were getting nowhere until Angel Huggins came into the case. She's the estranged wife of John Huggins."

"I wanted to ask you about her. Is she credible?"

Weir settled back in his chair and focused his sharp brown eyes on Ashton. "We were wary of her at first, but we followed up everything she told us, and it proved to be reliable. Then her sister also provided credibility to Angel's information."

Detective Weir reviewed in detail the call from Faye Elms about how she discovered Carla's jewelry in a wall box in her shed.

The two men went over each detail of the case, with the

detective meticulously explaining and the prosecutor listening attentively and making notes, shaking his head and mumbling, "Incredible, incredible."

Finally Ashton put down his pen and leaned back in his chair. "Cam, you and John did a fantastic job putting this case together. I certainly appreciate your efforts."

"Thanks, Jeff. We sure put our hearts in it."

In long sessions with other members of the investigating team, and with various individuals who would be called to testify, the two prosecutors instilled confidence and inspiration in everyone on their side, creating a united front and positive approach in trial.

CHAPTER 22

Monday, January 25, 1999, was a dreary, sunless, rainy day in Jacksonville, one of the largest cities in Florida. A brisk breeze from the nearby St. Johns River chilled the air outside the downtown Duval County Courthouse, where the murder trial of John Steven Huggins was set to begin.

Jacksonville, a metropolitan city situated on the northeasterly coast of Florida, is unique to the state. The climate is more northerly than the rest of the tropical state. Named for Andrew Jackson, the town sits on the edge of the St. Johns River, the nation's longest north-flowing waterway.

The city is actively engaged in trade that stretches throughout the world, and huge oceangoing vessels provide a picturesque setting in the downtown area of Jax.

Mayport, a U.S. Navy base, is alive with military operations, and the Jaguars professional football team has established a high place in the sports world. All in all, Jacksonville is a vibrant, energetic city with varied cultural activities that extend in many diverse directions.

In the courthouse ASA Jeff Ashton and ASA Ted Culhan entered the assigned courtroom and headed for the cordoned section where the prosecution would sit during the trial.

Ashton's eyes swept across the large room in a quick survey of the physical aspects of the playing field, where he and Ted would be using all their know-how and experience to convict the man they viewed as a vicious killer.

Ashton felt the chill of the dimly lit, cheerless courtroom and commented to Culhan, "Not exactly the Great White Way."

"Maybe it's an indication of the future that Mr. Huggins has to look forward to," Culhan answered, smiling.

Ashton told Culhan, "That tall deputy near the entrance told me that they call this courtroom 'the Dungeon.' "

"And rightly so," Culhan responded. "I'm glad that we're here only for this trial."

The two prosecutors continued to survey the courtroom, where they would be spending most of their time for the next few weeks.

Ashton said, "I understand that this building is only about thirty years old. I'd think that the architects would have done a better job of lighting."

Culhan smiled. "We're just spoiled by Orlando's posh new courthouse with its superb lighting."

"You're probably right." Jeff Ashton laughed.

The two prosecutors viewed the spectators who were filing into the room and recognized several individuals from Orlando. Ada Larson, Jim's smartly dressed mother, entered the shadowy, bleak courtroom, followed by Phyllis and Mert Thomas, Carla's parents. They walked to the prosecution side of the courtroom, took seats on the hard oak bench and held each other's hands for comfort. They knew this was going to be a very difficult time for them. They were all aware that some of the testimony that they would hear would be painful for them, and they hoped that they could maintain control.

Fashionably dressed Phyllis Thomas tilted her head, looking around at the others already seated. Her husband, Mert, tall and strong, dressed in his nicely tailored business suit, sat quietly staring straight ahead, patiently waiting for the trial to begin. After so many months of waiting, the three parents were eager finally to see John Huggins answer for killing their beloved child and bringing such misery into all their lives.

Jim Larson, who would appear as a witness, was awaiting his summons to the courtroom, in a separate room.

There were also a number of fellow workers of Carla Larson's, from the Centex Rooney Company at the Disney World building site, who came for the proceedings.

Reporters for the various media, who would relate what happened here, filled many of the seats.

By this time attorney Bob Wesley, just under three hundred pounds, basically bald, blue-eyed and trim bearded, took his place at the defense table along with his co-counsel, Tyrone King.

Wesley looked around the Duval County Courtroom, assessing the battleground in which the life of his client would depend on his expertise.

The opposing attorneys nodded and greeted each other cordially.

All heads in the room turned and watched as the defendant, John Steven Huggins, entered the courtroom, escorted by a guard. The large, burly man made a quick survey of the room, his green eyes noticing all who were there to judge him. For the important occasion, Huggins was clean shaven and dressed in a conservative dark blue suit. His long, normally straggly brown hair was now trimmed and neat. His overall appearance was of a man who could be dressed for his college reunion dinner.

His two lawyers rose to seat him at their table. For the rest of this day and the weeks ahead, he would be the center of all the activities that unfolded here. There was no expression on his face that revealed his thoughts. His attitude was an almost indifference to the gravity of his situation.

At the direction of the bailiff, everyone in the courtroom rose as Chief Circuit Judge Belvin Perry entered and approached his seat at the bench. This highly regarded African-American criminal court judge had been in the legal profession for more than twenty years, as had the two prosecutors for the state. Both Jeff Ashton and Ted Culhan, who knew the judge for many years when they all were part of the state attorney's staff in Orlando, nodded respectfully to Judge Perry, who in turn politely acknowledged them.

The interrupting gavel sounded throughout the courtroom. "Hear ye, hear ye, this court is now in session: The Honorable Judge Belvin S. Perry presiding."

For a day and a half, the four opposing attorneys slowly but zealously questioned the men and women called as possible jurors; they ultimately agreed on the selections, which both sides described as balanced.

A wave of quiet satisfaction drifted across the room in anticipation at the start of the upcoming battle.

When the trial opened, prosecutor Culhan addressed the jury, explaining what evidence the state would present to them to prove the guilt of John Steven Huggins. He detailed the case against the defendant, concluding with his assertion that there could be only one verdict: guilty of all charges.

Defense attorney Bob Wesley declined to make an opening statement.

ASA Culhan rose and announced, "The state of Florida will now call its first witness, Mr. James Larson."

In the witness room, where he was waiting, Jim Larson nervously wiped his palms. *This is it,* he thought. He entered the courtroom and moved slowly but deliberately toward the witness stand, where he would be sworn in to recount the worst horror of his life. He looked around the room until he saw his mother, Ada, who smiled encouragingly, as did his in-laws, Phyllis and Mert Thomas.

The room grew silent as the husband of the victim, Carla Ann Larson, faced ASA Ted Culhan, who would question him about everything relative to the events that brought him here for this trial.

Culhan walked slowly to the podium and faced Larson. Standing quietly and assembling his thoughts before he began his interrogation, Ted Culhan, a stocky man with a pleasant, confident smile, usually described by his friends as a teddy bear with gray hair, presented a portrait of quiet power.

After the preliminary questions of Larson's name, his address, who lived at that address with him and when he was married, the prosecutor asked for the date of daughter Jessica's birth.

Defense attorney Wesley, who had been sitting quietly, sprang to his feet. "Objection to relevance, Your Honor. State shouldn't ask questions that evoke an emotional response from the jury."

Judge Perry straightened in his chair and said, "Overruled at this time."

Ted Culhan returned to his questioning, asking politely, "When was your daughter born?"

With his mind obviously rattled by the intensity of the situation he was in, Jim Larson answered, "I can't remember— right now." He waited, thought a moment and then said, "She is two and a half years old."

Sensing the pressure that his witness was experiencing, prosecutor Culhan walked over to the prosecution table and exchanged a few words with co-counsel Jeff Ashton, considerately giving Jim Larson a few moments to collect himself and settle down.

Hoping his witness was a little calmer, Culhan returned to simple questions, establishing where Jim worked, where Carla worked, the routine the Larsons had in the mornings for going to work, what time they left for their jobs and who dropped Jessica off at the day-care center.

As the session continued, reporters busily made notes and drawings of the scene.

In his careful questioning the prosecutor provided the surviving husband an open door to show the Larson family's happy daily life. Jim also could portray his wife, Carla, as an exceptionally talented woman, who was an engineer working with a major company, Centex Rooney, building a fabulous resort hotel at Walt Disney World.

The prosecutor then turned to specifics. "I direct your attention to June 10, 1997. Do you recall that day?"

What a question, Jim Larson thought. *How could I ever forget the day my wife vanished? It is emblazoned into my mind.* A shadow crossed his face with the memory of that dreadful day.

"Yes," he answered tensely.

Culhan asked, "Do you recall the last time you saw your wife that day?"

"Yes."

"When was that?" the prosecutor asked.

Larson looked down, hesitated and, obviously saddened, said, "That was in the morning. I kissed her good-bye and told her I loved her."

There was a buzz in the court, and Wesley, like a jack-in-the-box, was on his feet again. "Your Honor, I object, basis of relevance. Ask it be struck."

The defense scored with Judge Perry, who ruled, "Sustained." He turned to the witness and admonished, "Mr. Larson, listen carefully to the question. Only answer what is asked."

Jim Larson nodded. "Yes, Your Honor," he answered in a barely audible voice.

Ted Culhan resumed the questioning, asking about Larson's work in June, his hours on the job, when he became aware that his wife was missing, when he notified authorities and filed a report.

Culhan continued, asking Larson about the events of June 10 and 11, delving into Larson's participation in the search for Carla.

The prosecutor then introduced the subject of Carla Larson's jewelry. With this line the courtroom sat silently as Jim Larson described his wife's jewelry. Although Larson knew that Carla's jewelry would take a prime position in this trial and had steeled himself for the ordeal, nonetheless, he winced at its introduction by the attorney.

Larson tugged on his tie as though suddenly it was too

tight, then stared down at the floor. He looked as though he would much rather be anywhere than here in this courtroom at this time, forcing his mind back to the happy time when he gave Carla those pieces of jewelry.

Culhan wanted the details of Larson's purchases of her engagement and wedding rings, so he asked, "Did she customarily wear those, for example, when she went to work?"

"She never took any of them off," Larson answered.

The prosecutor asked if Larson bought Carla some diamond earrings. He confirmed he did.

"Where did you purchase the diamond earrings?" Culhan pursued.

"In Ohio. At a place—one second." Larson paused to clarify and to be specific. "It was in Akron, Ohio. That's where I purchased them." He waited and apologized. "I'm trying to think of the name of the place." He scanned across the courtroom. "It will come to me."

The jury seemed entranced by the questions and by Jim Larson's earnest answers.

Culhan continued: "Was your wife wearing that jewelry the last time you saw her?"

"Yes," he answered somberly.

Culhan asked Larson if he saw the jewelry again in July 1997.

Larson stated that he had, and when asked to specify where, the troubled husband mumbled, "The police department . . . or the . . . I guess it was the police station." He shifted in his chair and added, "They had them."

The prosecutor moved away a bit from the lectern and faced Judge Perry. "Your Honor, may I approach the witness?"

"You may."

Stepping in front of the witness, the prosecutor said, "Mr. Larson, for the record I'll show you state's exhibit 'W' for identification. Also, for the record, I will now break the seal with this pair of scissors."

All attention in the courtroom was focused on Ted Culhan as he cut open the sealed evidence package.

Continuing, Culhan said, "Mr. Larson, I'll hand you this article, one of state's exhibit 'W.' Sir, I ask you if you recognize what's in that plastic bag?"

With his complexion slowly turning a mild shade of red, Jim Larson managed to answer, "It looks like Carla's wedding band."

There was a whispered sigh from the onlookers in the courtroom.

Ada Larson lowered her head when she saw Jim's emotional distress, which matched her own. Phyllis and Mert Thomas held hands tightly, mentally sharing the agony Jim was facing. Tears welled in their eyes and the women dabbed at them with tissues.

One by one, Culhan took his witness through a series of identifications of the various jewelry pieces that Jim Larson had purchased and given to his wife, including earrings and rings. Finally he offered Larson a last item, asking if he recognized it.

"Yes," the witness almost whispered, "that's her chain."

The prosecutor entered into evidence receipts for the purchases of the jewelry before turning the subject to the Larsons' vehicle.

Step by step, in carefully phrased questions, Culhan elicited information about the Ford Explorer, where it had been purchased, the model year and its full description.

Culhan then showed Larson a photograph of a vehicle, which was marked as state exhibit "CC" for identification, and asked if he recognized it. Larson said it was an accurate representation of the white Ford Explorer that he and his wife owned in 1995.

The prosecutor placed it into evidence.

Culhan asked further questions about the interior of the automobile, the air-conditioning, the controls, the vents and the leather seats, and Larson gave a full description of each.

The prosecutor asked about the radar detector. Larson paused, took a deep breath and said, "We bought a radar detector for it and I had the dealer hardwire it in for me. I didn't want to take a chance on messing something up."

Culhan asked, "Did you go in the store and buy it, or was it mail order?"

Larson stated that it was a mail order purchase.

With a glance to Judge Perry, sitting firmly upright in his black robe, absorbing the examination, Culhan turned to the witness. "For the record I'm going to show you state's exhibit 'AA' for identification. Also for the record, I'm going to break the seal at this time."

The prosecutor handed the package to the witness. "Sir," he said, "take a look inside this bag. You can pull it out if you want to. Do you recognize that item, Mr. Larson?"

"Yeah, that looks like it." Larson nodded.

After his witness identified the radar detector, Culhan asked Larson how it was used and Larson explained. The piece was then moved into evidence.

On cross-examination Bob Wesley asked many detailed questions about the description of the Ford Explorer, comparing it to other SUV models made by other manufacturers, and asking Jim Larson if he was familiar with them. He was not.

Wesley had many more questions about the vehicle. "This car has sort of a remote-control configuration that came with the key ring, correct, sir?"

Larson nodded his head. "Yes."

"And from a distance a person could operate or unlock buttons to the doors, correct?"

Again Jim Larson agreed that was true.

The defense lawyer's bright blue eyes pierced into Larson, and he asked sharply, "And the panic button, how did that operate? Tell the jury, please."

"You press the button, the horn and lights flash."

"Have you ever seen that in action?"

"Oh, yeah."

The defense lawyer pressed on, asking what kind of noise the Explorer horn made.

Larson stated, "It's just a beep, beep, beep; the lights flash—"

Wesley interrupted, following through. "All the lights flash on the car?"

"Yes."

"And that's a key ring feature of that truck that you had?"

Larson told him that was correct.

Several courtroom viewers were puzzled by Wesley's questions. Since Carla evidently didn't press the alarm button, was Wesley implying she left the parking lot voluntarily? This woman who was so safety conscious that she didn't speak to strangers? Or was the more likely scenario that the man approached Carla as she opened her car door with her arms filled carrying the grocery bag, punched her in the stomach, and when she doubled over helplessly, shoved her inside the vehicle and took off?

Wesley turned to another subject. "Her work as an engineer, Mrs. Larson worked for Centex Rooney, correct?"

"Yes."

"And more of her coworkers, at least from a professional basis, were men, is that correct?"

"That's correct," Larson answered, a puzzled expression on his face.

Bob Wesley pressed on. "And so your information was that she would often go to lunch with men, or had meetings with other men, is that correct?"

"Yes."

Wesley looked around the courtroom as he formed his next question. "Sometimes"—he paused dramatically—"even after-hours activities that involved coworkers who were male."

Ted Culhan sprang to his feet. "I object to this, Your Honor, as irrelevant, beyond the scope of direct examination."

Judge Perry leaned forward at the bench and stated, "Overruled at this point."

The burly defense counsel proceeded. "Some after-hours functions involved male coworkers, correct?"

"Yes," Larson answered, perplexed.

Wesley asked the judge for a moment, and after conferring with his co-counsel, Tyrone King, announced, "Nothing further. Thank you."

James Larson was excused from the witness stand.

Judge Perry announced that there would be a fifteen-minute recess and instructed the jury there was to be no discussion of the case

When court reconvened, Judge Perry nodded to the bailiff to have the next witness brought in. Angel Huggins, estranged wife of the accused John Huggins, would be the final witness on this second day of the trial.

The courtroom filled with whispers as the tall, very pretty, nicely dressed woman came into the courtroom. Her oval face was carefully made up, and her reddish blond hair was arranged attractively. She exuded an air of confidence and a pleasant personality, although she was somewhat hesitant in the unfamiliar and solemn surroundings. Angel Huggins was sworn in and took the witness chair, where she sat quietly, with an inquiring expression on her face.

One of the reporters could be heard whispering to a colleague, "She's tagged as a key witness."

His friend shrugged and whispered back, "Why would such a looker fall for such a loser?"

Prosecutor Jeff Ashton asked Angel to tell the jury and the court how she, her estranged husband John Huggins and their collective children shared the day of June 10, 1997, staying near Walt Disney World at the Days Inn, across the road from the Publix market, where Carla Larson was last seen alive.

In answer to the questions, Angel testified in a clear, sharp voice, bringing out that John Huggins vanished for several hours that day.

Ashton asked Angel Huggins to describe her husband's

appearance when he finally came back to the motel, where they were staying.

"When he returned, he acted strangely. He appeared like he had been running. He was sweating. He was clammy and his T-shirt was clinging to his body."

In her continuing testimony Angel Huggins stated, "He disappeared again." She said in her clear, confident voice, "The next time I saw him, he was driving a white Ford Explorer."

The courtroom viewers stirred and whispered to each other.

Court recessed, concluding the first full day of testimony.

CHAPTER 23

When Wednesday, January 27, 1999, dawned, the Florida sun beamed through curtained windows of the Jacksonville Residence Inn, starting the new day brightly for the Orlando lawyers, who were pleased with the new sunny day replacing the previous dreary weather.

"Hey, Ted," Jeff Ashton called out to his partner. "Time to rise and shine if we want breakfast before court. You know Perry can be a stickler for punctuality."

"Ain't that the truth," Culhan agreed, appearing in the doorway, knotting his necktie. "At least we've got some sunshine today."

Ashton replied, "Things do appear better. Look out the window and see the beauty of the river. They really get some big ships coming into this port."

"Yeah, too bad we have to spend the day in that dungeon. I never saw a courtroom so dark and dingy. It's depressing."

"You've got that right," Ashton replied.

After a hearty breakfast and several cups of coffee, Ashton leaned back in his chair. "Are you ready for a big day?" he asked.

"Yes, I am. I'm anxious to hear Angel Huggins continue her testimony. She's doing a good job."

"I agree. And she's sure adding some feminine charm to the proceedings. She's certainly very attractive. I've heard that people see a Marilyn Monroe resemblance, but I don't see it."

"Oh, well, I don't, either, but she's on our side. That's what matters." Ted Culhan laughed.

Jeff Ashton checked his watch. "We'd better move it. Don't want to be late."

When court convened, the intensive cross-examination began. The defense pressed Angel Huggins, accusing her of masterminding a frame-up of her husband, John.

Angel, stretching her seated position to her full height, indignantly disputed the accusation. "I never framed John in any way," she flung back at the defense counsel.

The defense attorney contended that Angel, blistering with rage that her sister had an affair with John Huggins, was determined to have her revenge against him.

Defense lawyers Bob Wesley and Tyrone King also came up with a side issue, accusing Angel of seeking an escape of pending charges of drunk driving against her by testifying against Huggins.

Angel Huggins vehemently denied that she requested or received any special treatment.

Her testimony was concluded.

In December 1998, in preparation for the trial, Jeff Ashton went to Sumter County to take a deposition from Jonathon Huggins, John Huggins's eleven-year-old son.

In his deposition young Huggins stated that John Huggins, his estranged wife, Angel, and their kids came from Melbourne to Orlando in June 1997 in Angel's car on a visit to Gatorland. They stayed at the Days Inn on Route 192, which was across the street from the Publix market.

Importantly, Jonathon stated in his deposition to Ashton that his father was not with them on the afternoon of June 10 when they left to return to Melbourne.

Before the trial began, defense counsel Bob Wesley requested of Ashton that young Jonathon not be put on the witness stand and subjected to the stress of testifying.

As a father, Jeff Ashton readily agreed, but he got approval and consent to read into the record the deposition that Jonathon gave him.

In that deposition, the boy also described the SUV his father was driving later that day, giving details of the vehicle and describing it as a Ford Explorer.

John Huggins sat stolidly through the reading of the deposition, showing no reaction to his son's words.

The state called in a steady parade of Centex Rooney employees, Walt Disney World workers, various landscapers and others who saw a white Ford Explorer on June 10 coming out of the woods, driving along the highway or traveling rapidly over the territory near the site where Carla Larson was last seen and where her body was later found.

Among the great number of witnesses were Centex Rooney employees Cindy Garris, Gary Wilson and son Brad, and Barry O'Hearne and Milton Johnson of Dora Landscaping, all accounting what they saw. Also testifying was Disney World's Reedy Creek serviceman in charge of roadway maintenance, Tommy Sparks.

Culhan showed an aerial photo of the area to Barry O'Hearne, who was landscaping in the area on June 10, 1997. He also had seen the vehicle, and he stated that it was driven by a white male.

When defense lawyer Bob Wesley cross-examined O'Hearne, he dwelled on whether the male driver wore sunglasses.

"Yes, it looked like he was."

"And you also described him as being dark-skinned, is that correct?"

"Well, that was probably just from the windows."

Wesley continued questioning. "Okay, but you told the police that this individual had a dark complexion, is that correct?"

"Well, that isn't how I meant it. Maybe kind of looked tanned. Not dark as a dark person."

"Okay, so this person was kind of tanned to you, had a darker complexion, wasn't a pale person?"

"Right."

Over several days other Centex Rooney employees, as well as Disney World workers, testified, recounting the search for Carla Larson and the subsequent discovery of her body.

Questioned by Jeff Ashton, John Ricker described how he and Michael Munson went about their arduous trek through the brush, then met the Disney employee Tommy Sparks, who had seen a white vehicle parked in the brush and directed them to the area. Ricker talked about the foul odor and their using the cigarette lighter to follow the wind direction to the final discovery of Carla's body.

The prosecutors and defense attorneys argued over the admission into evidence of photos of Carla Larson's body as it appeared when the witnesses found her.

Wesley's objection was to the use of color pictures. "I think it can be described without photographs. Or (with) alternatives, such as black-and-white photographs, which make less prejudicial impact on the jury."

Culhan countered, stating, "This photograph depicts the condition the body was discovered in. The body is covered up with debris and is fairly accurate, without being a gruesome photograph of what they saw when they came upon the body."

Judge Perry ruled, "Okay. As to this picture, objection will be overruled."

In his cross-examination, Wesley asked Ricker for a total review of his search of the area, without any mention of the discovery of the body.

The courtroom spectators stirred with interest and speculation when the bailiff called the next witness. They whispered, asking, "Who is he and why is he here?"

ASA Ted Culhan greeted him and asked, "Could you please tell us your name?"

"Jeffrey Alan Shrader."

"How are you employed?"

Shrader said that he worked in landscaping at Disney World and that he was employed there in December 1997.

Culhan asked that Shrader identify the location where he and others worked on December 24, 1997, and to explain the cleanup work that his crew did.

Shrader described the area where they worked that day as the grassy section leading onto Osceola Parkway. Culhan elicited from Shrader that in the course of his cleanup, he came upon a discarded purse.

Shrader said he opened the purse and saw that it contained Carla Larson's driver's license and a Discover credit card. When Shrader realized what he found, he set the purse back down, called his supervisor over and showed him the purse, explaining his find.

Culhan asked, "Other than the driver's license and the Discover card, did you touch anything else?"

Shrader shook his head. "Not that I am aware of."

With permission, the prosecutor approached the witness, showing him a photo that was marked state's exhibit "GG." "Do you recognize what's contained in that photograph, sir?"

Shrader nervously clenched his hands, recalling the incident of his find. "Yes, sir." He named the driver's license and Discover credit card.

He identified another state exhibit as the purse he found. He also confirmed that these items appeared to be as he initially saw them.

In answer to a question about any other items discovered, Shrader described finding an empty prescription bottle with a November date on it. (Subsequent investigation revealed it had no connection to the Larson case. Someone had simply thrown it away.)

The prosecutor showed Shrader a photograph of the area where the landscapers were working and had found the purse.

It was the area where many eyewitnesses had seen the Ford Explorer entering Osceola Parkway. Shrader identified the photo as accurate.

The witness, who had never been involved in anything as serious as this case, sat uneasily and faced the prosecutor, hoping for the conclusion of his ordeal.

Prosecutors showed Shrader an aerial photo of the specific area, and he stated that it was an accurate depiction.

Culhan asked that these photo items be admitted into evidence.

The prosecutor then asked Shrader to point out on the photograph exactly where he found the purse.

Silently Shrader complied.

Culhan followed with a request to introduce the actual purse, complete with its contents as it was discovered.

Defense attorney Wesley objected, stating, "The purse, if full of baby pictures, receipts, other things, might be prejudicial to Mr. Huggins because they tend to evoke sympathy from the jury."

Culhan responded, "I think the jury has the right to see the purse the way it was discovered on the side of the road."

The defense answered, pressing the point, "Some of those items are inflammatory. The things inside, the baby pictures, notes and things like that, go back to the jury room and cause the jury to make a decision based on emotion rather than facts."

Defense attorney King, anxious to add his weight to his partner's protestations, voiced his objection. "Your Honor, the defense objects to all of the exhibits. There is argument as to each piece."

Judge Perry called the attorneys to the bench for a sidebar. They reached an agreement to have a study made of the individual items from the purse.

In Wesley's cross-examination of Shrader, he asked questions about the landscaping of the area leading to the finding of the purse. He went on with further questions about the contents. When asked, the witness admitted that when the purse was opened, "things came out. I think like lipsticks and stuff."

At the conclusion of the testimony, the court broke for lunch. Judge Perry gave the jury the usual admonishment not to discuss the case.

Ashton and Culhan left the courthouse and headed for a nearby restaurant. As they walked briskly together, Ashton said, "It's good to be getting even this little exercise. It feels great to be outdoors, to breathe some fresh air."

"Yeah, but that wind coming off the river can go right through you. I'm glad the restaurant isn't far," Culhan replied.

"You must be living too soft a life." Ashton laughed.

"Maybe." Culhan chuckled in agreement. "Anyhow, we'd better stoke up. We've got a long, detailed afternoon facing us."

"Don't remind me."

CHAPTER 24

Jeff Ashton addressed his next witness. "Would you please state your name and your position?"

The tall, well-structured, dark-skinned man, best described as an authoritative person, said, "I'm Shashi B. Gore, chief medical examiner of District Nine, Orange and Osceola Counties, Florida."

When asked, Gore outlined his medical education. "Basic medicine and surgery in Bombay, India. I completed my baccalaureate in medicine and surgery and pursued it with pathology, microbiology, in 1963, University of Bombay. Further on, I specialized in forensic pathology and toxicology at Johns Hopkins University in Baltimore, Maryland, in 1969. I've been working as a medical examiner or associate for the last eighteen years."

The audience shifted in their seats, impressed with the doctor.

Ashton continued his examination. "Are you qualified as an expert to give opinions in the area of forensic pathology, in Florida?" Gore answered affirmatively.

After a short exchange with defense counsel, Judge Perry accepted Dr. Gore to render opinions in the discussed field.

Ashton's questions revealed that Gore responded, when

summoned, to the Disney site of the body, on June 12, 1997. The ME said that he had the body removed to the special mortuary facility for the autopsy, during which he supervised the taking of pictures of various aspects of the procedure. He had the pictures produced as slides to be presented here. After Gore confirmed that the slides showed the remains as they appeared when the ME arrived at the scene, Ashton asked the doctor to describe the findings to the jury.

The courtroom grew still at the sight of the slides, and there were more than a few gasps. The Larson and Thomas families held each other's hands for comfort as they steeled themselves for the dreaded ordeal ahead.

John Huggins stared curiously at the slides, his face totally expressionless.

Ashton asked Dr. Gore to explain what the picture slides showed. Pointing to the first one, the doctor said, "This is the basic picture, the first one we take normally as a routine practice, which tells the name of the victim as well as the time and the number.

"This is for identification of the site only. You can see on this area the growth of some vegetation."

The next slide, Gore explained, "was the picture we took that shows the left leg and part of the foot." He stated, "It does not show any peculiar pattern of injury."

He took the next picture after the remains were moved to the morgue. Gore noted, "It shows the front of the face. This is what we call an identification shot." He pointed out, "Unfortunately, the body was not identifiable because of the decomposition changes."

The jury reacted with quiet shock as they viewed the beaten, battered, unrecognizable face of the young woman. The Larson and Thomas families averted their eyes, but not quickly enough, to avoid seeing their beloved wife and daughter's last agonies. Tears filled their eyes, but they hung on grimly.

Moving to the next slide, Dr. Gore explained clinically how "it shows the torso complete, the breasts, the abdomen and part of the neck and chin." He pointed out a reddish area on the left breast region, "which is different from the area with no injuries." He suggested, "There could have been some injury prior to death."

Ashton, with the curiosity of a nonmedical expert, asked about the difference in appearance before and after death.

Gore responded in great detail, explaining antemortem (before death) and postmortem (after death) trauma.

With a change in slides, Dr. Gore stated, "This gives a complete idea of what happened. . . . This is the genitalia, the thighs," he indicated, pointing out specifically, "this area shows definite evidence of antemortem injury, antemortem trauma." He moved his head, silently conveying the sad situation he was presenting.

Ashton asked the doctor, "What type of antemortem injuries do you think would cause that?"

After thoughtful consideration the doctor responded: "As common sense . . . one would expect this could be as a result of sexual intercourse or molestation or attempt at sexual intercourse."

The audience whispered comments; the jury seemed visibly shaken by this information.

Gore elaborated, pointing to the slide. "This is the posterior end, the buttocks; this is the anus, the perianal region."

Prosecutor Ashton, trying to bring the attack Carla Larson suffered into sharper focus, interrupted to ask, "Are there any internal injuries to the sexual organ?"

"No."

Jeff pressed, "So what you see is the external?"

"Internally," Dr. Gore answered, "there were no tears or lacerations of the vagina or the anus, the rectum."

Again a wave of whispers drifted through the audience. "Was she raped, or was there an attempt at rape?" they asked each other. The judge rapped his gavel for quiet.

Dr. Gore continued, next showing a slide displaying the hyoid bone, in the front of the neck. "You can see the area of hemorrhage." He pointed with his marker. "There is evidence of antemortem traumatization, of antemortem injuries. Injuries that the victim received prior to death."

The doctor went into a long explanation about another slide that showed the insect activity on the body. "The animal activity . . . immediately after the death, they come up there and start taking the pieces of flesh. But you don't see any reaction," Gore emphasized, "because there was no life." Gore stressed that "reaction is very important, because reaction means life."

The families' grieving reactions were clearly visible on their faces. Members of the press wondered how long the families could stand to see and hear these awful details.

The ME showed a slide exhibiting the left hand of the victim. He pointed out that the wedding band was clearly in view on the finger, with no major lacerations or abrasions.

One member of the press leaned over to a colleague and said sardonically, "Wonder why he didn't rip off that ring." The other answered cynically, "Must have been on too tight and he didn't have a knife to cut off the finger."

Ashton, continuing to focus on the brutal attack on the victim, asked, "What you have shown us here in the photographs are all the areas of antemortem injury that you believe exist, is that right?"

"Yes, sir."

"When the body was found," Jeff asked, "do you recall whether the earlobes for earrings were torn in any way?"

"No."

"They were not?" Jeff asked in surprise.

"No," replied the doctor firmly.

Continuing on the same track, Ashton asked, "Were there holes for pierced earrings?"

"Yes, sir" was the positive answer.

Again the reporter whispered to his colleague, "He removed the earrings, not ripped them out." And the other one answered derisively, "Probably didn't want to harm the diamonds."

"Was there anything on the body, other than the one ring that we saw in the photograph . . . the wedding ring?"

"No."

The prosecutor was subtly stressing the importance of the victim's jewelry and its relation to this case, and bringing out the fact that the killer took every bit of the victim's clothing, as well as her jewelry.

Ashton went on, in another direction. "Is there anything to indicate that the body was dragged to the area where it was found?"

Dr. Gore tilted his head and stared upward before answering. "I did not see any drag marks on the body that would have indicated to me linear antemortem, that is before death, scratches, either on the buttocks or on the front of the abdomen or anywhere on the legs. I did not see those." He paused, and after consideration, added, "The legs were clean and clear."

"If the body after death was dragged, can that still leave some evidence?" Ashton asked.

The doctor settled back in the witness chair and answered calmly, "There will be some evidence indeed."

Ashton continued: "Did you see anything to indicate that after death the body was dragged or scratched or abraded in any way?"

"There was no indication," Dr. Gore affirmed.

Still pressing to establish the facts and leave no doubts, Ashton asked, "Anything to indicate in any way that this body was moved after she died?"

"I did not see any indication," Dr. Gore answered in a quiet but firm voice.

Ashton stepped back from the podium and in a clear, strong voice asked, "Based upon your examination in this case, do you have an opinion as to the cause of death of Carla Larson?"

The courtroom grew totally silent, awaiting the doctor's response. "Yes, sir" was the firm, positive answer. "Yes, sir."

Ashton asked, "And what is that opinion?"

"In my opinion," Dr. Gore began, aware of how important his answer would be, "the cause of death in this particular case is asphyxiation." He halted to define what he meant. "That is the common word, meaning depriving of oxygen to the human body as a result of severe neck injury and strangulation. So when that is inflicted, naturally the fresh oxygen to the body is curtailed, and that is the state we call asphyxiation, asphyxia."

Ashton questioned the doctor: "Is it possible scientifically for you to give a precise time of death?"

Gore shook his head emphatically. "No."

Ashton tried again. "Based upon what you saw, is it possible to give estimates as to whether certain dates and times are consistent with being the time of death?"

"Yes, sir."

The prosecutor asked, "Would what you saw be consistent with Carla Larson dying sometime between noon and one on June 10, 1997?"

"It is not inconsistent with that."

Ashton continued: "Would, in fact, the potential time of death be much broader than that hour?"

"Yes, sir. That's the reason that we gave the cause of death that early time, from noon to maybe two or three o'clock. But we can't be a hundred percent certain. Nobody can, in fact."

For the record Jeff Ashton had achieved a reasonable time frame of the actual killing.

Bob Wesley rose and strode commandingly to the podium. He initiated a series of detailed questions about antemortem and postmortem trauma, Gore's record keeping, taking of photographs and how the ME went about making his tests.

The lawyer asked a preponderance of questions, in hopes of countering the accuracy of the medical testimony.

Wesley asked, "Dr. Gore, another test that you performed

is to remove a semen sample from the vagina of Ms. Larson, is that correct?"

"Yes, sir."

"And that was obtained with a swab?"

"Correct."

"And the purpose of taking that sample was for testing or comparison, correct, sir?"

The doctor agreed.

Wesley asked the doctor the procedure of how the work was done, if he was the person who retrieved the sample or if it was done under his direction. "Was it the standard pathological exam?"

The doctor answered yes.

Strangely, Wesley did not pursue this line, especially since the investigation found that the semen taken from Carla's body did not match Huggins's. Testing determined that it was from her husband, Jim Larson.

Wesley asked a series of detailed questions about trauma to the genital area, which Dr. Gore answered fully.

Wesley added, "And there was no trauma to the perianal region, is that correct?"

"That is correct."

Wesley moved their attention to defensive wounds.

"Doctor," Wesley asked, "when you examined Ms. Larson's body, you did not find any broken fingernails, did you?"

When Gore told him that was correct, Wesley continued: "There was no skin or debris underneath the fingernails, is that correct?"

"Yes, sir."

"Nothing," Wesley went on, "to indicate that there had been a struggle, that she used her hands to defend herself, is that correct?"

This disclosure brought a buzz of whispers among the people attending: "Where was Wesley heading? Was he implying that Carla didn't try to fight back? Why didn't she? Maybe, for whatever reason, she wasn't able to defend herself?" they asked. Judge Perry rapped his gavel, silencing the noisy comments.

The doctor thought for a moment and then stated, "My findings only tell me that I did not find anything between the nails and the finger beds. Now, whether it was washed off, whether it went off, we don't know. But my finding is that I did not see anything, any skin tags, blood or fiber."

"Okay, Dr. Gore, when you do your work, when you go to a crime scene, isn't one of the procedures that you place bags over the hands of the victim?"

When Gore agreed, Wesley asked, "What is the purpose of placing bags over the hands?"

"The reason is simple. That we should not lose any trace evidence."

"And that is because your job is to collect, preserve, every bit of evidence, correct? So the hands of Ms. Larson would have been bagged at the scene, correct? Could you have put bags over the feet also?"

"Yes, sir."

Wesley, satisfied that he made points about evidence, continued asking detailed questions about defensive wounds, blood discoloration, abrasions.

One of the issues that defense raised involved the question of breast cancer, which Ashton vehemently objected to, arguing, "It isn't relevant to this case."

After heated discussions Judge Perry agreed.

Despite Judge Perry's ruling on the breast cancer issue, Bob Wesley continued to bring up irrelevant issues with the clear intention to confuse and complicate the proceedings.

Ultimately Dr. Shashi Gore's testimony concluded and he stepped down from the stand, obviously tired and glad to be finished.

After Ashton and Culhan gathered their files and papers together and secured them for the night, they went to dinner to unwind from the pressures of the day.

"I don't know about you, Ted, but I'm bushed," Ashton said as they looked over the dinner menu.

Culhan held up his thumb in agreement. "What are you going to have, Jeff? I think we earned a good dinner." He smiled.

"I'll stick with a steak."

"Me too. Can't go wrong with that."

While they waited for their food to arrive, Ashton said, "I don't think today would have been so intense if our friend Shashi Gore were not so thorough and meticulous. He does run on sometimes."

"Hey, he was a great witness. I agree that he tends to be a bit too technical sometimes, but overall he presented his information and was very effective."

"He always is," Ashton agreed. "He's a nice guy and you can depend on him to do an excellent job. He knows his business. But he can wear you out." Ashton grinned. "It's early to bed for me tonight."

"That is an excellent idea."

CHAPTER 25

After a restful night the two prosecutors were totally revived and ready to continue when court convened; they were dressed in their well-tailored suits and sober neckties.

Ronald Weyland was the next witness. He is a specialist in forensics and is seriously devoted to his work. He has a pleasant, friendly smile, and is a trim, 5'9", well-built man, with a round face and healthy reddish complexion.

Prosecutor Ted Culhan, in his usual clear voice, asked the witness for his name, occupation and his special assignment.

He answered, "Ronald Weyland," and stated that he was a deputy with the Orange County Sheriff's Department for six and a half years, working with the forensic unit.

Asked to explain his work, Weyland replied, "I respond to crime scenes; I take notes, photographs and document the scene, process evidence."

"Were you assigned to be the crime scene technician on June 10, 1997, in the murder case of Carla Larson?"

"Yes," he answered, very self-assured.

The stocky prosecutor asked a series of questions relating to Weyland's procedures in the case, and the witness explained that a command post was set up on that date, composed of a large number of deputies, Disney employees and civilians, as well as canines, along with several specially trained persons with vehicles and a metal detector to search the wide area.

"We were prepared and determined. We had a major area to examine, and we were going to go through all of it thoroughly."

After a number of questions about the search, the finding of the body and the subsequent investigation, Culhan asked, "Did you assist employees of the television show *America's Most Wanted?*"

"Yes, I did."

"And for what purpose?"

The forensic specialist thought for a moment and answered, "To re-create the scenario and the scenes to depict what might have happened, and possibly develop leads that could be used in solving the case."

Culhan moved to questions about Weyland's work on the burned Ford Explorer, which he explained in detail.

The prosecutor asked about the search of Faye Elms's home, where Angel Huggins was living. Weyland explained the purpose of the search.

Culhan had Weyland relate the removal of the jewelry and photographing of the electrical box in which the jewelry was discovered. Weyland explained how earlier they searched two electrical boxes in the shed but not the one low to the floor where the jewelry was found. He emphasized that when an investigation is under great pressure, sometimes something can be overlooked.

Ted Culhan turned the focus to the area where the purse was found, and he established that this purse was Carla Larson's. The prosecutor inquired if the witness took pictures of the purse, and also if he took the item into evidence.

"Yes, I did," Weyland answered.

After receiving permission from Judge Perry, Culhan showed the purse to the witness, who nodded his head, confirming that it was the purse being discussed.

"Did you take any of the contents out?"

The witness replied affirmatively and described several items that were in the purse.

Defense lawyer Tyrone King objected and an exchange ensued about the contents of the purse. The prosecution and defense teams wrangled back and forth until Culhan, feeling that the arguments were impeding the flow of his questioning, finally suggested, "I can move on to something else. We can do this tomorrow morning."

Judge Perry looked at the defense, then made a quick appraisal of the prosecution and in a low voice said, "Okay."

Culhan returned to questioning Weyland, asking various questions about photographs that the witness took of the contents of the purse. The defense objected to almost every question.

Mercifully, Judge Perry, seeking a way out of the endless cross fire, asked, "Is this a convenient point for you to stop?"

When it was agreed, the judge sent the jury out of the courtroom.

After the jury left, Ted Culhan rose and announced, "Let's take up the contents of the purse now."

Tyrone King stood and stated, "Your Honor, the defense objects to all of the exhibits. There is argument as to each piece. Our objection is to the relevance of the miscellaneous paper contents in the purse."

Ted Culhan, speaking directly to Judge Perry, responded that the relevance was that the prosecution believed that the purse was discarded intact, hastily thrown out the window of the car while the defendant was speeding away from the scene. He said that from the evidence it was reasonable to infer that the defendant tossed the purse out the window as he was going down off the ramp of the parkway. Culhan argued that apparently nothing was removed. This was in keeping with the theory that the defendant made a very quick movement back to the Days Inn, which the prosecution thought was a reasonable inference from the evidence.

The defense argued that there was no evidence to show

that nothing was removed from the purse, or that the purse was discarded in a quick manner.

The judge overruled King's objection, but the wrangling continued, with the defense attorney still objecting as to relevance.

Culhan's argument was that the purse contained credit cards, which a thief would take if he rifled through the purse.

The arguing went on and on, with the judge overruling the defense on each point.

As the fray continued, the crowded courtroom became more and more restless, until Perry once again rapped for order with a threat to clear the room.

When court resumed, Deputy Weyland was still on the witness stand. The questions asked of him were about the items he ID'd that were inside the victim's purse, including a four-leaf clover, Carla Larson's driver's license, a pen and her Social Security card. Culhan asked the court to admit these items into evidence.

Defense lawyer King objected vehemently, but he was overruled by the judge.

King's cross-examination concerned Weyland's search of the Elms house, his methods and specifically on the electrical wall boxes. He asked countless questions that finally began to tire the witness.

King asked, "Did you find any jewelry?"

"No," he answered tersely.

The defense lawyer asked about other items collected by the investigator. He concentrated on some envelopes of letters written by John Huggins to Angel, asking about their use for DNA. He also asked about blood samples, including one taken from Jim Larson.

Culhan sprang to his feet. "Your Honor, I object to this as being beyond the scope of direct examination." There was a low fire in the prosecutor's voice.

Judge Perry ruled, "Sustained."

King asked interminable questions about items taken into

evidence: fingerprints, swabs, items from the purse, jewelry, tests made for latent prints, trace evidence, hair fiber.

Finally Culhan objected, and the judge sustained his objection.

After a short requestioning session by Culhan, and another brief cross-examination by King, Weyland left the witness stand.

As the two prosecutors ate their lunch, Culhan suggested, "I'm thinking maybe we can drive down to Orlando for the weekend. What do you think?"

"That sounds great," Ashton answered. "I sure would like to spend a little time with my family, get caught up on all their activities. I feel like we're totally isolated, out of touch with the rest of the world. I haven't read a newspaper or seen TV news in so long; I haven't the foggiest idea of what's happening outside of that courtroom. A change of subject would be a welcome relief, give me a chance to recharge my batteries." He laughed.

"It all depends on the way the trial goes. If the judge calls a Saturday session, it wouldn't be practical to go just for Sunday."

"I know, and he's pretty determined to move this trial along expeditiously," Ashton said wistfully.

"We'll just have to play it by ear. Now, to more practical matters, I'm starved. Gotta keep up my strength." Culhan grinned.

"Yeah, I could do with something hearty." Ashton laughed. "And when we get back to the suite this evening, I'm going to call home."

Deputy Todd Howard of the Brevard County Sheriff's Department took the stand and was sworn in.

Ted Culhan questioned him about the blazing destruction of the Explorer on June 26, 1997. He asked about the fire and the condition of the burned vehicle. Then he showed the witness a photo of the destroyed automobile, asking him to confirm whether that was the way it looked when the fire was out.

"Yes, sir, that's it," Howard confirmed, nodding his head.

With permission from the judge, Culhan introduced an aerial photo of the area where the vehicle was burned. He asked the witness to point out the location of the vehicle, which he did. The photo was entered into evidence without objection.

In his cross-examination, defense attorney Wesley viewed the photo with Deputy Howard and asked specific questions about the location, trying to establish it specifically. "For the jurors' reference, this is the same general area as Kennedy Space Center? And right here to the south would be Patrick Air Force Base?"

"Yes, sir."

After a number of follow-up questions, the attorney concluded.

Prosecutors Culhan and Ashton called several expert witnesses for technical questioning about the destroyed Ford Explorer.

The first was Charles LaCorte, identified as a lieutenant with the Bureau of Fire and Arson Investigation, Division of State Fire Marshal. He testified to his findings about the vehicle. In his distinctive voice LaCorte gave an involved account, relating the technical observations that he made about the obvious arson and the condition of the vehicle, specifying the open doors, raised hood, burned interior, melted submerged tires and the dent in the rear left side of the body.

He was followed by Virginia Casey, crime scene investigator and latent fingerprint examiner with the Brevard County Sheriff's Department, who explained how her collecting of evidence involved the burned SUV. Casey made clarifying statements, further explaining the arson destruction to the Explorer, plus detailing her extensive work in the search for fingerprints.

Next came Sandy Cawn with the Orange County Sheriff's Department, assigned to the forensic unit. Her testimony dealt with her participation in the collection of Carla Ann Larson's jewelry at Faye Elms's residence in Melbourne, Florida. This aspect of their work with the jewelry evidence would prove to be of greatest importance in the case against John Huggins.

At the conclusion of the technical experts' testimony, the state called Annette Moore, the neighbor who lived across the street from Faye Elms's home in Melbourne. Moore, a fortyish woman with dark brown eyes and hair, eagerly recounted seeing the white Ford Explorer parked at the Elms residence on June 11, 1997. She seemed like the kind of person who missed nothing in her neighborhood.

The solemnity of the courtroom changed to levity with the appearance of the next witness, Derek Hilliard, who shared a home with Annette Moore. Before testimony began, defense attorney Bob Wesley objected to the T-shirt that the witness was wearing. Printed on the front of the shirt was REAL FEAR and on the back HE WHO DIES WITH THE MOST TOYS, STILL DIES.

Wesley stated, "It's prejudicial." He claimed that it was a religious message and "deals with the subject of death."

After heated discussion the objection was overruled.

Hilliard's testimony, which supported Moore's observations, was that he also saw the Ford Explorer parked at the Elms home, across the street from his residence, on June 11, 1997.

CHAPTER 26

Jeff Ashton and Ted Culhan relaxed at dinner that evening while waiting for the food. "I think it's going well, don't you?" Culhan asked.

"Yes, I do. We're getting in all the main points we needed to make, and while it's slow, it's rolling like a tank, nice and steady."

"We've got Kevin Smith tomorrow, which might be lengthy," Culhan said.

"But good," Ashton said. "That poor guy—he's Wesley's target for reasonable doubt."

"Yeah," Culhan agreed. "Wonder how he'll like that."

"Probably not his first choice." Ashton smiled.

Prosecutor Ted Culhan walked slowly, deliberately, to the podium to face witness Kevin Smith, a tall, thin-faced man in his thirties, with long brown hair, worn in a conspicuous ponytail.

"Sir, could you please tell us your name?"

"Kevin Smith."

The prosecutor lost no time in tying this witness to John

Steven Huggins. "Mr. Smith, is John Huggins an acquaintance of yours?" he asked.

With Smith's positive answer, Culhan continued questioning. "Did you know him in June of 1997?"

Smith said that he did. Culhan asked a number of questions, establishing where Smith lived, providing the Cocoa Beach address of the duplex and who lived with him.

"Kim Allred," he answered.

Responding to employment questions, Smith stated that he worked for a lawn service, adding, "I'm a crew leader."

Culhan continued with questions about Smith's work hours, the stretch of territory along the Atlantic coast that he serviced—Titusville (twenty-five miles north of Cocoa Beach), south to Palm Bay (about forty miles south of Cocoa Beach)—as crew leader of a two-man crew.

Culhan's questions brought out that at this particular time in June 1997, Smith was visited by family members, which included his parents and brother who came from Oklahoma City.

In answer to further questions, Smith stated that John Huggins arrived at his home on June 12, driving a white SUV, which he left there, after asking permission to do so. He volunteered, "It was a pretty neat vehicle and made me wonder about where and how John came by it."

John Huggins scrutinized Smith with a piercing stare, his eyes unblinking, his expression inscrutable. Smith did not look at Huggins.

Culhan produced a photo of the section where the white Explorer was torched, and he asked Smith many questions relative to the vehicle and the territory where it took place, a short distance south of his home.

With that, Culhan concluded his examination of the witness.

Defense attorney Bob Wesley opened his cross-examination with a question about Smith riding a motorcycle in the area where the Explorer was burned.

Smith responded, "I've ridden there."

There was a new wave of audience reaction. The surprise element of the motorcycle set the people buzzing.

Wesley asked Smith, "You had around your duplex a lot of motorcycles and motorcycle parts, didn't you?"

Upon Smith's agreement Wesley asked abruptly, "Who is Derek Smith?"

"He was a friend of mine," Kevin answered. "Also rode bikes."

"And did he live across A1A from you?"

"Yes," Smith said, leaning back in the chair with a wary expression.

In the next series of questions that Wesley asked, he learned from the witness that Derek Smith, who was not related to Kevin, drove a white Ford Explorer. And Kevin Smith answered that Derek's was identical to the SUV belonging to Carla Larson. Smith shifted in his chair, his manner somewhat defiant.

A tense silence fell over the courtroom.

The witness waited, a questioning look on his face.

Wesley had Kevin identify Derek Smith's white Ford Explorer from a photo that he produced. The jury could see it later and identify it.

As Bob Wesley kept up his barrage of questions to Kevin Smith, the reporters began to speculate about the defense lawyer's intention, and the agreement among the press was that Wesley was creating inklings of doubt for his client, John Huggins. By Kevin Smith's admission that Derek's SUV was identical to the vehicle that John Huggins parked at Smith's home, which was later destroyed by fire, he was creating uncertainty for the jury by focusing instead on Derek Smith.

The defense lawyer stretched to his full height of 6'6" and continued with seemingly endless questions to Kevin Smith about June 10 and June 12, the days he worked.

The result was that Smith, hopelessly confused, stammered his answers senselessly. "It seems like that . . . I don't know," Smith babbled, "if I was or not (referring to the date), but I took that day off to get ready for my incoming family."

"You just took Friday off?" Wesley sounded surprised.

"Yeah, you got to work—I mean, I'm having trouble with our accommodations—and Monday—since I'm in Jacksonville," Smith prattled.

The defense lawyer continued without letup to press the totally confused Kevin Smith for answers, which failed to make much sense.

Wesley made an abrupt turn in his questions, asking, "You knew John Huggins because you were a drug supplier to John Huggins, is that right?" He waited, the courtroom frozen into silence.

"That's a good way to put it," came the meek reply.

John Huggins never took his eyes off Kevin Smith, but his face was impassive.

Wesley continued: "And your source for drugs was Derek. Is that right?"

"Yeah, it's marijuana is what we're talking about. Marijuana."

"And that's how you made your money, correct, sir?"

"No, no," Kevin Smith denied. "It's not correct," he protested with a new spark of life.

Standing back from the lectern, Wesley asked commandingly, "Well—was Derek a drug dealer?"

With his eyes casting about the courtroom as though looking for a way to escape from this ordeal, Smith managed to say, "No, actually he was involved in the lawn business, too."

As Kevin Smith sat mute, awaiting the next salvo from the defense lawyer, he wiped his perspiring forehead, undoubtedly wishing that he were any place other than here. Wesley followed up relentlessly. "What role did you play in distributing drugs for Derek?"

Ted Culhan, who listened silently to the haranguing of Smith by Wesley, reached the point of "enough." He sprang to his feet, objecting, "Irrelevant. Impeachment by prior bad acts."

In quick order Judge Perry ruled, "Sustained."

Wesley turned the direction of his attack, asking Kevin Smith about his residence and the general area, which resulted in another confusing discussion. At the attorney's direction Smith left the witness stand to approach a displayed photograph of the locale. The lawyer continued with repetitive questions before Kevin Smith was permitted finally to return to the witness chair.

John Huggins sat watching the barrage on his friend as though he were simply a disinterested spectator, not personally involved in this whole thing.

After a renewed merry-go-round of questions, Wesley asked Smith about knowing Angel Huggins. Kevin said he knew her as John's wife, had seen her only once or twice.

Wesley asked, "In the summer of '97, you were aware John Huggins was charged with this crime, correct?"

"Yes," he mumbled, barely audible.

"And then after that time, Angel Huggins moved in with you and Kim, is that right?"

"No, that's not correct, either," Smith answered smugly, shaking his head.

Wesley asked, "She moved in with Kim?"

"I've heard so," he responded in a sullen tone.

More rounds of questions continued, until Wesley asked, "Have you met with Angel Huggins in the past two months or so to talk about testimony in this case?"

Culhan objected but was overruled.

Smith stated flatly that when they met, there were no discussions of the case.

After a brief recess, court was resumed with the defense attorney continuing his examination of Smith.

Wesley showed Kevin a photograph and asked if it accurately depicted his appearance in 1997. Smith responded that it did, and he smiled proudly.

"In the summer of 1997, were you employed in the land-scape business?"

"Yes."

"You worked outside?"

"Yes." He tilted his head, a questioning expression on his face that seemed to ask silently, "Where the hell would you work in the landscape business?"

"You usually have a dark suntan?"

"Yeah, I would say so."

"All right. Also you and your girlfriend, Kim, liked to go across to the beach, too, when you had time to lay in the sun?"

The witness stared at the lawyer and, in a puzzled tone, answered, "Yes, we did."

"So your personal preference was to have a suntan or a dark tan?"

Nodding his head, he stated, "Yes, I'd say so."

"By your work and by your hobby?"

"Just kind of goes with it, yeah."

"Okay. Mr. Smith, you wear your hair long, is that correct?"

"Yes, I do." He straightened in the witness chair and answered defiantly.

"Is it in a ponytail right now?"

"Yes, it is." He smiled.

"How long have you worn your hair in a ponytail?"

Smith rubbed his head, searching his mind. "Probably like six or seven years. Ever since I got out of the military, I started letting it grow. Had a lot of regulations there. I just quit cutting it."

"And in June of 1997, was your hair that long?"

"Yes, it would be."

Wesley asked about the sunglasses in the photo and Kevin said that he usually "put them on my visor."

"Of your cap?"

"Yes."

Murmurs in the courtroom by the onlookers speculated

whether the defense attorney was trying to establish that Kevin Smith, not John Huggins, fit the description given by eyewitnesses of the man driving the Explorer on June 10, 1997.

Wesley turned to the subject of the Orange County Sheriff's Department detectives questioning him.

"First evening they showed up I wasn't there." Smith explained that a card was left with his girlfriend and he called the OCSD and met with them the next afternoon.

Wesley charged that Smith was "not there because you were directly across the street watching them, is that right? At Derek's house?"

"No, no, but I did go over to Derek's house."

"So there was not a time when law enforcement officers came to your home, you left?"

"No," he answered vehemently.

Wesley changed course again. "What date was it that you say that John Huggins brought the truck to your house?"

"I think we all talked about it being the twelfth."

"It was on a Friday?"

"Yeah." (Actually June 12 was on Thursday, but no one seemed to catch that.)

"And you were just hanging out in your yard that day?"

"Well, yeah, I was finishing the last of my prep for my family coming to town. We were having a big Father's Day party."

Wesley asked about a man named Mike Varcadipane and was told that he was the owner of the lawn service Kevin worked for.

The defense attorney continued to question and confuse the witness, until finally, after repetitive introduction of the same questions, the session came to an end.

Kevin Smith walked out of the courtroom, passing John Huggins but avoiding making eye contact.

Prosecutor Jeff Ashton confidently moved to a position facing Detective Cameron Weir, who took the witness stand and was already sworn in to testify.

"Please state your name," Ashton requested.

"Cameron George Weir."

After identifying Weir as a detective with the Orange County Sheriff's Department, Ashton asked him many questions regarding the crime area where Carla Larson's body was found.

Weir gave a long description about the details of the crime and his investigation.

Turning to another subject, Ashton asked if Weir had occasion to meet with Kevin Smith in the summer of 1997.

"Yes, I did," he responded, his bright eyes alert.

Ashton then followed with a series of questions that included seeing Smith today and details about the length of Smith's hair today, as compared with what it was in July 1997.

"If I recall correctly," Weir projected, "his hair is longer at this time than it was then."

The prosecutor, deeply interested in Kevin Smith's hair and overall appearance, drilled away at the detective, asking, "Did the hair extend down below the collar, noticeably below the collar?"

"Yes, sir," Weir confirmed with surety.

Ashton inquired, "When you met with Mr. Smith, did he have his hair in a ponytail as he did today?"

"At various times," the detective responded. "I believe that he did."

Ashton asked, "Now, did Mr. Smith give you the name of the person that he was working with on June 10, 1997?"

"Yes, he did."

"And did you find that person?"

"Yes, I did." Weir told him that it was Mike Varcadipane.

"Okay, sir. Now, did you speak to Mr. Varcadipane about Mr. Smith's whereabouts on June 10, 1997?"

"Yes, sir," Weir confirmed, nodding his head.

"And after that conversation, did you do any further investigation of Kevin Smith as a suspect in the murder of Carla Larson?"

"No, sir," he answered in a positive, assuring voice. Weir was satisfied in his thorough investigation of this murder case that Kevin Smith had no part in the killing of Carla Larson.

Wesley began his cross-examination by referring to the photo of Kevin Smith that was previously displayed. He asked Weir, "Does that appear to be the way that Mr. Smith presented himself on June of 1997?"

"Yes, sir," Weir affirmed authoritatively.

After more reexaminations and more cross-examinations over various fine points of Weir's testimony, he was excused, the last witness of the day.

It was Friday, almost the weekend that Jeff Ashton and Ted Culhan were anticipating, hoping to get away for a trip home to Orlando.

"Well, Jeff, it looks like we're going to be stuck here working all weekend."

"Yeah, I had that feeling. If we plan to finish presenting our case on Monday, Wesley will start with his witnesses and his technical experts, so we have to be prepared." Ashton sighed. "And I was so looking forward to a change of pace, time to clear my mind."

"Oh, well, it will soon be over and we can go home to stay," Culhan comforted.

"I can hardly wait."

CHAPTER 27

In the wrap-up of the state's case on Monday, February 1, 1999, Jeff Ashton, after securing permission from Judge Perry to show it to the jury, nodded to the bailiff to start the videotaped television interview conducted by TV reporter Steve Olson with Huggins while he was incarcerated in the Seminole County Jail.

Huggins on the videotape was quite a contrast from the defendant who sat here on trial neatly dressed in a conservative blue suit, white shirt and subdued necktie, his hair trimmed and combed.

The jury watched with rapt attention as the defendant asserted that he didn't think he killed Carla Larson because "I'm not that kind of a guy." They heard him talk about his blackouts from his medications coupled with drug and alcohol abuse. And they listened attentively as he said, "Inside myself I feel I didn't kill her."

When the tape concluded, the courtroom was still. The jury automatically turned to look at John Huggins as he sat quietly with his head lowered. His expression remained bland, unreadable.

Ted Culhan rose and announced that the state rested.

* * *

Defense lawyer Bob Wesley stood before the jury, confidently asserting that his client, John Huggins, was innocent of the crime of which he was accused and now being tried.

As his attorney began to present the defense's evidence, Huggins sat silently, watching everything with full attention.

The crowded, almost to capacity, courtroom listened as Wesley presented a forensic scientist who contended that hairs found with the body of Carla Larson did not match hair from John Huggins, the accused. The implication was that the hairs might belong to Huggins's friend Kevin Smith, who the defense was hinting was the real killer.

A wave of reacting comments drifted across the room and the judge rapped for order and quiet.

ASA Jeff Ashton made the point that the defense never compared hair from Smith to the hair found at the murder scene. He also contended that the absence of Huggins's hair at the murder scene did not prove that he was not there.

By presenting nine expert witnesses over Monday and Tuesday, February 1 and 2, Wesley and King tried to convince the jury that Kevin Smith of Cocoa Beach could be the killer. They said Smith resembled the early drawings of the possible killer. They also made note of the fact that Smith had the radar detector from the Larson vehicle.

Wesley said, "And there's nothing to support what Kevin Smith says, except Kevin Smith."

The defense team continued to stress the lack of physical evidence to link Huggins to the crime. There were no fingerprints, no DNA, no hair, no proof of any connection that their client had anything to do with it.

In their presentation the defense concentrated on instilling reasonable doubt into the minds of the jurors. If the jury bought that premise, John Huggins conceivably could walk away from the murder charge.

The defense attorneys tried to cast doubt on Angel Huggins's testimony about the time that she said her husband was gone from the motel on June 10, 1997.

The onlookers were curious about how the defense would explain away the prosecution's key evidence of Carla Larson's jewelry found at Huggins's mother-in-law's house, but the defense skirted the issue and finally rested.

Closing arguments were set for the next day, Wednesday, February 3. The judge, after admonishing the jury about discussing the case with anyone, told them to bring a packed bag, because if they did not reach a verdict by the end of the day, they would be sequestered in a hotel.

CHAPTER 28

The following morning, Jeff Ashton wore a conservative blue suit, and his lightly gray streaked brown hair was carefully combed. As his bright brown eyes panned across the faces of the jurors, he began in a confident voice: "Ladies and gentlemen of the jury, you have listened to the case of the prosecution. . . ."

He went into a long review of the tragic, brutal murder of a lovely young wife and mother, who had the misfortune to be at the wrong place at the wrong time.

Step by step, Ashton outlined the state's case, recalling the statements of the witnesses who saw the accused driving the white Ford Explorer that belonged to the victim, the fact that the defendant was in the area where Carla Larson was last seen, and citing her jewelry, which was found in the shed behind Huggins's mother-in-law's home, tying it directly to the accused.

In his dramatic closing Ashton declared absolutely that the man who killed Carla Larson was the man seated at the defense table, defendant John Huggins. Jeff pointed directly at him. Huggins stared back at him, unblinking, impassive.

The defense's presentation of its case alluded to a frame-up of Huggins by his estranged wife, Angel, and his friend Kevin Smith.

Jeff Ashton scoffed at that argument. "I haven't heard a conspiracy theory like that since I took my children to see *The X Files* movie," he asserted to the jury.

Following the conclusion of this day in court, Kevin Smith was contacted at his home in Cocoa Beach, where he said that he was disgusted being called a killer and that he was shocked to learn that he was being blamed for something that he didn't do. He couldn't believe his friend John was doing this to him.

After the judge's instructions to the jury, the nine-woman, three-man panel began its deliberations.

The jury was out for four hours, coming back with a verdict of guilty on all counts.

John Huggins seemed to have no visible reaction when the verdict was read. Onlookers staring at him marveled, and one said, "He looks like he expected it."

The jury would return the following Tuesday to begin the sentencing phase and to make its recommendation.

When the jury announced the verdict, the mothers of Jim and Carla wept. The families were emotionally drained from the stress of the trial. The guilty verdict was small comfort after their terrible loss, but there was some satisfaction that the perpetrator of the horrendous trauma Carla suffered would be punished. And maybe they could finally have some closure.

"It still really doesn't change a whole lot," said Jim Larson. "It's not like the movies, where Carla gets up and we go home and we get to be happy. I want to move on to the next step. If we can put another one on death row for the Larson family, maybe they'll start a wing for us," he said bitterly, referring to Danny Rolling, who is on death row for killing Sonja Larson and four other students in Gainesville, Florida, in 1990.

Carla's mother, Phyllis Thomas, said, "It is a relief to know this sad human being will get what he has coming to him."

In the hearing on Tuesday to determine what penalty should

be imposed on the convicted John Huggins, Carla Larson's family members were allowed to talk about what her loss meant to them and to the community.

They were not permitted, however, to mention the crime or what penalty they might suggest.

The defense attorneys proposed that the convicted Huggins should receive life imprisonment without the possibility of parole, rather than the death penalty.

Bob Wesley and Tyrone King argued that Huggins could minister to prison inmates. "He did much missionary work in Haiti, helped the homeless and donated money and cars to charity," Tyrone King pleaded passionately.

The jury listened carefully to all arguments, then deliberated for more than two hours, after which they voted eight to four that Huggins be executed.

Huggins sat frozen, again no reaction showing on his face, shocked silent.

Judge Perry stated that he would render his decision on Friday, February 26, 1999.

On that Friday, in the crowded Orange County Courthouse in downtown Orlando, the black-robed Judge Belvin Perry entered and took his seat behind the expansive mahogany bench.

With an austere expression on his face, the judge acknowledged the prosecution and the defense, whereupon the bailiff announced, "This court is in session." A grim quiet settled over the courtroom while the judge shifted his fourteen-page sentence order that lay before him.

"One could only imagine," he said in a deep, somber voice, "the alarm, the anxiety, the apprehension, the fright and the terror that Carla Larson felt as she was forced to ride to her demise."

Perry paused, and the family and friends of the deceased blotted the tears that welled in their eyes.

"What fear and horror she must have felt when she was forced to walk from her vehicle into the wooded area ... Carla Larson's own death march to Bataan."

The judge stopped again, wanting his portrait in words to affect the courtroom audience.

"No one can truly know," he continued, "the emotional strain and physical pain she had to endure as she struggled to breathe, as the defendant strangled her to death."

After the judge completed the thirty-minute, most compelling speech of his professional career, he asked the convicted Huggins to stand before him at the bench.

In grim prison attire, shackled hand and foot, the convicted killer stood like a frozen bleached statue before the judge, in whose hands was his right to live or die.

Judge Perry looked down at the career criminal who stood before him, thinking back to the fact that both his and Huggins's fathers had been police officers serving in Winter Park, Florida, a small, exclusive city adjacent to the city of Orlando. He thought, *It's amazing. Our fathers were both lawmen, and here I'm a judge and this fellow has no respect for law or decency, has a record a mile long. And now it's my duty to sentence him.*

"John Steven Huggins," Judge Belvin Perry began, his voice cutting through the still of the courtroom like a razor-sharp blade, "you have forfeited your right to live at all. . . . You shall be put to death in the electric chair by having electrical current passed through your body . . . until you are rendered dead."

Judge Perry paused. The people in the overcrowded courtroom seemed to have stopped breathing to absorb the judge's pronouncement of death.

The judge continued his speech. "John Steven Huggins, may Almighty God have mercy on your soul."

Court was adjourned and officers from the courtroom led the expressionless Huggins away.

CHAPTER 29

Subsequent to the death sentence for John Huggins, the attention of the defense attorneys focused on the automatic appeal to the Florida Supreme Court.

Then came a surprise twist. Within weeks following the conviction, Preston Ausley, an engineer at the Orange County Courthouse, contacted attorney Bob Wesley and informed him that before Huggins's trial, he had approached the state attorney's office, giving them some important information.

Ausley explained, "I informed investigators that a blond woman driving a Ford Explorer cut me off in traffic a day after that Larson lady's disappearance." He explained that he was very bad with dates and came to the conclusion that he encountered Carla Ann Larson's vehicle on June 11, 1997, by verifying the date through other sources. He added that he wrote down a partial license plate number, which was verified within one digit of Carla's Ford Explorer.

Somehow in the transmission of Ausley's account to the investigators, the written report stated that Ausley saw a "man" driving the Explorer. This information was included in Lead Sheet 302 in the evidence file, then turned over to the defense during discovery.

Subsequently on February 1, 1999, the day after seeing

Angel Huggins on television during coverage of John Huggins's trial in Jacksonville, Preston Ausley contacted the state attorney's office again. He gave a taped interview to an investigator there, with more details about the woman driver. Ausley said that when he saw Angel Huggins on television, it struck him that she resembled the white female with blond hair he saw driving the white truck, with a license plate that matched Carla Larson's within one digit, on the morning of June 11, 1997, on International Drive in Orlando.

After he gave his statement to Investigator Pat Guice, he was asked to return the next day so that the attorneys, who were at that very time in Jacksonville prosecuting the Huggins case, could speak with him by telephone.

The next morning, Jeff Ashton in Jacksonville spoke to Ausley via telephone. After their conversation, ASA Ashton determined that Ausley's name and information were already given to the defense in Lead Sheet 302. Therefore, Ashton did not turn the interview tape over to defense.

After defense counsel Tyrone King studied Ausley's statement, he reported the situation to Judge Perry.

The judge appraised the facts, and after studying all aspects, he found that the state violated the dictates of a Brady violation, in that the government possessed evidence favorable to the defendant and didn't turn it over to the defense.

After serious consideration Judge Perry threw out Huggins's conviction and death sentence.

This decision upset the prosecution, and Jeff Ashton appealed Perry's decision to the Florida Supreme Court.

In early June 2001, in an unexpected ruling, the Florida Supreme Court upheld Judge Perry's decision overturning the verdict. The court ruled in a seven-to-nothing opinion that the information provided by Ausley clearly conflicted with Ms. Huggins's testimony at trial. It could have been used to impeach Angel Huggins, the state's star witness. Angel insisted that she did not ride or get into the truck. The state supreme court ruled that had the jury been presented with Ausley's statement of seeing a woman resembling

Angel driving the Ford Explorer, Angel's testimony concerning the truck could have been severely undermined.

The state asserted that it did not suppress the information, and contended that it turned Lead Sheet 302 over to the defense.

Meanwhile, defense counsel Bob Wesley stated that he had plans to file a motion with the state supreme court to prevent any retrial. The defense lawyer would cite "protection from double jeopardy." Wesley's argument would be that "the state should be barred from a second trial, because its misconduct led to a reversal."

The powerhouse lawyer said that he was concerned that Huggins could not get a fair trial after so much time had passed. He stressed that "it's a horrible disadvantage. We showed our cards, the state created an error and the only impact is that they think they can do it all over again."

Later in June 2001, the Florida Supreme Court, on the strength of the dispute regarding the evidence withheld, ordered a retrial of John Huggins.

In complying with the high court, Judge Belvin Perry set December 6 as the new trial date, which he ordered to be held in Osceola County, Florida, just eighteen miles from Orlando.

In his reaction to the developments of a new trial, which he hoped to avoid, defense counsel Bob Wesley offered, with a concerned smile, that his case might benefit from a jury familiar with the area.

Wesley also said he wanted ASA Jeff Ashton, who, he said, made the error, removed from the case. "It's not fair for Mr. Huggins that the state caused an error and then has the benefit of a new trial. If you don't play by the rules, you shouldn't get to play again."

In court Judge Perry announced that Bob Wesley, who since was elected to his position of Orange/Osceola public defender (with a staff of more than eighty lawyers working under his direction), could continue to represent Huggins.

As the weeks rolled along, the general interest in the case

mounted. On Thursday, August 23, 2001, John Huggins, the accused, with sheared hair, cleanly shaven, looking reserved in his red-and-white-striped jail uniform and trimmed down a bit in weight, appeared in court with attorney Wesley at his side.

Standing obediently and politely before the bench of Judge Belvin Perry, the career criminal stated that he was there to complain about prosecutor Jeff Ashton. He presented a bailiff with a two-page letter for the judge. It read, "I assert this matter causes a grave personal conflict between myself and Jeff Ashton, and I urge you to bar him from doing any further work on this case in hopes I may receive a fair trial this time."

Chief ASA Bill Vose, of Orange County/Osceola County, appearing for the state, rose and addressed the court. In a potent response to the defendant, the capable professional flatly stated, "Assistant State Attorney Ashton has shown no prejudice against the accused."

In a speedy response the judge agreed. He ruled that Jeff Ashton could remain on the case for the second trial, scheduled to begin December 6, 2001.

Then looking directly at Vose, he added, "I hope that you will assign an additional prosecutor to the case." He smiled, nodding for the ASA's endorsement. Enjoying the spotlight for the moment, Perry added, "It's like riding in a car without a spare tire. I hope the state attorney's office, in its infinite wisdom, will travel with a spare tire."

Vose stated that he was pleased with the judge's decision, expressing his confidence that Jeff Ashton was the best-qualified prosecutor. Vose waited moments for his appraisal to sink in, and then continued, "We're concerned about the defendant getting a fair trial and the best way is to get the most experienced prosecutor." He paused and added, "While the defendant may not think so, we think Jeff Ashton is the best person."

CHAPTER 30

While the attorneys for both sides and the judge were involved in their various activities preparing for his retrial, John Huggins was busily engaged in writing poems and requests for pen pals, and drawing cartoons in his cell on death row. They were surprisingly good but derogatory about law enforcement, sort of "gallows humor."

He dispersed his works using a Web site provided by the Canadian Coalition Against the Death Penalty. The CCADP publicized internationally that it offers free Web pages to over three hundred death row inmates. The convicted John Huggins was busily using one to his advantage.

His main Web site carried a flattering photo of himself, along with his name and address (Death Row, Florida).

It began:

Hello. My name is John Huggins, I am the single father of three children. I have been wrongly convicted and sentenced to die for a crime I did not do. Florida has had to let more people off death row, than any state in our country. Why, because innocent people do get sent to death row.

Huggins argued that if a defendant didn't have money for a total defense, he had trouble. Citing his own case, Huggins offered that his defense was poor, emphasizing that they did not have resources to defend him. He said his court-appointed lawyers had a limited budget, which resulted in his poor defense.

But he contended there was more to his story and said the prosecutor was now under investigation by the Florida Bar for lying and hiding key evidence from a witness in his case. He said that they knew that he was innocent, but because this case was in the news so much, they were eager to win, so, according to Huggins, they lied and broke the law by hiding key evidence.

Huggins said a judge ruled that he should get a new trial because the judge found out what they did to him. He said the prosecutor was fighting his getting a new trial, but he asked what good was a new trial if he still didn't have resources for a fair defense?

He asked for help to hire an independent expert DNA lab and an independent investigator to interview witnesses he claimed were never before questioned in his case. He also asked for help from an expert lawyer who would keep him from death row for a crime he insisted he did not do.

Huggins said that the prosecutor's office would use every trick they can get away with rather than let him come back from death row and show everyone that they do send innocent people to be executed.

He explained that he could never repay for the help, the only thing would be the knowledge that they helped save an innocent man from death.

Huggins asked people to write and tell him what they thought. In a postscript he asked that they visit the Florida Bar Web site and express their opinions about the prosecutor's lying and hiding key evidence in his case. He also requested they ask the bar to disbar his prosecutor.

His appeal was followed by a drawing of a piece of barbed wire and below was another paragraph:

PENPAL REQUEST—Please Write!

Hello I am looking for pen pals to share my thoughts, feelings and time with. I am 37 years old, I have three children. I am from Orlando, Fla. I like the outdoors, swimming, fishing, boating. I love music from the soul.

He said that he spent twenty-four hours every day in a small cell and needed someone with whom to exchange letters. He pleaded, "If you have room in your life for a new friend, then please write."

He concluded with the same photo of himself and his address.

His copyrighted poems on another page consisted of his thoughts on deaths of inmates and he seemed to "dedicate" each to a specific individual, naming each man and the date of his execution, including Terry Melvin Sims, the first man to die by lethal injection in Florida, (2/23/00), Anthony Bryan (2/24/00), Bennie Demps (6/07/00), Thomas Provenzano (6/21/00), Dan Hauser (8/25/00), Edward Castro (12/07/00), Robert Glock (01/11/01). The titles of the poems were grim, perhaps macabre: "Gallows," "Soul Injection," "Don't Murder Me," "Gray Skies," "Hurry Hurry," "Smoke or Choke," "Where Dead Souls Swim."

CHAPTER 31

As occurs in many important murder cases, the case against John Huggins continued to create sundry problems. When Judge Perry decided to move the trial to Osceola County, he felt it would provide a venue outside Orange County and save the expense of moving the second trial outside of the circuit. He set it for the first week in April 2001.

When the trial began there, for three days the prosecutors and the defense went through the rigors of attempting to seat a jury, but without success.

They questioned 150 potential jurors, 75 filled out detailed eight-page questionnaires, and 15 of these persons were individually interviewed. Most remembered the case and had strong opinions regarding the guilt or innocence of John Huggins. Many of these prospective jurors said without qualm that they believed that the man on trial was guilty. One said he was a Jehovah's Witness and could not impose the death penalty.

It soon became obvious that a jury could not be seated in this county. Osceola County was not far enough from Orange County, and evidently not enough time had passed since the crime.

Judge Perry stated that he would consider a move to Broward County or Palm Beach County.

After much deliberation and consideration, as well as negotiating the arrangements for the moving of the Huggins trial, Judge Perry selected Tampa as the site for the retrial. The judge set Monday, July 15, 2002, as the starting date.

Ada and Jim Larson's attention was diverted from the Huggins retrial by the news that Danny Rolling, infamous killer who brutally murdered the five college students in Gainesville, among them Sonja Larson, was to appear on Tuesday, April 2, 2002, before the Florida Supreme Court, appealing his five death sentences.

The Larsons religiously attended all the hearings on Danny Rolling.

At this hearing Ada and Jim listened attentively to both sides arguing whether the killer should be put to death. Rolling's attorney included the argument that his five death sentences were recommended by a jury biased by fear.

The decision by the court would be forthcoming.

Press coverage of the Huggins retrial continued, with news of two new witnesses for the prosecution scheduled to appear at this second trial. One was Christopher Smithson, a thirty-seven-year-old construction specialist whose company, Electric Construction and Erection Company, was involved at the Coronado Springs Resort site, near Blizzard Beach at Walt Disney World.

Smithson's story was that just before lunchtime on that fateful June 10, 1997, he saw Carla Larson, whom he knew, walking to a work trailer. Smithson described her wearing a hard hat and sunglasses.

Smithson stated that later that day around 2:00 to 2:30 P.M., which was later than the reports other witnesses had given, he saw a man matching the description of John Huggins coming out of the woods and driving a white Ford Explorer, the same kind of vehicle Carla Larson drove, heading east on Osceola Parkway.

Chris Smithson said he noticed because "the Explorer jumped across the westbound lanes and took a place in the median, before falling in behind my Jeep."

In a subsequent interview, Smithson added to his account that "I'm an observant person, and I noticed this shiny white Ford Explorer coming out of the woods. I thought it was someone with a new car showing off."

Smithson said that when he heard that Carla Larson was missing, he put two and two together: "Then I saw John Huggins's photograph on the news." Smithson said that he tried to call authorities but never reached them, and later, when he saw that John Huggins was convicted of first-degree murder, he didn't pursue it.

With assurance Smithson explained, "I wouldn't be doing this if I were not sure. I am not out for recognition. I am here out of civic duty."

The second new witness was a Brevard County resident, Charlotte Green, who came forward in 1999 and claimed that she saw John Huggins driving the white Explorer, badly overpainted black in places, in her area near Eau Gallie.

On June 27, 2002, Ada and Jim Larson were relieved to hear that Danny Rolling lost his second sentencing appeal in the Florida Supreme Court.

The High Court of Florida rejected the issues raised by Rolling's lawyer. His five death sentences stood.

CHAPTER 32

Another important element that arose for the judge with the Huggins retrial was a new factor regarding the legality of the death sentence in Florida. The question involved whether a judge had the authority with restrictions to hand down a death sentence.

Judge Perry was unwilling to wait many months more for a decision from the Florida Supreme Court to decide whether Florida's death penalty was constitutional before going ahead with the Huggins case.

While the brouhaha continued over the intricacies of constitutionality and state interpretation of the law, Judge Perry stated, "I can't rewrite the statute. I'm going to do the best I can to see that Mr. Huggins has his day in court and receives a fair trial."

But the judge described the situation as similar to "putting a person in a room with no windows and no lights, and asking him to navigate through the room with no flashlight."

A reporter simplified the judge's position: "Perry will tell the jurors in the trial that starts on Monday, July 15, 2002, in Tampa that they will have the final say on whether John Huggins gets life in prison or death if he is convicted."

Huggins, staying abreast of the supreme court situation

and vitally interested in avoiding the death penalty, made a request of Judge Perry to remove execution from consideration in his trial, on the basis that Florida's capital sentencing procedure was now unconstitutional.

Judge Perry, with no hesitation, denied the request.

In a strong-voiced objection to the judge's ruling and decision, public defender Bob Wesley argued that Judge Perry did not have the power to change the statute.

The press ran stories expressing different opinions from both sides of the Huggins case, commenting and exchanging views on this death penalty issue that captured their full attention, as well as having profound effect in courtrooms throughout the country.

The defending lawyer Wesley vehemently stated, "I understand the frustration of the judge because this is a complex issue, but philosophically we are at odds. We think that once the Arizona case was decided, that means that Florida's statute is flawed and a judge can't save it. That is a job for the legislature."

The arguments in the Arizona death penalty statute before the United States Supreme Court raised the issue that in a first-degree murder case in Arizona, the jury heard the evidence in the guilt phase of the trial and rendered a verdict, but they were not allowed to hear the penalty phase. The judge alone heard the penalty phase and rendered the decision.

In declaring Arizona's procedure unconstitutional, the United State Supreme Court ruled that the jury must hear and decide the penalty phase as well as the guilt phase. The judge then makes the final decision and imposes sentence.

In Florida the jury hears the guilt phase and delivers a verdict and then also hears the penalty phase before deciding the sentence.

But the similarity between Arizona's death penalty statute and Florida's caused the Florida Supreme Court on Monday, July 8, 2002, to halt executions until the matter could be resolved.

Prosecutors and defense offered different opinions, with no clear conclusion. The impact of this unresolved death penalty question flooded the entire judicial system of the nation.

An organization of state prosecutors made it known that they would do their jobs as if the death-penalty-sentencing guidelines were constitutional.

The Florida Prosecuting Attorneys Association decided to move forward cautiously on death penalty cases. Jerry Blair, president of the association and state attorney for the 3rd Judicial Circuit in Florida's Panhandle, stated, "We are going to proceed as prosecutors on the assumption that we have a valid death penalty statute."

Blair said they would decide on a case-by-case basis, but would seek continuances or stays in as many cases as they could, until the Florida Supreme Court decided whether the state's death penalty statute was constitutional.

In the Huggins situation Jeff Ashton said that he would not ask for a continuance and did not anticipate asking Judge Belvin Perry to postpone the sentencing portion of the Huggins trial if Huggins was convicted.

The argument about the death penalty expanded across the nation involving other states' laws, defense lawyers, prosecutors, various legal organizations, legislators and the general public.

On Tuesday, July 9, 2002, Governor Jeb Bush of Florida announced that he would continue to sign death warrants for condemned inmates.

Specifying, Bush decreed, "If appeals have been exhausted by death row inmates, I will sign death warrants." He emphasized, "I have an obligation and duty to do so. And then we'll let the courts respond."

CHAPTER 33

Judge Belvin Perry selected Tampa for Huggins's second trial, which was to commence on July 15, 2002.

Tampa is an old and colorful city situated on the shores of the Gulf of Mexico, and it covers about sixty-five square miles with inland waterways. Since the 1920s Tampa has been a popular tourist attraction, with appealing hotels and motels. Crowds followed railroad magnate Henry Plant to Tampa, where he built his Tampa Bay Hotel and extended railroad and steamship lines, developing the city as a fashionable winter resort, which it remains today.

A great pleasure for the American male is the hand-rolled cigars made in Tampa. Vicente Martinez Ybor brought their production to Tampa and he rolled them into high favor throughout the nation. An older section of this town is Ybor City, named for him, where the art of hand-rolled cigars still continues.

Tampa is also known for its shipbuilding, the Henry Plant Museum on the campus of the University of Tampa, and the Florida Symphony Orchestra. The popular Tampa Bay Buccaneers professional football team finally made it to the Super Bowl XXXVII, in San Diego, on January 26, 2003, beating the Oakland Raiders, by a score of 48–21, to the wildly cheering city's delight.

In the quiet of the staid courtroom, on Monday, July 15, 2002, Bob Wesley and Jeff Ashton questioned more than fifty would-be jurors for the trial.

All went well, and the indication was strong that a jury would be seated by Tuesday afternoon, with the actual trial beginning Wednesday morning.

Both prosecutors and defense attorneys seemed satisfied with the panel.

Ashton's co-counsel was Jim Altman, a fellow in his early fifties, about 5'10", with thinning gray hair. He migrated from New York City to Florida and was a public defender in Seminole County prior to joining the Orange County/Osceola County State Attorney's Office.

In Tampa the two prosecutors shared a suite in the Residence Inn: two bedrooms, two bathrooms, a living room and kitchen.

"This is very nice, a little apartment." Ashton smiled. "A great place to stay."

"Yes, we should be very comfortable," Altman agreed.

"And convenient. We're right next door to the Courtyard Marriott, where we're putting all of our witnesses, so it's very handy."

Consideration was shown to Judge Perry by providing a newly refurbished courtroom, apparently the best one in the system.

(One practical problem they discovered was that there were only two working rest rooms available on the floor. Jeff Ashton put it laughingly, "We had a consistent problem when taking a break, trying to find a rest room. The jurors were always lined up at the two on this floor, so we would have to go up or down a couple of floors.")

On Wednesday, July 17, 2002, a day that the defendant

hoped to avoid, Jeff Ashton and his co-counsel, Jim Altman, sat at the prosecution table, a stack of papers and notes before them, whispering last-minute comments before the start of the retrial of the case against John Huggins.

In moments Chief Judge Belvin Perry took his place in the courtroom while a bailiff announced authoritatively, "This court is now in session."

A sudden blanket of quiet fell over the chamber, then Assistant State Attorney Jeff Ashton, with a serious demeanor, broke the silence. "Your Honor, ladies and gentlemen of the jury, I thank you for your participation in this important trial."

Scanning the members of the jury and pausing for a moment to ensure their attention, the confident attorney told the gripping story of a beautiful, young woman engineer working for the construction company Centex Rooney, who left the work site of a new luxury hotel at Walt Disney World on June 10, 1997, for a simple journey "to buy some things for lunch at a nearby Publix market."

In dramatic fashion Ashton stated that the devoted wife, and mother of a one-year-old girl, vanished and "was never seen alive."

Ashton continued in a grim, detailed narration, describing the intensive, tireless search orchestrated with a great number of varied persons, including sheriff's personnel, Centex Rooney employees, landscape specialists, friends, helicopter pilots and cadaver dogs with their handlers, with no immediate success in finding her.

He told of the two grueling days of scouring the highways, the byways, the woods and all of the immediate area before her coworkers happened on her nude body. He described the condition of the body and the area in which she was found.

The courtroom was deathly quiet, spellbound by Ashton's portrayal of the facts of the dreadful murder.

In a strong, emotional presentation, Jeff Ashton told the jury that this defendant took the victim's clothing and jewelry, as well as her white Ford Explorer, which he parked at a friend's house and later spray-painted black before destroying it with fire. He added that Huggins took the victim's purse, which he discarded as he drove along in the Ford Explorer. He said that Carla's jewelry was found at Huggins's mother-in-law's house in an electrical outlet in a shed behind her home.

Ashton stressed that John Huggins premeditatedly, brutally, unmercifully, murdered Carla Ann Larson.

Letting his voice drop into silence, the prosecutor turned his head to view the accused seated with his counsel at the defense table. The jury's eyes followed the prosecutor to focus on John Huggins, who sat unmoved, unaffected and undisturbed.

Ashton concluded by telling the jury, "You must do your duty, which you have sworn to do."

A murmur rippled across the courtroom as Ashton took his seat.

Orange/Osceola public defender Bob Wesley rose, and facing Judge Belvin Perry, he addressed, "Your Honor, the defense offers no opening statement." He returned to his seat.

Wesley's attitude was that his client did not need to provide a defense. The big man later explained confidently, "Our defense is that the state cannot prove Mr. Huggins's guilt beyond a reasonable doubt."

The prosecution began its case as they did in the first trial by presenting Jim Larson, describing his family's lifestyle, and specifically their activities on and subsequent to June 10. The trial proceeded on course, and Ashton set forth his case methodically, step by step.

On Thursday, July 18, 2002, the courtroom buzzed as a sixteen-year-old boy took the witness chair. His blond straight hair was in a bowl cut, and he had a diffident expression. Jonathon Huggins, son of the accused John Huggins, sat with his heavy, round face slightly tilted, his eyes focused into the distance, and awaited whatever questions would be asked of him. In this second trial he would testify against his father in person instead of having his deposition read by the prosecutor, as in the first trial.

A few rows away sat his seventy-two-year-old grandmother, Joanne Hackett, who was raising him and his sister. Her eyes were focused on the boy, and it was clearly evident she was concerned about his appearance in the courtroom.

Outside the courtroom earlier that day, she had asserted with motherly insistence that she didn't think her son, John, had participated in the murder of Carla Larson. "I don't think he did it. I just don't think he could do that to anybody. He's a good guy." She said her son didn't want her in court, because he thought all the lies told about him would upset her. She acknowledged that her son was a career bank robber, but she said he did that to support his drug habit, for which she blamed Angel. "We're talking about a real treacherous person here," she said. "But he was in love with her."

Outside the courtroom Jeff Ashton explained the situation with Jonathon Huggins, recalling the deposition he took from the young Huggins in December 1998. "He gave some testimony that was helpful to us, the most important part was that when Angel and the children left the Days Inn in Kissimmee on the day of the murder to go back to Melbourne, John was not with them, which dovetailed with our theory that Huggins murdered Carla Larson, then drove back to Melbourne in her truck."

In the first trial, when Huggins asked that Jonathon not be forced to testify in person, Jeff Ashton agreed, not wanting to put the boy in the position of testifying against his father.

Despite his hard-line approach to his profession as a prosecutor, Ashton was the father of sons himself, and he had a compassionate feeling for this lad whose father was on trial for his life. The state attorney felt it would be traumatic for Jonathon to be put in the position of saying something against his father that might contribute to his conviction.

In this second trial the ASA put the ball in Bob Wesley's court, asking the defense if they wanted to do the same this time.

Without consulting his attorneys, John Huggins decided that now he wanted his son to testify in person.

Ashton accepted that decision and had Jonathon come to Tampa to testify.

On Thursday, before Jonathon testified, Ashton provided him with a copy of his 1998 deposition, asking him if there was anything that he didn't remember or anything that was different from what he remembered.

The boy assured the prosecutor that essentially there was not anything different.

Ashton and his co-counsel, Jim Altman, discussed the potential testimony of Jonathon Huggins, and they agreed to put him on the stand.

When the young boy testified, he claimed that he pretty much had no memory of anything.

Prosecutor Ashton skillfully got him to acknowledge that in his deposition in 1998 he made the statement about going back to Melbourne without his father, the defendant. Ashton was pleased to get that important information in front of the jury.

When Bob Wesley began his examination of Jonathon, he asked, "Did anything happen between the date of the crime and the date in December when you gave the statement that affected your memory?"

Jonathon began to say, "My stepmother told me—"

Ashton sprang to his feet and objected.

Judge Perry ordered the jury removed, and a hearing was held.

When questioned, Jonathon claimed Angel Huggins told him to say those things in his deposition, but they were not true.

Bit by bit, the truth slowly emerged. The court found out that this supposed new testimony was never told to any defense attorney. Jonathon never discussed it with any of the prosecuting attorneys. Less than surprising, the only person that he talked to about it was his father, and it became evident that he was lying. His father put him up to it.

Everyone was surprised that Huggins would put his son up there to lie, and in a not very clever way. Ashton felt bad for Jonathon, because he got the impression from the way Jonathon was acting that he really didn't want to lie, but that his father pressured him to do it, and it backfired on him.

Judge Perry explained to the defense that if they wanted to put Jonathon on and ask him these questions, he was going to let the state cross-examine the boy about his conversations with the defendant.

Public defender Wesley agreed that the jury should not hear Jonathon's new statement.

Judge Perry also said that as punishment for the defendant basically surprising everyone with this development, the judge was going to allow the state to read Jonathon's testimony from 1998 to the jury.

So this jury heard the same important information as the first jury. Jeff Ashton was elated with this important victory for the state.

Continuing his deft structure against John Huggins, Ashton presented his slate of witnesses, with one after the other testifying to seeing Huggins driving a white Ford Explorer identical to the victim's, and racing out of the Disney woods from the area where the strangled body of Carla Larson had been discovered.

As in the first trial, Dr. Shashi Gore, the ME, showed his slides of the victim and explained the injuries, as well as the cause of death.

Phyllis Thomas's lips trembled and she averted her eyes from the graphic display of her beloved daughter's body.

Detective Cameron Weir told of the disappearance of Carla Larson, the search for her and the thorough investigation that ensued.

Jeff Ashton did not call Angel Huggins to testify at this trial. He felt that he could make his case without her, taking the wind out of the defense charge of Angel trying to frame her husband.

CHAPTER 34

At the lunch break Jeff Ashton and Jim Altman walked to a nearby restaurant. Ashton smiled at his partner. "Whew! This Tampa heat sure gets to me. We've walked two blocks and I'm wringing wet. My shirt is sticking to me."

"Me too. It seems to me that Tampa is so much hotter than Orlando. Or is this just a heat wave or something? Either way I'll be glad to get inside and cool off."

When seated, Ashton reached for the menu. "What looks good to you, Jim?"

"Something cold," he answered.

"Yeah, and a big glass of iced tea with lots of ice." Jeff Ashton laughed.

Back in the courtroom, Judge Belvin Perry eased into his bench seat and nodded to the bailiff, who called the court to order.

In the quiet tense courtroom, Ashton showed the jurors the videotape of the John Huggins and Steve Olson interview that took place in the Seminole County Jail.

This jury was as surprised as the first at the contrast of the suspected killer, in his navy blue jail garb, unkempt hair and generally coarse appearance on-screen with the defendant sitting at the defense table, properly attired in a neat dark business suit, hair trimmed and neatly combed.

The jury watched spellbound and listened to Huggins as he talked about his blackouts and his medicine, his alcohol and drug abuse, telling that he didn't think he was the kind of guy to do such a thing. He never, however, flatly denied that he committed the murder.

When the tape was finished, the courtroom was hushed; then whispers rippled across the room. The jury stared at Huggins, transfixed.

Defense lawyer Bob Wesley, attempting to play down the effects of the tape, said, "It's obviously rambling and confused. Mr. Huggins was in poor medical condition then." He added that Huggins was very ill and "jail officials had to hospitalize him several times in the days before the Olson interview."

Prosecutor Ashton, however, saw the tape "as a powerful piece of evidence because John Huggins does not deny involvement in the killing. Plus, he places himself near the scene of the crime at a hotel where he was on vacation at the time."

Kevin Smith, Huggins's friend, took the witness stand. He repeated his testimony from the first trial about Huggins driving the white Ford Explorer, and again told about his friend leaving the unfamiliar vehicle on his property for what he thought was going to be a few hours but turned out to be several days. He also recounted finding the radar detector from the Explorer deposited mysteriously at his home.

Wesley's cross-examination replayed his inferences about Smith. He stressed Smith's resemblance to the artist's composite sketch, his long hair and deep tan, and his knowledge of the area of the burned vehicle. He questioned Smith's alibi, hoping the jury would find a reasonable doubt about Huggins's guilt.

When Wesley concluded, he excused Smith.

After a weekend spent poring over their notes and making

last-minute adjustments, the participants in the Huggins trial returned to the Tampa courtroom on Monday, July 22.

Ashton and Altman, nearing the end of their presentation, would probably rest their case that morning.

The Larsons and the Thomases were all present, hanging on grimly, following the court proceedings with unflagging interest, quietly anticipating the end with their hoped-for verdict.

Also in court were Huggins's mother with his two children and his stepdaughter. Seated at the defense table next to his two attorneys, Huggins smiled and waggled his fingers at his family. He seemed totally relaxed, as though all of the proceedings going on around him had no connection to him.

Ashton's witness Faye Blades (formerly Faye Elms), mother-in-law of John Huggins, confidently answered the prosecutor's questions about finding Carla Larson's jewelry.

She explained in detail about the electrical wall box in her shed with two screws missing from the cover plate, which made her curious. She said that after unscrewing the remaining two screws, she was stunned to find a stash of jewelry wrapped in a paper towel stuffed inside. The jewelry was identified as Carla Larson's.

Upon completion of her testimony, the prosecution rested its case. Judge Perry announced a recess, after which the defense would present its case.

Following the recess when the bailiff announced that the court was now in session, public defender Bob Wesley leaned his body toward Huggins and made some comment to his client, then turned to address the court and the jury.

The assembly fell quiet as everyone waited to hear Wesley address Judge Perry and the jury. He began with a flat pronouncement: "The prosecution has no physical evidence to directly link John Huggins to the crime." He paused dramatically while his statement was absorbed. The members of the jury sat quietly, listening attentively.

As the defense lawyer calmly opened his presentation, designed to counteract and destroy the state's case, Phyllis and

Mert Thomas watched with hardened eyes focused on the attorney who was fighting for the life of the man they saw as the demon who stole their beloved child's life.

Shaking his head to negate the prosecution's evidence, Wesley continued in a low-toned voice. "No physical evidence, but they presented a series of circumstances that supposedly support their case."

The defense lawyer brazenly suggested that Angel Huggins, the estranged wife of his client, angered because he was having a sexual relationship with her sister, Nancy, conspired to frame him for this crime.

Wesley began the defense case by calling scientific and technical authorities as witnesses, maintaining that there were no fingerprints of Huggins on or near the body, no matching DNA to the hair found on the body or the jewelry, no footprints, nothing to tie John Huggins to the crime.

In order to discredit the eyewitness testimony and create reasonable doubt, defense attorney Bob Wesley implied that the description of the man seen driving the Explorer matched Kevin Smith, not John Huggins.

On Wednesday, July 24, an unexpected bombshell blew up at the trial.

Earlier in the trial, prosecutors had claimed that Huggins shaved his hair in the jail, including his pubic hair, to keep detectives from collecting a sample for evidence.

To refute that testimony, assistant public defender Greg Hill, who was assisting Bob Wesley, brought Orange County Corrections Officer Mark Thornton to the witness stand to question him about the reason John Huggins shaved his hair. Thornton was to testify that Huggins claimed to have a plausible explanation for it, and Thornton confirmed that there was an outbreak of lice in the jail at that time.

The devastating misfire for the defense attorney occurred when he asked Thornton, "How did you find out the reason Huggins shaved his pubic hair?"

"He told me" was his simple answer.

Jeff Ashton leaped to his feet, objecting. He was anxious to introduce the question of Huggins's credibility and stated firmly, "Your Honor, because the jurors will have to make a decision whether they believe Mr. Huggins's explanation to the jail officer, we ask the judge to reveal to the jury the record of John Huggins's felony convictions."

Like an unexpected thunderclap, the courtroom reacted with whispered comments and opinions. The judge rapped his gavel for order.

With no hesitation Judge Perry agreed with the prosecutor.

Normally, any previous convictions or records of a defendant are not allowed to be used or mentioned in a current trial. Jeff Ashton, though, was aware of an evidence provision, which is not well known. He said that it's in the book, but very few people have noticed it: "It basically says that if you offer somebody's statement through another witness, it will be called hearsay, that you can then attack the person who made the statement, just as if he or she testified in person. So our basic argument was that since the defendant tried to put in front of the jury his own statement about whether he had lice or not, that made his credibility an issue. If his credibility is an issue, then his prior conviction record is an element of that credibility. And Judge Perry ruled in our favor. I believe he was absolutely right and I don't think it's even a debatable question."

Judge Perry explained the situation to the jury and began to read a statement to the panel in which he cited nine felony convictions, admonishing that they "may consider in deciding the credibility of Mr. Huggins on the issue of his shaved pubic hair."

The judge did not detail that Huggins's record also included dozens of arrests since 1975, on charges of burglary, grand theft, aggravated battery, forgery, and that he was currently serving seven life terms and four thirty-year terms for bank robberies in Orange County and Brevard County in Florida.

In his Monday-morning quarterbacking account, assistant public defender Greg Hill sorrowfully stated that he did not expect Thornton's statement.

Bob Wesley summed up his reaction with the simple statement "I wish it hadn't happened."

Jeff Ashton wouldn't comment on whether he thought the mistake was a break for the state. He said only, "I'm sure the jury will follow the judge's instructions and limit its use to that one comment."

During this downturn for the defense, John Huggins sat soberly, with a weak, sickly, smile, staring into a scratch pad on the table before him. His family in the first row—his seventy-two-year-old mother, Joanne, his son, Jonathon, daughter, Ruth Anne, eleven, and stepdaughter, April Saunders, twelve or thirteen, all watched with grim expressions.

The press and electronic media burst out of the courtroom, individually contacting their various home bases to deliver full accounts of what took place in court. They had a field day with the story, the newspapers carrying banner headlines, and the TV and radio declaring it "breaking news" and giving it the top spot on newscasts.

The defense rested its case.

Observers commented later that it seemed odd that Preston Ausley was not called to testify. After all, it was his statement about seeing a woman driving the Ford Explorer that caused the original verdict to be overturned in the first trial, resulting in this new trial. They speculated that perhaps after checking out his story, it didn't hold up.

Judge Perry recessed for the day. The spectators filed out of the courtroom, aware that the next day would be important, perhaps crucial, with the closing arguments.

Jeff Ashton and Jim Altman sat at their table, intensely scanning through their notes and papers, considering what references they should take back to their hotel for some last-minute cramming for the important close.

"I don't want to miss the boat on this one, Jim," Ashton said.

"You've got that right. After all that's gone into this, we don't want to overlook anything."

"And we're not going to. We'll have a session later. Most importantly, I want both of us to get a good night's sleep, like boxers do before a championship fight."

"Gotcha."

CHAPTER 35

Thursday, July 25, 2002, was a lovely, sunny, typically hot summer day. The crowded Tampa courtroom eagerly awaited the final arguments of the murder case against defendant John Steven Huggins.

An atmosphere of expectancy permeated the courtroom, which included an expanded number of media personnel.

The short, heavyset bailiff rose and announced, "All rise, this court is now in session." Slowly and deliberately Judge Belvin Perry took his place and opened the proceedings.

Seated close to the area of the prosecution team were Jim Larson and his mother, Ada Larson, along with Phyllis and Mert Thomas, parents of the victim. Across the aisle there were several family members of the defendant.

John Huggins and his defense attorneys sat quietly at their table.

Prosecutor Jeff Ashton, speaking for the state of Florida, would be followed by public defender Bob Wesley, who would plead for the life of his client. Ashton would be allowed to speak again after Wesley concluded.

As Ashton rose, the room grew silent, awaiting this climax to the long trial. Respectfully he nodded his head to the judge and greeted, "Good morning." Turning to the members of the jury, he said, "Good morning," and they responded in low tones, "Good morning."

In a confident manner Ashton began his presentation. He explained that he wanted to give an overview of the case in a chronological order, then proceeded to name each witness in turn. He guided the jury step by step from the disappearance of Carla Larson, through the search, to the finding of her body.

He detailed the meticulous police investigation, ultimately leading to the suspect, John Huggins, and his stay at the Days Inn, across the street from the Publix market, where Carla Larson was last seen.

There was a slight interruption of Ashton's progress when a tall, thin, bronze-haired reporter pushed his way to a seat on the crowded news bench and was greeted with quick handshakes and welcome words.

The judge banged for order. The prosecutor panned across the jury, making eye contact with each panelist. He picked up his narrative, noting that it was approximately 12:16 P.M. when Carla Larson left the Publix, presumably to go back to work. He continued to follow the timeline, from the first sighting of the white Explorer, through all the witnesses who saw the vehicle driven out of the wooded area.

The hard-driving prosecutor paused. Scanning the jury to ensure their continued attention, he went on to the descriptions given by the various witnesses who saw the driver of the SUV.

Defense counsel Bob Wesley sat busily scribbling notes as his opponent rolled on with his presentation. Huggins listened with an attentive expression on his round face.

Ashton consulted his notes and continued. "The one thing that everyone who saw the man driving the SUV is certain of is that it was, in fact, a man. No one has ever, ever suggested that this could have been a woman." He hammered home: "It was clearly a man who everyone saw."

Ashton stated that one of the witnesses particularly noticed the driver's eyes.

Showing to the jury the composite that was drawn by the sheriff's department artist, prosecutor Ashton pointed out the eyes, and then asked the panel to compare them to John Huggins's eyes on the videotape.

Ashton described the killer's path from Osceola Parkway, getting off where he dumped Carla's purse, on a route that would take him back to Highway 192, back to the Days Inn. "Why is Days Inn important?" Ashton asked. "Because we know from documentary evidence that on June tenth Angel Huggins, the defendant's wife, was registered at the Days Inn directly across the street from the Publix, which is the last place that we know Carla Larson was."

Ashton showed the jury photographs of the Publix and a receipt for Carla's purchases specifying the time, 12:16 P.M., on June 10, the last day of her life. He told the panel they would have copies of the receipt to take to the jury room. This would show that she charged it to her Discover credit card, the same card later found in her purse.

He emphasized that John Huggins, by his own statement, was at the motel across the street with Angel, and that on the morning of June 10, 1997, John Huggins was staying within one hundred yards of where Carla Larson disappeared.

John Huggins, obviously disturbed by Ashton's systematic recap, leaned over and grabbed his attorney Wesley's arm. The lawyer nodded supportively to his client, which seemed to pacify him somewhat. But there remained a grim expression on the defendant's face.

In the nearby press section, a flurry of whispers broke out again, and the judge rapped his gavel for quiet.

As the courtroom hushed, Jeff Ashton continued, point by point, listing the witnesses. He emphasized that Jonathon Huggins said that when they left the Days Inn to go home to Melbourne, his father was not with them and that he appeared later, driving the vehicle that impressed the boy.

Ashton stressed the point that Jonathon's father did not leave with them. He questioned: "How did Huggins get from Osceola County to Brevard County? And why didn't he go back with his family? The evidence shows that he went in a white SUV."

Jeff Ashton stood quietly, waiting for the impact of this statement to score with the jury. Confidently following through in his methodical presentation, the prosecutor stated positively, "The family left the hotel, according to the record, without John Huggins."

Ashton turned his attention to statements from Christopher Smithson, the witness who saw Huggins at the wheel of a white Explorer, coming out of the Disney woods, between 2:00 and 2:30 P.M.

Jeff Ashton paused and explained that Huggins was there at that time because he was taking care of the evidence.

There were a few gasps and some whispers among the gathered group in the courtroom: What did that mean? Taking care of what evidence?

Ashton said that Carla Larson's body was very meticulously stripped of all of her clothing and jewelry, every bit.

He said the killer returned to the murder site later in the afternoon when there were no workers around having lunch, and he disposed of each piece of the victim's clothing. That was when Smithson saw him leaving the area.

The prosecutor reminded the jury of the testimony of Angel's mother seeing the Ford Explorer parked in her drive on June 10, driven by her son-in-law. Two neighbors across the street also saw the vehicle. Ashton stated that this vehicle was described as identical to Carla Larson's in all respects.

The prosecutor recalled Kevin Smith's testimony about the SUV, that his friend Huggins left it at his home for several days and that it was identical to Carla's car.

Ashton looked at the jurors, who watched and listened, totally absorbed in what he was presenting. Scanning across their faces, he registered their attention and continued, bringing out the most incriminating piece of evidence in the case. He paused for dramatic effect and stated, "And then there is the jewelry."

Jim Larson put his arm around his mother's shoulders as

tears welled into their eyes. The Thomases held hands tightly.

Jeff Ashton stated that Carla Larson's jewelry was found in Faye Blades's shed, a place where John Huggins was known to store items. There is no question it was Carla Larson's jewelry, found by Faye herself, hidden in an electrical outlet.

He emphasized, "There is no way that anyone other than John Huggins could have put the jewelry in that shed." The prosecutor ticked off the important points. "We know the killer was a man. There is only one man that you have heard evidence about in this case who was near the scene where Carla was kidnapped, who has a connection to the area where the car was burned—and had the ability to hide the jewelry in the shed."

Shaking his head and moving back a step, Ashton declared, "There is no one else on earth that you have heard of in the evidence in this case that has all three. . . . The only person is John Steven Huggins."

Ashton reviewed the taped interview with Huggins and discounted his blackouts, pointing out that no evidence was presented to demonstrate that any of his claims were true. The prosecutor instructed the jury: "Watch that tape, ladies and gentlemen, when you are back in the jury room. . . . Ask yourself, 'Is this a guilty man trying to lie his way out?' "

Jeff Ashton looked at the individuals who held the fate of John Huggins in their collective hands.

Ashton brought up the matter of the pubic hair issue, telling how the court ordered Huggins to produce or allow pubic hair samples to be taken from his body. But the defendant shaved every bit of pubic hair off his body, making any hair analysis by the state absolutely impossible.

Ashton said that Huggins explained his shaving because of lice in the jail, but the prosecutor stated they had only his word for the reason. Ashton asked the jury to consider the credibility of the accused, stating, "You have to decide whether a statement made by a nine-time convicted felon is worthy of your belief." He added, shaking his head, "It's not."

The prosecutor concluded by denouncing Huggins's actions in destroying evidence. "It's like stripping the body. It's like burning the car. Every single thing that the killer of Carla Larson did is consistent, designed to make it impossible to find evidence to convict him, and that's exactly what John Huggins did."

ASA Jeff Ashton thanked Judge Belvin Perry, the members of the jury, and said that he would speak to them again, following defense attorney Bob Wesley's closing statement.

Judge Perry turned toward the defense table and addressed, "Mr. Wesley."

The defense lawyer rose to his full height and confidently began, "Please the court, ladies and gentlemen of the jury. Thank you for your attention and also thank you for your hospitality in Tampa."

He started by stating that his client entered a plea of not guilty to the charges, explaining that it was the obligation of the state to prove the case against an accused. Then he discussed reasonable doubt. He went into a lecture on the law about which he said Judge Perry would instruct them.

He moved on to the subject of witnesses and how they often disagreed after seeing the same thing. He questioned the value of some of their testimony about the description of the vehicle driver, and went into detail about his hair, its length and if it was worn in a ponytail.

Wesley characterized the two latest witnesses as Johnny-come-latelies, suggesting they only came forward to be involved in an important case. The defense attorney concluded that some of their testimony was indefinite and virtually worthless.

Wesley cited disputing statements, not only from some of the witnesses, but from some of the investigators and specialists as well.

He reminded the jury they were not to speculate, paying attention only to the evidence presented.

The defense attorney stated that the prosecution did not even prove the ownership of the burned vehicle, not through a license plate or the vehicle identification number. He said, "There is not even a showing that the burned vehicle is Carla Larson's."

Then Wesley turned to Kevin Smith. The defense attorney cited that the vehicle was on his property, burned on the same block where he lived, and Smith had the radar detector in his custody.

Wesley wove a strong scenario linking Smith to the case, reminding the jury of Smith's testifying on the stand. "You evaluate his demeanor. . . . You saw how relaxed he was." Bob Wesley took a step back from the podium and, in a voice as sharp as the crack of a whip, accused, "He was comfortable because he is getting away with murder."

The defense attorney continued with his review of Kevin Smith, questioning his testimony about his whereabouts on the day of the murder and when he saw John Huggins. He showed the jury photos of Kevin Smith, comparing them to the artist's composite drawing, which he said more closely resembled Smith than Huggins, telling them to examine both when they were in the jury room.

He continued to harp on Smith's statements, his alibi, his proximity to the burned car. Wesley stated that no one else was at his home on June 12 when Smith said Huggins left the car there, that they only had Smith's word for what took place, if anything. He questioned if there were other people around and said that the home was a duplex with a lot going on, but no one saw John Huggins at Kevin Smith's home. He asked the jury to determine whether Smith was telling the truth or not. Wesley said, "He tried to put together a good 'aw-shucks' story."

The defense attorney brought up the burning of the vehicle, explaining that Kevin Smith tried to sell the jury a bill of goods. He said, "We know his approximation to the burn. We know that he had the vehicle at his place. We know he is the logical candidate for the burn. We know nothing suggesting Mr. Huggins was involved in the burning."

Wesley introduced Carla Larson's jewelry, asking how it

got to Faye Blades's house. He laid out a scenario linking Kevin Smith, his girlfriend, Kimberly Allred, and Angel Huggins, implying there was a conspiracy to frame John Huggins by hiding it at Faye Blades's house.

He questioned why it was not found when the crime scene technicians searched the place. "It stretches credibility to say that that outlet box itself was not searched."

He scoffed at the prosecution's conjecture that the jewelry was related in any way to John Huggins.

The defense attorney described the area of the Publix market, raising the question of why no one saw an abduction taking place in that grocery store parking lot. It was in a busy tourist area in the Disney neighborhood at noon in the middle of a hot summer day, with workers going there for food and families picking up supplies. All of this going on, so many people, so much activity in the store and in the parking lot, yet no one saw Carla Larson leave. No one saw a struggle or a man attempting to force a woman into a car. He said there was not a single fact to support the kidnapping, and he concluded, "It cannot be shown that Ms. Larson left against her will."

He continued refuting the charges against John Huggins, explaining carjacking as a specialized form of robbery, that it means the car was taken by force or fear against a person's will. He said there was no proof of that in this case.

The defense attorney said that the state couldn't show when any of the events took place or where they took place or how they took place.

Wesley explained that the judge's instruction would include the area of alibi, "which is a sort of legal term to say a person wasn't present at the scene of the crime." He said that John Huggins's alibi was that he and his family were visiting in Kissimmee. The defense attorney told the jury if they had a reasonable doubt about whether the defendant was present when the crime was committed, it was their duty to find him not guilty.

Wesley turned to the subject of the purse found on December 24, implying that the purse and its contents were deposited in the brush at some point after November 11, the date on the discarded prescription bottle, which was long after Huggins was arrested and incarcerated.

He told the jury that this was a case of circumstantial evidence. And he emphasized that for the jury to find a defendant guilty of first-degree murder, it must show that he is guilty beyond and to the exclusion of every reasonable doubt: "Because you know as jurors you're bound by your oath to return a verdict based on the evidence." He stated firmly, "The evidence does not show John Huggins was involved. . . . Suspicions cannot convict a person of first-degree murder. Your verdict should be not guilty."

He thanked the jury for its attention and patience during the course of the trial and returned to his seat.

As the courtroom quietly waited, Judge Perry declared a ten-minute recess. Leaning forward, he stated to the jury, "I'll ask you not to discuss this case among yourselves nor with anyone else."

After the jury left the courtroom, the weary spectators rose to stretch. Some left the room; others milled around, whispering to each other.

Defense attorney Wesley rose and asked Judge Perry, "May I address the court on one matter briefly?"

Judge Perry nodded.

Wesley raised an objection to the state showing the videotape of Huggins's interview in rebuttal. He said he did not mention the tape in his argument, therefore it could not be used now.

The courtroom was silent as people drew near to hear the oral argument.

Judge Perry looked over at the prosecution table and addressed, "Mr. Ashton?"

Jeff Ashton rose and faced the judge, saying, "Mr. Wesley mentioned alibi. This videotape contains all the statements that were put before the jury as to the defendant's whereabouts at the time of the crime. That is directly relevant to that claim." Ashton waited for Judge Perry's response.

Wesley contended, "The issue is whether Huggins was present when the crime was committed." He asserted, "We don't know where the crime was committed. We know it wasn't at the Days Inn."

Judge Perry inquired, "Mr. Ashton, is it your intention to show the whole tape?"

Jeff Ashton responded, "Yes, sir, and discuss various aspects of it as they relate to the evidence."

Bob Wesley disputed the argument. The temperature in the courtroom elevated several degrees as the differences took over the proceedings.

Ashton countered, "I think I'm pretty much permitted—"

"Folks, folks," Judge Perry interceded. "I'm not going to tolerate that."

Family members of the victim exchanged looks, whispering comments to each other.

The defendant sat quietly, observing the volley between the two attorneys, his face impassive, as though the proceedings had nothing to do with him.

The discussion continued, both sides putting forth their arguments, hoping for a favorable decision from the judge. The word "alibi" was the catchword, with the defense saying Huggins had an alibi and the prosecution arguing that there wasn't any alibi.

Bob Wesley at his defense table shifted his massive weight in his chair, displaying his silent objections to the prosecutor's contentions.

The judge, adjusting his glasses, tipped his head slightly and judiciously cautioned the prosecutor: "As long as it is rebuttal, then you're fine."

After the recess, when the court reconvened and the jury was seated, Ashton began his rebuttal. In opening he indicated that the judge would instruct the jury on the law and that they would be provided with typed copies of instructions to take back to the jury room with them.

Ashton then began methodically to refute the points Wesley raised in his closing. He went over each one and recalled testimony that directly contradicted each, including the prescription bottle, which he said distracted from the case since it was found in brush seven to ten feet away from the purse.

Ashton asserted, "That prescription bottle was never tied to anything remotely having anything to do with this case."

He agreed with Wesley's cautioning not to speculate, but said, "There is a difference between a speculation and a logical inference." He gave examples of such difference and then became specific. "It is a logical inference that this lady went to the store and bought some grapes and pita bread. It is a reasonable and logical, almost undeniable, inference that she didn't end up out in the field of her own free will."

He turned to face Huggins, then gave his attention back to the jury. "Carla Larson did not voluntarily drive out in the woods with her killer. That," he emphasized, "is not speculation. That is a reasonable—and, in fact, the only reasonable—inference that you can draw from these facts, and there is absolutely nothing wrong with drawing logical and reasonable inferences from facts that are proven in the record."

The hard-driving prosecutor said, "There is an essential difference between a logical inference and a speculation."

He gave an example of speculation. He stopped, panned his eyes across the jury and picked up: "An absolute, complete, total speculation is the claim that Kevin Smith was anywhere near this Publix supermarket on June 10, 1997. There is not one single shred of evidence of that. Nothing." Ashton detailed Smith's workday hours on that day when he was one hour away, which were verified. "And you have not heard one single solitary fact that should make you doubt that. For you to believe that he was anywhere near this Publix is an absolute rank and totally improper speculation."

The prosecutor disputed the conspiracy theory of Angel, Kim, Kevin and Faye ganging up to frame John Huggins. "That's ludicrous. . . . That's speculation upon speculation upon guess upon speculation. That's not evidence." He paused to let his words sink in.

Judge Perry sat silently, staring owlishly through his large dark-rimmed glasses, watching the prosecutor unrelentingly destroy the defense that Bob Wesley had conjured up for his client, but he showed no reaction. The long-experienced jurist would in no way display his thoughts.

Ashton continued, stressing that only John Huggins fit the criteria of Carla Larson's killer. He cited the three factors that were important: that the person had to be in the area where Carla was kidnapped, had to have some connection with the burned vehicle and had to have access to the shed on Faye Blades's property, where the jewelry was found.

"And John Huggins," Ashton continued, "has all three. And John Huggins is the only human being on earth that you have heard about in this trial that has that connection." Shaking his head, he emphasized, "No one else."

Ashton told how the killer tried to destroy any possible evidence of his involvement in the case, stripping the body, hiding the jewelry, ditching the purse and finally burning the car to a cinder.

The prosecutor continued to gnaw away at the scenarios Wesley had tried to present: focusing on Kevin Smith as the killer, discounting state witnesses' testimony, trying desperately to create a reasonable doubt. One by one, Ashton refuted the defense attorney's points.

Carla Larson's family listened intently, watching Ashton's passionate presentation, clearly pleased at the prosecutor's step-by-step linking of John Huggins to the murder.

John Huggins sat as he had through the entire proceedings, emotionless, inscrutable, seemingly indifferent to the debate about his life swirling around him.

Jeff Ashton moved to face the jury, telling them that the evidence showed no alibi: "Nothing to show that Mr. Huggins was any place other than at the Days Inn or the Publix parking lot."

When he played the tape of Huggins's interview with the reporter, Ashton invited the jury to look at and review Huggins's taped statement and find anywhere in it that there was evidence of an alibi.

Ashton told the jury that when Huggins said, "I don't think that I am the person that killed Carla Larson," the prosecutor urged, "Look at his eyes."

Ashton concluded: "Your verdict, ladies and gentlemen, should be guilty of first-degree murder, should be guilty of carjacking, should be guilty of robbery, should be guilty of kidnapping, because that's what the evidence you received shows. Thank you."

Jeff Ashton turned and walked back to the prosecution table.

CHAPTER 36

Following a brief recess, the courtroom filled immediately and Judge Belvin Perry resumed his seat on the bench. The bailiff called the court to order.

All activity ceased as total quiet prevailed and the jury was seated.

The attorneys for the defense sat beside their client at their table, soberly awaiting the forthcoming charge from the judge.

The prosecutors listened attentively, satisfied that they did their job in presenting their case.

Judge Perry, sitting totally erect, began his address to the jury, pointing out its great responsibility in reaching their important verdict.

The judge reviewed step by step the separate charges that were made, and he instructed them how they were required by law to deal with each. He emphasized that their ultimate decision must be based solely upon evidence that had been presented in trial.

There were new complications in the law regarding the death penalty due to the United States Supreme Court's decision in the Arizona case, which ruled that the jury must hear and decide the penalty phase as well as the guilt phase in a trial.

In his own interpretation of the U.S. Supreme Court ruling, Judge Belvin Perry created and issued to the jurors a special verdict form. It basically listed every aggravating circumstance that the state presented that would warrant the death penalty. There were five in this case. The form would show how each individual juror voted on each of the five aggravating-circumstance factors.

The defense attorneys thought this would give Huggins strong grounds for appeal. "Those verdict forms were not authorized by the law," Wesley said.

When Perry concluded, he dismissed the jury to go into their room to deliberate.

After the jury filed out of the room, Judge Perry acknowledged defendant John Steven Huggins, who asked permission to speak to the judge.

Bob Wesley had a puzzled expression on his face, but he sat with his assistants watching and waiting for the next event and the judge's decision.

"You may speak," the judge allowed.

"Your Honor," Huggins began, "I have a request to make to you."

Perry sat up more attentively. "And what is that request, Mr. Huggins?"

"Your Honor," Huggins politely offered, "I would like your authorization to dismiss my lawyer Bob Wesley."

The courtroom came alive with whispers. What in the world was this development? Jim Larson looked askance at his mother and whispered, "What will this guy come up with next?"

John Huggins, the accused, stood before the judge, cleanly shaven, hair cut and combed neatly, dressed in a dark suit. He presented an impression of an ordinary citizen who just happened to be in court as an observer, not the man on trial for a heinous murder.

Judge Perry was taken aback by Huggins's request.

"I don't know" was his first voiced reaction.

Huggins responded, "Your Honor . . . I believe that it is my right to be represented by counsel of my choice."

Stiffening, the judge stared at Huggins momentarily and then assured him, "Mr. Huggins, none of your rights will be denied by this court, but at the same time it is the obligation of this court to recognize all proprieties. Mr. Wesley was your choice and yours alone. At this point there is question about the propriety of dismissing him."

"Your Honor," John Huggins stated, "Mr. Wesley and I have come to an impasse on the strategy for the penalty phase of this trial." Huggins stopped, permitting the judge to consider his request seriously.

"Your Honor," Huggins continued, "this is my life that we are discussing. This is a question whether I shall be permitted to go on living—whether I live or die." Huggins waited again.

A wave of whispers swept over the courtroom in reaction to Huggins's request. The reporters asked, "He's discussing the penalty phase. Is he conceding that he will be found guilty?"

Judge Perry shifted in his chair, grasped a pencil and scribbled a note as Huggins spoke again.

"Your Honor, may I please continue?"

The judge nodded his permission.

"Your Honor, I implore you. Please consider this pleading from me as a man who stands before you asking for your consideration."

Judge Perry tried valiantly to persuade Huggins that this was not a wise decision and he should carefully reconsider.

But John Huggins was adamant in his request.

Finally Judge Belvin Perry reluctantly granted John Huggins his desire to dismiss Bob Wesley as defense counsel and to represent himself.

"I thank you, Your Honor."

The judge addressed the defense attorney. "Mr. Wesley, I want you, along with your associates, to stand by in this court and function in an advisory capacity."

Wesley agreed and sat down again with his associate at the defense table, but they were silent. John Huggins was in charge of his own defense now.

This request created a rare circumstance. Acting as his own attorney put him in the unique position of being able to have direct contact with, and to question members of, the Larson family during the penalty phase of the trial.

Ada Larson turned to Phyllis and Mert Thomas in vexation and whispered, "It's a circus that he can represent himself and question our family."

Jim whispered back that he wasn't bothered by Huggins's doings. "He's trying to make a big flash. . . . Let him have his moment."

The court went into recess, awaiting the rendering of the verdict from the jury.

Just hours following his denigrating firing of his defense lawyers, John Huggins heard the verdict. The jury returned after five hours to pronounce Huggins guilty on all charges, convicted for the second time.

Ada Larson unabashedly pumped her fist into the air.

John Huggins requested the jury be polled, then sat stone-faced, watching as the jurors were individually asked about each one's decision.

The jury would return the next day, Friday, July 26, 2002, to consider and determine the sentencing portion of their verdict. The now-convicted Huggins faced the penalty of death or a prison term of life with no parole, which would be decided by the returning jury.

Jeff Ashton stated that he felt vindicated.

Jim Larson, in his usual subdued but serious manner, said, "I'm happy with the verdict. We got what we wanted."

Mert Thomas, father of the victim, said, "I'm glad it went the way it did." He paused and then continued. "If we can get the next days behind us, then maybe we can get the whole thing behind us."

Phyllis Thomas's view was emotional. "We were thinking that Carla was with us today, guiding us through this." She dabbed her eyes. "We just hope this shows that the system is working . . . maybe a little too slow sometimes, but I guess it's working and these people cared. They believe in what they heard and followed through."

CHAPTER 37

It was Friday and most people in the courtroom were looking ahead to the weekend break after this penalty phase of the trial.

Jeff Ashton, confident of the progress of the prosecution, rose and called Phyllis Thomas to testify, asking her to express in her own words how her daughter's death affected the family.

The bereaved mother spoke emotionally about her beloved daughter, how the family was forever changed and how much they all missed her. There was great sympathy in the courtroom for the woman as she spoke lovingly about how special her daughter was and what she meant to all of them.

Ashton also called Carla's dear friend Kristi Lovell, who spoke tearfully of their friendship over many years and what it meant to her.

John Huggins did not ask any questions of either Phyllis Thomas or Kristi Lovell.

Jim Larson was next on the witness stand. He spoke in a subdued voice about how devastating the loss of his wife was to him and their daughter. When he concluded, he sat calmly, prepared to face the self-appointed defender John Huggins.

The tension in the courtroom was heavy, and it was so quiet it was as if every person in the room were holding his or her breath.

Huggins strode to the podium proudly, like a gladiator who had triumphed in a life-challenging contest.

One reporter observed, "Look at that son of a bitch. He's got a helluva nerve. You'd think that he just won a seat in the senate." His fellow writers snickered in agreement. But the big questions in their minds were "What in the world is he going to ask Jim Larson? What can he possibly ask him?"

In a friendly approach, as though the two men were life-long dear buddies who had only a minor difference of opinion, Huggins inquired affably, "How long have we been going around in circles with this case?"

The quiet, soft-spoken Jim Larson, a bit startled by the question, hesitated and then responded, "Quite a while . . . five years."

Taking a step closer to the husband of the woman he brutally murdered, Huggins directed defiantly, "Please look at the jury and tell them what sentence would be appropriate in this case."

Like an unleashed tiger sprung from its cage, Jeff Ashton was on his feet. "Objection," he shouted.

Judge Perry quietly sustained him.

Ignoring his setback, the convicted Huggins brazenly continued, "Was there a plea offer made in this case?"

Again Jeff Ashton was on his feet, objecting. And again Judge Perry sustained the prosecutor.

The reporters, who immediately picked up on that question, whispered to each other, "Did you know about that? Do you think it's true? What could he have been offered?"

Huggins didn't ask Jim Larson any further questions, but he successfully imparted to the jury that the state offered him a deal that he turned down.

He cockily turned from the jury and sat down.

The courtroom remained quiet, still shocked by the bizarre sight of Huggins questioning the husband of the woman he was convicted of killing. It seemed almost a travesty of justice for Huggins to have any contact at all with Larson.

Huggins had only one witness speaking for him, Sandra Jo Huggins, his sister. The thirty-six-year-old woman was currently serving time in the Levy Forestry Camp near Ocala, Florida, for a DUI manslaughter conviction. In January 1999 Sandra Jo lost control of her truck at Lake Panasoffkee, killing her thirteen-year-old passenger. She is scheduled for release in May 2010.

In a clear-cut bid to create sympathy for John and the Huggins family, the testimony brought out that their father suffered from colon cancer, but his death occurred in a fire. And another Huggins sister died in a car accident.

At the conclusion of her testimony, John Huggins gave only a brief forty-second summation to jurors and sat down.

Prosecutor Jeff Ashton addressed the jury, explaining this second phase of the trial, which was to determine the sentence for John Huggins.

The defendant, representing himself, pushed his chair back from the defense table, prepared for whatever Ashton was about to suggest or propose.

Bob Wesley and Greg Hill, Huggins's former attorneys, sat silently beside him, alert and ready to consult if called upon.

At the front-row audience section, Jim and Ada Larson gripped hands, as did Phyllis and Mert Thomas. It was the end of a long ordeal for these family members, and they were simply glad to see the light at the end of the tunnel.

Jeff Ashton continued explaining to the jury that they had to think of the two phases of the trial separately, because they had to do those two acts separately.

Ashton went on to specify the issue of aggravating circumstances, pointing out that in this case there were five, and indicating that the jurors would be required to determine whether the state proved them beyond a reasonable doubt.

One by one, Ashton defined the five separate aggravating circumstances in full detail, and specifically gave examples of Huggins's involvement in each.

Jeff Ashton fervently described the horror Carla Larson suffered in her last hours and minutes, asking the jury to imagine not just how she was killed, but the terror that she went through from the time she met up with Huggins through the time her life ceased. "And that's very difficult, because to think about what Carla went through is to imagine one's worst nightmare."

Huggins interrupted, "Objection, Your Honor."

In a quiet voice Judge Perry asked, "Basis of objection?"

Huggins answered, "Improper statement."

Judge Perry said, "Overruled."

Ashton went on describing the agony the victim went through emotionally.

This brought Huggins to his feet again. "Objection, Your Honor."

With a patient tone the judge asked, "Same objection?"

"No."

Judge Perry inquired, "Basis of objection?"

Authoritatively Huggins stated, "State of mind of the victim is not a material fact."

"Overruled," declared Judge Perry.

Ashton continued, "It's not just physical pain, it is emotional and psychological torture that you must consider. You must ask yourselves, 'What was Carla thinking?' "

Phyllis Thomas's head dropped as she dabbed the tears from her eyes, envisioning her lovely daughter's painful last moments of life.

Ashton watched the jury as they absorbed his dramatic words, and then he described for them his reasonable inferences as to how and where Carla was murdered.

He dramatically painted a word picture of her strangulation, how she was conscious and aware of what was happening to her. "We know that she had time to think. And we know that when Mr. Huggins put his hands around her throat, she was awake, she was alert and she knew what was going on."

Interrupting Ashton's graphic and explosive presentation, John Huggins rose and said, "Objection. Can we approach?"

With the judge's permission, Huggins spoke at the bench with all the bravado of a "jailhouse lawyer."

"Judge, I believe this is improper argument. Going to the state of mind of the victim, in *Stone versus State,* his case was overturned on the basis of improper argument. The state of mind of the victim at the time of the offense."

Ashton responded, citing other cases that disputed Huggins's argument. Again Judge Perry overruled the objection.

The prosecutor continued reviewing all of the aspects of aggravating circumstances, as well as mitigating circumstances, stating, "It will be your duty to determine whether any mitigating circumstances have been proven."

Ashton told the jury that the weight of the evidence presented to them in aggravation in this case was overwhelming. "You have a man with a lengthy record of violent criminal conduct going back to 1979, with eleven convictions for armed robbery; you've got a man who kidnaps a woman, murders her in a way that I do not want to further describe. For financial gain. To take her car. . . . The death of Carla Larson is beyond comprehension."

The prosecutor concluded: "Based upon the laws and based upon the facts that you have seen, the only reasonable verdict is to find that the aggravating circumstances in this case so far outweigh any mitigation presented, that the only reasonable, the only legal, recommendation you can make is death."

Ashton thanked the jury and returned to his seat at the state's table, satisfied that he did his best in presenting the state's case. Now it was up to the jury.

The jury filed out to begin their deliberations.

John Huggins sat motionless in his chair, silent and passive.

Jeff Ashton was weary from the strain of delivering his arguments, but he was also keyed up. This was the culmination of so many months of preparation.

He turned to Jim Altman. "I wonder how long the jury will be out."

"There's no telling," Altman replied.

Ashton stood up. "C'mon, let's stretch our legs. I'm too antsy to just sit here and wait."

"I know how you feel. These waits for juries can be agony."

"Yeah," Ashton agreed, then grinned. "But not as bad for us as for Huggins."

"You got that right," Altman replied.

It was only a few hours, but they seemed to drag. Finally word came that the jury was ready.

The courtroom settled into an expectant quiet as the jury silently returned to their box, looking straight ahead, avoiding eye contact with any of the adversaries, giving no hint or clue of their verdict.

Jim Larson gripped his mother's hand, the pressure revealing his anxiety. The Thomases also held each other's hands, awaiting the pronouncement that would spell the end, they hoped, of this ordeal that they had lived for the past five years.

Breaking the tense silence, Judge Perry asked, "Have you reached a verdict?"

The jury foreman stood, faced the judge and answered, "Yes, Your Honor, we have."

The verdict paper was passed to the judge by the bailiff. Perry studied the form, then passed it back to the foreman.

"How say you?" the judge inquired.

The foreman quietly told the judge that the jury voted John Steven Huggins the death penalty.

A burst of chatter from the spectators, in reaction to the verdict, broke out over the entire courtroom as Judge Perry gaveled for order.

As quiet finally emerged, Judge Perry courteously thanked the jury for their devoted service and excused them. Accordingly, they filed out of the courtroom.

As the jurors departed, heading for different exits, the press swarmed around them, jabbing microphones into their faces and holding recording devices before them, to get first-hand accounts of what transpired in the jury room.

It became known through the continuous pressing of the jurors that as a body they voted nine to three that John Huggins should be executed.

During the melee of the postsentencing activities, John Huggins managed a weak smile and a wave to his mother and his children before he was escorted, cuffed and restrained, from the courtroom back to a jail cell.

Jim Larson, in his subdued manner, showed little reaction to the jury decision that he had hoped for. One of the men from the press approached Larson and asked for a comment. The widower studied him and then said, "I want him dead so he can't hurt anyone else." The reporter scribbled notes and asked, "Is there anything more you want to say?" Larson rubbed his hand across his face and added, "We can't stand in the middle of the street with our guns drawn, so it has to be done like this." He turned and walked away from the reporter.

Mert Thomas was more vocal. "It would be a relief if I could say that I never have to deal with this again, but I feel there is something else brewing. I hope I'm wrong. If it comes back again, I will come on crutches or a wheelchair or I'll crawl, but I will be there."

CHAPTER 38

For the next four weeks John Huggins sat in his solitary cell, working feverishly and more intensely than a law school graduate preparing for his bar examination, in his attempt to persuade Judge Perry to overturn the sentence and spare his life.

On Monday, August 26, 2002, one month to the day after the jury voted that Huggins should pay with his life for taking the life of Carla Larson, Huggins was permitted to return to court and once again face Judge Belvin Perry.

In the grave atmosphere of the solemn room, Huggins stood before the same judge who would pronounce the final order of these courtroom ordeals in a few weeks.

Continuing to serve as his own attorney, John Huggins was fully expected to present witnesses favorable to him, who would offer reasons that his life should be spared and that he be sent to prison for life, instead of being executed.

As usual, Huggins had a surprising response and told the court that he had no witnesses to present in this hearing.

The convicted murderer stood before Judge Perry and stated assertively that prosecutor Jeff Ashton should be disqualified. He denounced the prosecutor for his conduct in representing the state in the case against him.

Judge Perry passed over this and had Huggins move on.

Rising to his full six-foot-height, Huggins implored Judge Perry to have the death penalty barred from his case.

The judge patiently listened without commenting to everything Huggins presented.

In a stirring plea the convicted Huggins went into a long commentary on the witnesses who appeared in his trial. He finally asked the judge to have each and every one of the witnesses be given polygraph tests.

Judge Perry stared at Huggins in surprise and quietly rejected his request once more.

With this rebuff, the ever-inventive murderer requested that he be permitted to interview the jurors himself. He told Judge Perry that this petition should not be denied, but the judge was unimpressed by Huggins's arguments and ruled against any interviewing of the jurors.

Seated in the front row, close to the proceedings, Phyllis Thomas leaned over to her husband, and with an expression of dismay, she whispered into his ear, "Just listen to him. . . . This is disgusting." She pulled his arm and asked, "How can he do this?"

Mert put his arm around his wife and calmed her with his own whisper: "He's getting what he deserves."

Huggins spoke for three hours, presenting various arguments why his life should be spared, including his pitiable childhood. But after receiving no positive response from the judge, he finally halted his pleas.

Prosecutor Jeff Ashton sat through much of the hearing and said simply that it was a waste of time.

Jim Larson, who also attended the hearing, said that he stopped listening to Huggins. He said his mind was focused on picking up his little daughter, Jessica, and having dinner. "I'm not angry," he stated. "I have to get on with my life. I've stopped worrying about it."

At the conclusion of the proceeding, Judge Perry announced that he would hand down his sentence for John Huggins on Thursday, September 19.

Subsequently Judge Perry considered that since John Huggins presented no witnesses to speak on his behalf, there was no convincing presentation of mitigating circumstances. The judge wanted to ensure that every measure be taken to prevent any question arising about John Huggins not receiving every consideration for his submission.

With the constitutionality of the death penalty issue still uncertain in Florida, the judge was extremely cautious.

Accordingly, he ordered a presentence investigation that would look into the question of mitigating circumstances for John Huggins.

CHAPTER 39

As the late-summer August days drifted into September, the participants in the John Steven Huggins trial returned to their everyday lives, tensely awaiting Judge Belvin Perry's designated date of September 19.

John Huggins remained in jail, filling his time corresponding with his pen pals via e-mails, just whiling away the hours until his fate was decided.

Jim Larson quietly resumed his daily routine at his College Park home, caring for his little daughter, Jessica, dressing and feeding her, transporting her to and from her day-care center. He returned to work at his job at Home Depot, still adjusting to his life without his beloved wife, Carla. His evenings were spent tending to Jessica.

Ada Larson and the Thomases returned to their homes in Pompano Beach, Florida, attempting to readjust to their lives as best they could. Their only comfort was the visits they had with Jim and their granddaughter.

ASA Jeff Ashton and public defender Bob Wesley continued in their legal practices, patiently awaiting the final judgment from Judge Belvin Perry.

They all felt the heavy pall hanging over their lives every

day. They were all just marking time until that all-important September 19.

Judge Perry found himself in one of the most trying ordeals that a criminal-court judge must face. The dedicated jurist continued with his other judicial responsibilities, carrying on his official duties, presiding over the various cases that came before him. At the same time he devoted himself to considering the various pros and cons of the death penalty for John Huggins.

He spent hours poring over the trial transcripts, the report from the presentence investigators, meticulously studying each factor of the aggravating circumstances and the mitigating circumstances, and weighing the values of each.

The September weather in Florida was ideal, with its sketchy white clouds floating in the soft blue skies, emphasizing the beauty for which Florida has become known.

On September 19, in the quiet of his Orlando courtroom, Judge Belvin Perry prepared to announce his decision.

From his seat at the bench, he looked down over the gathered group. At the state's table Jeff Ashton and Jim Altman nodded to him. Sitting at the defense table was convicted killer John Huggins, dressed in navy blue coveralls; the guards removed his handcuffs. Beside him were his former defense attorneys public defender Bob Wesley and associate Greg Hill.

As he expected, Judge Perry saw Ada Larson seated in the front row beside her son, Jim, along with Phyllis and Mert Thomas. Members of the Huggins family sat somberly in another part of the courtroom. Assorted representatives of the media sat poised with their pens ready. All were gazing at the judge attentively, waiting for his pronouncements.

Judge Perry adjusted his large black-rimmed glasses and began to read from his eighteen-page decision.

He began with a history of the case from the grand jury's indictment of John Huggins through the first trial, conviction, sentencing and overturning of that verdict, and the granting of the new trial. The judge explained each change of venue for the two trials. He then launched into details of the jury's findings of the present trial, how they voted on each issue.

Judge Perry explained that he fully examined the testimony, evidence and all other matters in this case as to the presence or lack of aggravating and mitigating factors.

Additionally, the judge examined other aspects of the defendant's character, record and other circumstances of the offense. He said he also carefully considered the presentence investigation report.

The judge pointed out that he did not consider any evidence or testimony presented at the previous proceedings, other than that offered for mitigation.

Having established the background for forming his opinion, the judge launched into the details, taking each item separately.

He went into the specifics of the five aggravating circumstances that the state enumerated, meticulously explaining their meaning:

1. The capital felony was committed by a person previously convicted of a felony and placed on felony probation.

The judge cited Huggins's conviction in Osceola County for passing a worthless check, for which he received probation. There was also a conviction for possessing an unauthorized driver's license, for which Huggins also received probation.

The court found that the state proved this aggravating factor beyond a reasonable doubt.

2. The defendant was previously convicted of a felony involving the use or threat of violence.

Judge Perry enumerated Huggins's nine convictions for robbery with a weapon, resisting arrest, battery on a law enforcement officer in Orange, Seminole and Brevard Counties.

According to the judge, the state of Florida proved this aggravating factor beyond a reasonable doubt.

Judge Perry looked up from his reading to face the courtroom, perhaps to gauge the reaction to his message so far, then continued:

3. The capital felony was committed while the defendant was engaged in the commission of the crime of kidnapping.

The judge recited a résumé of the details of what took place on June 10, 1997, with the disappearance of Carla Larson and concluded, "The record in this case clearly supports that Carla Larson was taken by force or threat of force, against her will and taken to the place where she was murdered and robbed." Judge Perry found that this aggravating factor was present and proven by the state.

4. The capital felony was committed for pecuniary gain.

Judge Perry's explanation delved into the theft of the Ford Explorer and Carla Larson's jewelry. He asked, "Were these items—the Ford Explorer, the diamond ring, diamond earrings and necklace—just taken as an afterthought, and merely to facilitate the defendant's escape? Or rather, were they purposely taken as a means of improving his financial worth and providing a benefit to the defendant?"

His conclusion was that the murder was committed for pecuniary gain, and found this aggravating factor was present and proven by the state beyond a reasonable doubt.

5. The capital felony was especially heinous, atrocious or cruel.

Judge Perry gave his interpretation of the meaning of those words and asked, "Was the murder of Carla Larson a

conscienceless or pitiless crime and unnecessarily torturous
to her?" He went back over the medical examiner's description of what happened to Carla in those last moments, then
quoted Henry David Thoreau, "Nothing is so much to be
feared as fear." He decided that the crime met the definition
of heinous, atrocious or cruel, and found that the state
proved this aggravating factor.

At the conclusion of the reading of the aggravating circumstances, the judge continued on to the next phase, explaining that mitigating circumstances were any aspect of
the defendant's character, record or background, and any
other circumstances of the offense, that would affect the imposition of the death penalty.

Judge Perry stated that at the penalty proceeding the defendant presented one witness, Sandra Huggins, his sister,
who testified that John Huggins provided some care to their
father when he was ill with cancer. Huggins made a decision
not to use life-sustaining measures with their father, but that
decision was not necessary since the father died as a result
of a fire. The judge cited that the defendant offered no other
evidence of mitigation. He said he asked Huggins if he
wanted his defense attorney Bob Wesley to come back into
the case and present any mitigating evidence, but the defendant refused and said that he was satisfied.

The presentence investigation Judge Perry ordered was to
ensure fairness to the defendant. The judge considered the
fact that the defendant's parents were divorced, and at the
age of nine, when his mother was unable to control her son,
he was moved over to live with his father. The investigation
revealed that the father was a heavy drinker and a strong dis-
ciplinarian. John lived in this home situation, with a stepmother who detested the boy and did not want him in her
house.

Judge Perry learned that the defendant, as an adult,
abused alcohol and drugs.

In reviewing the records, Judge Perry confirmed that Joanne Hackett, John's mother, indicated that the defendant became known as a troublemaker. She felt that his contact with the juvenile system at age twelve caused him emotional damage.

Although she had constant contact with her son, she said that she was unable to make the situation better for him.

His mother confirmed that John had two failed marriages. The wives, the judge learned, also sometimes abused drugs and alcohol. Hackett felt that his wife Angel was the cause of some of his problems.

She stated that her son was a good man, who helped to establish and finance a church.

The judge considered that the defendant's sister supported her mother's statements about John Huggins's childhood. She added that the defendant had a very close, loving relationship with his father. She said that her brother "was a good father, a good man, that his problems were caused by women."

As Judge Perry continued reading his statement explaining his consideration, the audience in the courtroom shifted in their seats. Although they were intensely interested in what Judge Perry was saying, it was taking a long time and they were getting restless.

But the judge was not going to be rushed. He had worked very diligently over his decision, and was going step by step to show how he arrived at it.

The judge considered statements from Bobby and Sherry Burnette, friends of Huggins's, who talked about his involvement as a missionary in Haiti, working in the medical clinics treating children. Their opinion was that John Huggins was a good man, with a good heart.

The judge also read a statement from the Reverend Arlene Colter, pastor of Resurrection Ranch in Melbourne. Reverend Colter indicated that she first met Huggins when he helped baptize some people. He was quite young, but he stopped at the ministry periodically and brought food and clothing for the needy. She added that the defendant helped start a church in Oviedo, and she felt that he was a Christian.

Also speaking for John Huggins was Susan Irbin, a friend of his through the missionary trips to Haiti. She knew Huggins for about fifteen years, and talked about his alcohol problems and his two former wives.

Reverend Sandy Stafford was another friend of John Huggins's who spoke up for him. She went on three or four missionary trips to Haiti with the defendant. She felt that Huggins was a good person.

The judge read a letter from Barbara Parker, a novelist and pen pal of Huggins, in which she stated: "At my present age, I believe that I have acquired a certain sense about people, an ability to recognize what might be called evil when I hear it or see it. I've never sensed it in John Huggins. Without regard to his guilt or innocence in this or any other case, I can see that his lifestyle in the early to mid-1990's took him on a decidedly downhill path." She also felt the defendant had a definite talent in art.

The judge summarized what the presentence investigation had uncovered, that the defendant had a troubled early life, followed by bad marriages and alcohol abuse. He also had a side of him that showed compassion for his fellow man, evidenced by his missionary work in Haiti and his work with Reverend Colter.

The judge gave little or no weight to two factors submitted: that there was no sexual attack and no weapon was used, nor to the fact that Huggins was fifteen years old when sentenced to an adult-male prison.

Other mitigating factors submitted were Huggins's positive attitude toward people of other races, offering as proof his mission work in Haiti. Also the suggestion that John Huggins could contribute to the prison community if given a sentence of life without parole. Judge Perry found that these constituted a mitigating factor and gave it some weight.

Offered as mitigating factors were the facts that John was struck by his father and may have been abused as a child, that he may have witnessed violence toward his mother, that he endured difficult family separation as a child, that he was as an adult a caring parent, a loving stepfather and the sole surviving parent of his two children. The court gave those some weight.

Several other factors put forth as mitigating showed that Huggins was an active participant in religious functions, that he contributed his inheritance and more to the church, that he was active in the "Love a Child" ministry in Florida, that he served sick children and the poor in Haiti, that he served the homeless through contribution and labor. The court gave some weight to all of those factors.

Finally Judge Perry arrived at the awaited moment—his conclusion after the lengthy, detailed presentation.

He explained that he carefully weighed and considered each aggravating circumstance and the mitigating circumstances in attempting to decide the appropriate sentence to impose in light of all the evidence presented at the trial and sentencing hearing. He also considered the jury's verdict as to imposition of the death penalty for the first-degree murder of Carla Larson. The judge, very mindful that a human life was at stake, found that the aggravating circumstances greatly outweighed the mitigating circumstances heard by the court.

Officially, he ruled on Count I, "John Steven Huggins, you have not only forfeited your right to live among us as a free man, but under the laws of the state of Florida, you have forfeited your right to live at all.

"The court concluded that death is the appropriate sentence in this case for the murder of Carla Larson.

"Therefore, John Steven Huggins, having adjudged you guilty of the first-degree murder of Carla Larson, I hereby sentence you to death. It is the order of this court that you, John Steven Huggins, be taken by the proper authorities to the Florida State Prison or any other facility of the Department of Correction and there be kept in close confinement until the date of your execution is set.

"That on the date set for your execution, you shall be taken to the death chamber and you shall be put to death in the manner prescribed by law, until you are rendered dead."

Judge Perry also pronounced sentence on Huggins for Count II, the carjacking, for which he gave thirty years.

For Count III, the theft of the jewelry, the sentence was sixty days.

For Count IV, kidnapping, Judge Perry sentenced him to life imprisonment.

Judge Perry concluded his long dissertation by announcing for the second time, "John Steven Huggins, may Almighty God have mercy on your soul."

When Judge Perry completed his painstaking presentation, a hush fell over the courtroom. Everyone seemed to be overwhelmed by the solemnity, the finality of the sentence, even though it was not unexpected. Judge Perry looked at the assembled group owlishly, then began to gather up his papers.

As soon as Judge Perry exited, the courtroom came alive, the press scrambling to get near the principals, hoping to record their reactions.

John Huggins sat very still, his face as expressionless as it was throughout the entire proceedings. It was impossible to gauge what he was feeling, whether the sentence was expected or if he had hoped for prison. He turned to look at his family, trying to summon a smile for them. His mother was in tears. His children were visibly disappointed and crying. Their hopes were that their father's life would be spared.

John Huggins was led out of the courtroom in handcuffs, to be transported to the Florida State Prison at Raiford, to death row, to await his fate.

Outside the courtroom a reporter asked for Jim Larson's feelings on the sentence. Larson said in his usual quiet voice, his deep blue eyes focused into space, "I think it's fair." He added, "I just wish it could have been a little quicker." He brushed back his brown hair and said sadly, "I'm not looking to hang this guy. I just don't want him walking around so he can hurt anybody else."

Larson turned away from the reporter, obviously finished with this brief, unwanted interview.

The reporters pressed on to the nearby parents of Carla Larson. Dabbing her eyes, Phyllis Thomas murmured through her tears, "It's not a happy day. But it's a relief. It's what we hoped for."

When questioned, ASA Jeff Ashton stated that the United States Supreme Court's ruling should not affect the Huggins case, because jurors voted unanimously on the aggravating factors that led to his sentencing. With the strong confidence that Ashton displayed throughout the trial, he said that he did not see a third trial on the courthouse calendar.

Ashton explained, "It all depends on what the Florida Supreme Court says. But I am very confident that the guilt issue will not have to be readdressed."

Public defender Bob Wesley, Huggins's former defense lawyer, on the other hand, stated, "Perry's decision will likely give Huggins an appeal opportunity."

The Larson and Thomas families left the courthouse to try to pick up their lives, hoping that this was finally the end to their long, harrowing experience. Now all their lives would revolve around the care and rearing of Jessica.

John Huggins sits on death row. As his automatic appeal goes through the channels, the Florida Supreme Court has not yet reached a decision on the constitutionality of Florida's death penalty.

Meanwhile, the state of Florida resolved to proceed with the long-delayed execution of convicted murderer Rigoberto Sanchez-Velasco, which was effected on October 2, 2002.

With this execution precedent established, on Wednesday, October 9, 2002, the infamous Aileen Wuornos, one of the nation's first-known female serial killers, the so-called "Highway Hooker," who pleaded for the cessation of her life, was granted her wish by means of lethal injection.

After twenty-one years on death row for the murder of elderly Eatonville postmistress Catherine Alexander, Linroy Bottoson was executed on Monday, December 9, 2002.

All executions were on signed order of the governor of the state of Florida, who could at some future time sign the order to execute John Huggins.

However, the issue remains in limbo until the ultimate resolution is handed down by the United States Supreme Court.